APPRAISING THE IMPACT OF AN EVANGELISTIC CAMPAIGN

IN CAICÓ, BRAZIL

By

DANIEL CALEB KING

April 24, 2019

AN APPLIED RESEARCH PROJECT

Submitted to the Theological Faculty

in Partial Fulfillment of the Requirements

for the Degree of

DOCTOR OF MINISTRY

CHURCH MINISTRY LEADERSHIP

GRADUATE SCHOOL OF THEOLOGY AND MINISTRY

ORAL ROBERTS UNIVERSITY

DISCLAIMER

The beliefs and conclusions presented in this Applied Research Project are not necessarily those of the administration of Oral Roberts University, the Graduate School of Theology and Ministry, or the faculty.

APPRAISING THE IMPACT OF AN EVANGELISTIC CAMPAIGN
IN CAICÓ, BRAZIL

By

DANIEL CALEB KING

APPROVED BY   DATE

_____   12/11/18
Trevor Grizzle, PhD, Supervisor

_____   12/11/18
John Thompson, DSL, Director, Doctor of Ministry Program

ABSTRACT

Name: Daniel King   Date of Degree: 2019

Institution: Oral Roberts University

Location: Tulsa, Oklahoma

Title of Study: APPRAISING THE IMPACT OF AN EVANGELISTIC CAMPAIGN IN CAICÓ, BRAZIL

Pages in Study: 266   Candidate for the Degree of
Doctor of Ministry
Church Ministries Leadership

Supervisor: Trevor Grizzle, PhD

Scope and Method of Study: Are mass evangelistic campaigns effective? Who comes to an evangelistic campaign? Are local churches involved? How are attendees impacted by the event? Are people really being saved and healed? Is follow-up effective? How can the methods of evangelists be improved? The goal of this study was to use surveys of an evangelistic event in Caicó, Brazil to examine these important questions.

Findings and Conclusions: The surveys collected at an evangelistic event in Caicó, Brazil revealed the number of people in attendance, how many prayed for salvation, how many witnessed a miracle, and how many were discipled by local churches after the event was over. The participation of local believers was measured, and the opinions of local church pastors both before and after the event were recorded. The data collected illustrates the impact an evangelistic event had on a city. After evaluating biblical, theological, historical, and current literature on mass evangelism it was found that large evangelistic events continue to be a valuable method of evangelism, especially in the context of a developing nation.

All rights on this project are reserved by the author and nothing herein is to be used for publication without the express written agreement of the author or the Dean of the College of Theology and Ministry at Oral Roberts University.

Copyright © 2019 by Daniel King

All rights reserved

DEDICATION

I dedicate this project to my wife Jessica, my children Caleb and Katie Grace, and my parents Robert and Susan King. I am grateful for what God has done for my family in the past, and I am excited about what God will do through my family in the future.

ACKNOWLEDGEMENTS

I am grateful to the Oral Roberts University professors who helped me with my project, including Dr. John Thompson, Dr. Trevor Grizzle, and Dr. Kenneth Mayton. I am also grateful for the evangelistic insights of Dr. Tim Robnett from Multnomah University and for the editing help of Marlene Mankins.

TABLE OF CONTENTS

ACKNOWLEDGMENTS ....

LIST OF TABLES ....

Chapter

    1. THE PROBLEM 1

        Introduction 1

        Rationale 2

        Background and Significance 9

        The Setting of the Project 14

        Statement of the Problem 15

        Research Questions 15

        Definition of Terms 16

        Limitations of Study 19

        Assumptions 19

        Conclusion 20

    2. HISTORICAL REFLECTION 21

        Biblical Narrative 22

            Mass Evangelism in the Old Testament—Jonah 22

            Mass Evangelism in the New Testament—Philip 25

        Historical Narrative 38

Chapter

Early Mass Evangelism 38

The Reformation's Influence on Mass Evangelism 45

Mass Evangelism in the 1700-1800's 46

    John Wesley 46

    George Whitefield 48

    Jonathan Edwards 50

    Francis Asbury 51

    The Cane Ridge Revival 53

    Charles Finney 55

    D. L. Moody 57

Mass Evangelism in the Twentieth Century 60

    Billy Sunday 60

    Billy Graham 62

    Luis Palau 64

History of Evangelism in the Pentecostal/Charismatic Context 66

    John Alexander Dowie 67

    Aimee Semple McPherson 71

    Oral Roberts 71

    T. L. Osborn 75

    Reinhard Bonnke 78

Cultural Narrative 80

Chapter

       Evangelism in the Brazilian Culture 80

       Differences Between Brazilian and American Cultures 83

    Personal Narrative 87

3.   REVIEW OF RELATED LITERATURE.. 91

    Introduction 91

    Similar Research... 93

       250 Years of Mass Evangelism in America..................................... 94

       A Billy Graham Crusade in Europe in 1975 96

       Luis Palau and His Contribution to Evangelism 99

       A Luis Palau Festival in California in 1994................................... 102

       A Luis Palau Crusade in Chicago in 1996 105

       Mass Evangelism in the Philippines from 1969-1985 106

    Theorists and Theoretical Constructs 110

       What Is the Place of the Evangelist in Today's Church?............... 111

       Billy Graham's Methods of Mobilizing the Body of Christ 115

       Is There a Place for Mass Evangelism Today? 120

       What Are the Benefits of Mass Evangelism? 122

    Practitioners and Practical Applications.. 130

       Billy Graham Crusades 130

       Luis Palau Festivals.. 132

       T. L. Osborn Healing Crusades.. 134

Chapter

	Summary	136
4.	METHODOLOGY	137
	Introduction	137
	Rationale	137
	Rationale for the Project (for Topic)	138
	Rationale for the Method or Design (for Methodology)	138
	Procedures	139
	Sample Selection	140
	Construction of Questionnaire	142
	Additional Surveys	143
	Data Analysis	144
	Chapter Summary	144
5.	PRESENTATION OF RESULTS	145
	Introduction	145
	Data Presentation	150
	Friday and Saturday Night Crusade Survey	150
	Survey Question 1: Age of the Crowd	150
	Survey Question 2: Gender of the Crowd	151
	Survey Question 3: Prayer	152
	Survey Question 4: Why Did You Pray?	152
	Survey Question 5: Do You Need Healing?	153

Chapter

    Survey Question 6: Do You Feel Better? 154

    Survey Question 7: Is It a Miracle? 155

    Survey Question 8: How Did You Hear about Meeting? 156

    Survey Question 9: Why Did You Come to this Meeting? 158

    Survey Question 10: Distance Traveled 160

    Survey Question 11: Mode of Transportation 161

    Survey Question 12: What Is Your Religion? 161

    Survey Question 13: Are You Part of a Church? 162

    Survey Question 14: What Church Do You Attend? 163

    Survey Question 15: How Often Do You Attend Church? 163

    Survey Question 16: Would You Visit a Church if Invited? .. 164

Pastor's Pre-Crusade Survey 165

    Pre-Crusade Pastor's Survey Questions 1-4 165

    Pre-Crusade Pastor's Survey Question 5: Biggest Spiritual Needs 166

    Pre-Crusade Pastor's Survey Question 6: Is Your Church Evangelistic? 167

    Pre-Crusade Pastor's Survey Question 7: Evangelistic Methods 1-4 167

    Pre-Crusade Pastor's Survey Questions 8-12 168

    Pre-Crusade Pastor's Survey Question 13: How Is Your Church Participating in the Crusade? 169

    Pre-Crusade Pastor's Survey Question 14: Number of Volunteers 170

Chapter

    Pre-Crusade Pastor's Survey Question 15: Excitement About the Crusade 170

    Pre-Crusade Pastor's Survey Question 16: What Will Be Accomplished? 171

    Pre-Crusade Pastor's Survey Question 17: Concerns About the Crusade 171

    Pre-Crusade Pastor's Survey Question 18: Concerns About the Crusade 172

Pastor's Post-Crusade Survey 172

    Post-Crusade Pastor's Survey Questions 1-3: Number of Participants 173

    Post-Crusade Pastor's Survey Questions 4-5: Number of People Invited and Number of Visitors 174

    Post-Crusade Pastor's Survey Question 6: Follow Up? 174

    Post-Crusade Pastor's Survey Question 7: What Were the Positive Effects? 175

    Post-Crusade Pastor's Survey Question 8: Were There any Negative Effects? 175

    Post-Crusade Pastor's Survey Question 9: Would You Change Anything? 176

    Post-Crusade Pastor's Survey Question 10: Was the Crusade Worthwhile? 176

    Post-Crusade Pastor's Survey Question 11: Another Crusade. 176

    Post-Crusade Pastor's Survey Question 12: Are Crusades Effective? 177

Pastor's Post-Crusade Survey—Three Months Later 177

Chapter

    Post-Crusade Pastor's Survey, Three Months Later, Question 2: Weekly Attendance 177

    Post-Crusade Pastor's Survey, Three Months Later, Question 3: Follow Up.. 178

    Post-Crusade Pastor's Survey, Three Months Later, Question 4: Number of New Believers.......................... 178

    Post-Crusade Pastor's Survey, Three Months Later, Question 5: How Was Follow up Done? 179

    Post-Crusade Pastor's Survey, Three Months Later, Questions 6, 8, 9: Post-Crusade Church Involvement 179

    Post-Crusade Pastor's Survey, Three Months Later, Question 7: How Many Joined the Church? 180

    Post-Crusade Pastor's Survey, Three Months Later, Question 10: Positive Aspects of the Crusade 180

    Post-Crusade Pastor's Survey, Three Months Later, Question 11: Negative Aspects of the Crusade............... 181

    Post-Crusade Pastor's Survey, Three Months Later, Question 12: Was the Crusade Worthwhile? 181

    Post-Crusade Pastor's Survey, Three Months Later, Question 13: Another Crusade? 182

    Post-Crusade Pastor's Survey, Three Months Later, Question 14: Are Crusades Effective? 182

Church's Post-Crusade Survey 183

    Post-Crusade Church Survey Question 1: Age of Church Members 183

    Post-Crusade Church Survey Question 2: Gender 184

    Post-Crusade Church Survey Question 3: When Did You Go?.. 184

Chapter

        Post-Crusade Church Survey Question 4: How Did You Participate in the Crusade? 185

        Post-Crusade Church Survey Questions 5-6: Crusade Promotion 186

        Post-Crusade Church Survey Questions 7-9: Number of People Invited and Number Who Came 187

        Post-Crusade Church Survey Question 8: Who Was Invited? 187

        Post-Crusade Church Survey Questions 10-12: Rides, Salvation, and Miracles 188

        Post-Crusade Church Survey Question 13: Miracles Witnessed 189

        Post-Crusade Church Survey Question 14: Individual Impact 192

        Post-Crusade Church Survey Question 15: Church Impact 192

        Post-Crusade Church Survey Question 16: City Impact 193

    Chapter Summary 193

6.   RESPONSES TO FINDINGS 194

    Introduction 194

    Interpretation of Results 194

        The Prayer of Salvation 195

        Miracles 201

        Church Involvement 204

        Follow Up 208

Chapter

    Overall Impact 210

    Conclusions 211

    Theological Reflection 212

    Recommendations 214

    Summary of Chapter and Project 216

APPENDIX A: CRUSADE SURVEY 218

APPENDIX B: PRE-CRUSADE PASTOR'S SURVEY 222

APPENDIX C: POST-CRUSADE PASTOR'S SURVEY 226

APPENDIX D: POST-CRUSADE PASTOR'S SURVEY, 3 MONTHS LATER 229

APPENDIX E: POST-CRUSADE CHURCH'S SURVEY 232

BIBLIOGRAPHY 235

IRB 247

VITA 248

TABLES

Table

1.	Range of Ages of the Respondents to the Survey	151
2.	Gender of the Crowd on Friday Night	151
3.	Gender of the Crowd on Saturday Night	151
4.	Did You Repeat the Prayer? Friday Night	152
5.	Did You Repeat the Prayer? Saturday Night	152
6.	Answers to Question 4: Why Did You Pray?	152
7.	Do You Need Healing? Friday Night	154
8.	Do You Need Healing? Saturday Night	154
9.	Do You Feel Better? Friday Night	154
10.	Do You Feel Better? Saturday Night	154
11.	Is It a Miracle? Friday Night	155
12.	Is It a Miracle? Saturday Night	155
13.	How Did You Hear about this Meeting? Friday Night	156
14.	How Did You Hear about this Meeting? Saturday Night	157
15.	Why Did You Come to this Meeting? Friday Night	159
16.	Why Did You Come to this Meeting? Saturday Night	160
17.	How Far Did You Come? Friday	160

18. How Far Did You Come? Saturday 160

19. Mode of Transportation? Friday Night 161

20. Mode of Transportation? Saturday Night 161

21. Religion? Friday 162

22. Religion? Saturday 162

23. Are You Part of a Church? Friday 162

24. Are You Part of a Church? Saturday 162

25. How Often Do You Attend Your Church? Friday Night 163

26. How Often Do You Attend Your Church? Saturday Night 163

27. Would You Visit a Church if You Were Invited? Friday Night 165

28. Would You Visit a Church if You Were Invited? Saturday Night 165

29. Size of Local Churches 165

30. Is Your Church Evangelistic? 167

31. Questions about Evangelism Practices 168

32. How Is Your Church Participating in the Crusade? 169

33. Number of Volunteers 170

34. Excitement About the Crusade 171

35. I Have Concerns about the Crusade 171

36. Number of Participants 173

37. Number of People Invited and Number of Visitors 174

38. Our Church Is Planning to Follow up with New Believers 175

39. Was the Crusade Worthwhile? 176

40. Another Crusade	177
41. Are Crusades Effective?	177
42. Average Weekly Attendance	177
43. Did Your Church Follow Up on New Believers?	178
44. Number of New Believers in Follow Up Program	178
45. Questions About Post-Crusade Church Involvement	179
46. How Many People Joined Your Church?	180
47. Was the Crusade Worthwhile?	181
48. I Would Like to See Another Crusade in My City in the Future	182
49. Mass Evangelism is an Effective Method of Reaching People in Brazil	183
50. Average Age of Churches Surveyed	183
51. Gender of Church Members	184
52. Services Attended	185
53. Participation in the Crusade	185
54. Crusade Promotion	186
55. Number of People Invited and Number Who Came	187
56. Who Was Invited?	188
57. Rides, Salvations, and Miracles	188
58. Miracles Witnessed	189
59. Individual Impact	192
60. Church Impact	192
61. City Impact	193

CHAPTER 1

THE PROBLEM

Introduction

Large, public evangelistic campaign meetings are an important tool in the arsenal of the modern-day missionary evangelist. These meetings often attract large numbers of people and are reported to be a great success by the evangelist conducting the meetings. However, there is often a lack of scientifically verifiable statistics available for evaluating the success or failure of these events. In order to objectively evaluate the results of a typical campaign meeting in a developing nation, research tools are needed that accurately capture a snapshot picture of the crowd who attends the event and can measure the impact of the event on the local churches. The statistics gathered by these mechanisms can then be used by the evangelist to evaluate the preparation leading up to the event, the pre-event training of local churches, and the marketing and publicity required to organize and promote an evangelistic event.

For this research, an evangelistic campaign was held in Caicó, Brazil. Who attended this mass evangelism event and why did they come? What were the attendees hoping to experience at the event? Was the evangelist right in assuming that he is reaching the lost or was he just preaching to the proverbial choir? These are the questions this study answered by administering a questionnaire to ten percent of the crowd that attended an evangelistic campaign in Brazil, and by administering questionnaires to local pastors and believers who participated in the event. The answers provided in these questionnaires provided data that allowed the researcher to evaluate the effectiveness and impact of a mass evangelistic event in a majority world context. This research project examined the theological rationale for mass evangelism in the Old and New Testament, looked at the use of mass evangelism throughout church history, and interacted with current scholarship concerning the use of mass evangelism.

Rationale

The call of the evangelist is a mission that comes directly from the throne room of God. The concept of *missio Dei*, "the mission of God" goes back to the teachings of Karl Barth who "connected missions with the doctrine of the trinity."[1] The phrase refers to how the Father sends the Son, and how they both send the Holy Spirit. "All human mission . . . is seen as a participation in and extension of this divine sending."[2] God's desire to save people is the central theme of the Bible.[3] In the beginning of time, God walked and talked with Adam and Eve, but sin separated them from their Creator and caused death to enter the world. Despite the tragedy of sin, God promised that someday, the "seed of the woman" (Gen 3:15) would come and save humankind from the

---

[1] Christopher J. H. Wright, *The Mission of God: Unlocking the Bible's Grand Narrative* (Downers Grove, IL: InterVarsity, 2006), 62.

[2] Wright, 63.

[3] George W. Peters, *A Biblical Theology of Missions* (Chicago, IL: Moody Press, 1972), 9.

consequences of sin.[4] Christopher J. H. Wright describes the Bible as a "grand metanarrative":

> It begins with the God of purpose in creation, moves on to the conflict and problem generated by human rebellion against that purpose, spends most of its narrative journey in the story of God's redemptive purposes being worked out on the stage of human history, [and] finishes beyond the horizon of its own history with the eschatological hope of a new creation.[5]

He describes this four-point narrative as creation, fall, redemption, and future hope.[6] T. L. Osborn, the missionary evangelist, teaches this same concept using the terms: God's Creation, Satan's Deception, Christ's Substitution, and Our Restoration.

The Bible is the story of how the good news of God's salvation spread from one man, to a chosen people, to the entire world. God began His plan of redemption by calling a man named Abraham. God promised him, ". . . in you all the families of the earth shall be blessed" (Gen 12:3). Wright explains, "From the great promise of God to Abraham in Genesis 12:1-3 we know this God to be totally, covenantally and eternally committed to the mission of the blessing of the nations through the agency of the people of Abraham."[7]

Abraham's descendants became the nation of Israel. They were a chosen people called to become a vehicle for salvation to spread to the entire world. The nation of Israel

---

[4]Unless otherwise indicated, all English Bible references in this project are from the New King James Version (NKJV) (Nashville, TN: Thomas Nelson, 1982).

[5]Wright, 63-64.

[6]Wright, 64.

[7]Wright, 63.

went through cycles of sinful living and then turning back to God. Some kings, like David and Hezekiah, served God wholeheartedly, and other kings led the people away from God. Throughout the history of the people of Israel, God continued to demonstrate His great love and compassion. Judges, like Gideon, and prophets, like Samuel and Elijah, function as Old Testament evangelists as they call people to worship the one true God.

The book of Psalms is an intensely evangelistic book and it reveals the heart of God for the people of the world to be saved. The children of Israel sang songs of universal redemption: "How majestic is Your Name in all the earth!" (Ps 8:9) and "I will praise You among the nations" (Ps 18:49). God promises, "I will be exalted among the nations" (Ps 46:10). The Psalmist reminds his listeners, "God reigns over the nations" (Ps 47:8). It is promised that, "All the earth shall worship You and sing praises to You" (Ps 66:4) and "all the nations are Your inheritance" (Ps 82:8).

Throughout the Old Testament, God sent prophets as ancient evangelists to bring His word to the people of Israel and to other nations. They were called to "fill the earth with the knowledge of the Lord" (Isa 11:9) and "make known among the nations what He has done" (Isa 12:4). The prophets spoke of God's plan for the nations of the earth, "Many peoples will come and say, 'Come, let us go up to the mountain of the Lord, to the house of the God of Jacob'" (Isa 2:3). According to Donald Senior and Carroll Stuhlmueller, in Isaiah's Songs of the Suffering Servant, "the Old Testament reached its clearest expression of the universal salvation."[8] Jeremiah promises, "All nations will gather in Jerusalem to honor the name of the Lord" (Jer 3:17). Zechariah announces, "The Lord will be King over the whole earth" (Zech 14:9).

The New Testament tells the story of how salvation spread from the Jews (God's chosen people) to the Gentiles throughout the earth. John 3:16 reveals that God loved the world so much that He sent His only Son, that whoever would believe in Him would have eternal life. In the fullness of time, God sent forth His Son Jesus Christ as a missionary to the world (Gal 4:4). Jesus came to "seek and to save that which was lost" (Luke 19:10) and to "give His life as a ransom for many" (Mark 10:45). Jesus achieved His mission by dying on the cross to pay the price for the sins of humankind. But He did not stay dead. Three days after His crucifixion, Jesus rose from the dead (Matt 28:5-6). After appearing to His disciples over a period of forty days, He ascended into heaven to sit at the right hand of the Father (Acts 2:33).

Throughout His time on the earth, Jesus worked to train His disciples so they could continue His mission after He returned to heaven. Mark 3:14 reads, "Then He appointed twelve, that they might be with Him and that He might send them out to preach." In a parallel account in Matthew 10:1-7, Jesus "called His twelve disciples to Him, He gave them power over unclean spirits, to cast them out, and to heal all kinds of sickness and all kinds of disease . . . These twelve Jesus sent out and commanded them, saying . . . as you go, preach, saying, 'The kingdom of heaven is at hand.'" In

---

[8]Donald Senior and Carroll Stuhlmueller, *The Biblical Foundation for Missions* (Maryknoll, NY: Orbis, 1984), 126.

Matthew 9:37-38, Jesus tells His disciples, "The harvest truly *is* plentiful, but the laborers *are* few. Therefore pray the Lord of the harvest to send out laborers into His harvest." So, in this passage, Jesus points out the harvest fields of the world, asks the disciples to pray for laborers, and then sends them out to work in the harvest fields as the answers to their own prayers.

Initially, the disciples were to go to the "lost sheep of Israel" (Matt 10:6), but before Jesus ascended back into heaven, He gave His followers the Great Commission to go as evangelists into all the world (Matt 28:19; Mark 16:15; Luke 24:47; John 20:21). Between His resurrection and His ascension, Jesus had one thought on His mind: Repeatedly, He commanded His disciples to preach the Gospel to the whole world. Each of the Gospel writers and the book of Acts records this thought in a slightly different way. In Matthew, Jesus says, "Go therefore and make disciples of all the nations, baptizing them in the name of the Father and of the Son and of the Holy Spirit, teaching them to observe all things that I have commanded you; and lo, I am with you always, even to the end of the age" (Matt 28:19-20). In Mark, Jesus expresses a similar thought:

> He said to them, "Go into all the world and preach the gospel to every creature. He who believes and is baptized will be saved; but he who does not believe will be condemned. And these signs will follow those who believe: In My name they will cast out demons; they will speak with new tongues; they will take up serpents; and if they drink anything deadly, it will by no means hurt them; they will lay hands on the sick, and they will recover" (Mark 16:15-20).

In the Gospel of Luke, Jesus again mentions the mandate to preach repentance to all nations, ". . . Repentance and remission of sins should be preached in His name to all nations, beginning at Jerusalem" (Luke 24:47). In the book of John, Jesus said to them again, "'Peace to you! As the Father has sent Me, I also send you.' And when He had said this, He breathed on them, and said to them, 'Receive the Holy Spirit'" (John 20:21-23). Finally, in Acts, Jesus repeats Himself one more time, "But you shall receive power when the Holy Spirit has come upon you; and you shall be witnesses to Me in Jerusalem, and in all Judea and Samaria, and to the end of the earth" (Acts 1:8). These passages collectively are known as "The Great Commission." J. Hudson Taylor, British missionary to China, says, "The Great Commission is not an option to be considered; it is a command to be obeyed."[9] The Great Commission should be the believer's main ambition. David Livingstone, missionary to the heart of Africa, asks, "If a commission by an earthly king is considered an honor, how can a commission by a Heavenly King be considered a sacrifice?"[10]

The book of Acts is a history of the evangelistic efforts of the early Church. The idea of mission is central to "Luke's purpose for the writing of Acts."[11] In Acts 1:8, Jesus commissions the disciples to be witnesses to the "ends of the earth." They begin in Jerusalem on the Day of Pentecost. They continue to Samaria and Ethiopia in Acts 8 because of the ministry of Philip the evangelist. Salvation is extended to the Gentiles when Peter ministers to Cornelius in Acts 10. Paul goes on missionary journeys throughout the Gentile world until he is arrested and sent to Rome, the political center of the world in his time.

---

[9] Lee K. Ellenwood, ed., "Quotations on Mission," *The Living Pulpit 16*, no. 3 (2007): 45, *ATLA Religion Database with ATLASerials*, EBSCOhost (5 December 2017).

[10] Ellenwood, 48.

[11] William J. Larkin Jr., "Mission in Acts," in *Mission in the New Testament: An Evangelical Approach* (Maryknoll, NY: Orbis, 1998), 171.

The epistles were letters written to churches that had been established by evangelism. In his epistles, Paul extends the grace of God beyond the chosen people of God to the entire human race. Wright writes, "We confess, with Paul, that it is of the essence of the biblical gospel, first announced to Abraham, that God has indeed made such blessing for all nations available through the Messiah, Jesus of Nazareth, the seed of Abraham."[12] Paul shares the good news, "The Gospel . . . is the power of God that brings salvation . . . first to the Jew, then to the Gentile" (Rom 1:16) and looks for ways to take the gospel to "regions beyond" (2 Cor 10:16). Philippians 2:10 promises, "Every knee shall bow." God wants all people "to be saved and to come to a knowledge of the truth (1 Tim 2:4). According to Don N. Howel Jr., through his missionary journeys, Paul "became the catalyst for the planting of the Christian church throughout the urban centers of the eastern Mediterranean."[13]

The book of Revelation is the great culmination of salvation history. It promises that someday, "All the nations will come and worship . . . " (Rev 15:4). From Genesis to Revelation, God's love for the world and His desire for all people to be saved are revealed. The good news that salvation can be found in Jesus Christ is the message of the evangelist. The spread of this good news to people near and far is evangelism.

---

[12]Wright, 221.

[13]Don N. Howell Jr., "Mission in Paul's Epistles: Genesis, Pattern, and Dynamics," in *Mission in the New Testament: An Evangelical Approach*, ed. William Larkin Jr. and Joel F. Williams (Maryknoll, NY: Orbis, 1998), 63.

Background and Significance

The researcher is called by God to be an evangelist and he has conducted over one hundred evangelistic campaigns in nations around the world. These events have attracted from one thousand to fifty thousand people in a single service. Due to the scale of these evangelistic efforts, they can be classified as "mass evangelism" or evangelism on a mass scale. The researcher also trains other evangelists how to conduct large-scale evangelistic campaigns. The researcher believes that mass evangelism is biblical and is a legitimate and effective method of preaching the Gospel and building the kingdom of God. This project provided information that will help evangelists be more effective in how they promote and conduct evangelistic events. This research provided information that can be used to defend and promote the use of mass evangelism campaigns.

It is biblical to preach to large crowds of people. In the Old Testament, Jonah was commanded by God to preach to the evil city of Nineveh. At first, Jonah did not want to go, but after a roundabout journey, he finally made it to Nineveh. In response to his preaching, the entire city repented, including the king. Jesus frequently preached to large crowds of people (Matt 4:25; 5:1; 7:28; 8:1; 15:30; 19:2; 22:23; 23:1). "When Jesus saw the crowds, He had compassion on them" (Matt 9:36). Such "large crowds" came to hear Jesus that He was forced to retreat to a boat in order to preach (Matt 13:2). On one occasion, Jesus preached to a crowd of five thousand men, plus woman and children (Matt 14:21). With a wife and a child for each man, this yields a number of at least fifteen thousand people. Peter preached to a large crowd on the Day of Pentecost and three thousand people were saved in response to a single sermon (Acts 2:41). Philip, the only person specifically called an evangelist in the Bible, preached to "crowds" in Samaria (Acts 8:6).[14] Many people were healed and baptized because of his ministry. In Pisidian Antioch, the entire city gathered to hear Paul and Barnabas preach the Gospel (Acts 13:44). Later they preached to a large number of Jews and Gentiles in Iconium (Acts 14:1) and Lystra (Acts 14:18). Paul and Silas preached to "large numbers" of God-fearing Greeks in Thessalonica (Acts 17:4). In Athens, they preached in the synagogues and in the marketplace (Acts 17:17) and in front of the Areopagus (Acts 17:22). All of these references are biblical examples of mass evangelism in action.

Mass evangelism is an important method (although not the only method) for leading people to Jesus. In recent church history, men like George Whitefield, Jonathan Edwards, John Wesley, Charles Finney, D. L. Moody, Billy Sunday, Billy Graham, Oral Roberts, and T. L. Osborn gathered large crowds in order to preach to them. Today, there are many evangelists, like Franklin Graham, Luis Palau, Greg Laurie, and Reinhard Bonnke, who conduct large-scale evangelistic campaigns. Many people (including local church pastors, theology professors, and Christian authors) are openly critical of mass-evangelism efforts. It is often postulated that one-on-one evangelism is a better way of sharing the Gospel.[15] This is not a new sentiment. In 1966, TIME magazine called a Billy

---

[14]The fact that the evangelist engages in mass evangelism does not negate his call to also engage in personal evangelism. Philip preached to the masses in Samaria (Acts 8:5-8) and one-on-one to the Ethiopian eunuch (Acts 8:26-39). The evangelist is equally needed doing mass evangelism and one-on-one evangelism. The evangelist is also called to equip believers to evangelize (Eph. 4:11-12).

[15]Kirk Hadaway, *Church Growth Principles: Separating Fact from Fiction* (Nashville, TN: Broadman Press, 1991), 27.

Graham crusade a "redundant anachronism."[16] Ray Comfort argues, "Evangelical success is at an all-time low. Modern evangelism, from large campaigns to small gospel meetings, boasts only a 20 percent holding rate."[17] C. Peter Wagner says that ten percent or less of those who made first-time decisions at a crusade are involved in a local church one year later[18] and his analysis of an Evangelism-in-Depth campaign in the country of Bolivia found that the year-long effort had not resulted in the churches increasing their rate of growth.[19] Kirk Hadaway writes, "There is no evidence that mass evangelistic events help churches grow and there is limited evidence that they actually work against growth by draining time, money, and energy from the everyday activities of local churches— which do produce results."[20] George Barna, the Christian pollster, feels that the cost of mass media ministry is of dubious value when the low returns are considered.[21]

---

[16] "Billy's Victory in London," *Time,* 88, no. 3, 15 July 1966, n.p., *Academic Search Complete*, EBSCOhost (5 September 2017).

[17] Ray Comfort, *Hell's Best Kept Secret* (Springdale, PA: Whitaker House, 1989), 9.

[18] C. Peter Wagner, *Strategies for Church Growth* (Ventura, CA: Regal Books, 1987), 138.

[19] Wagner, *Strategies*, 140.

[20] Hadaway, 29.

[21] George Barna, *Marketing the Church* (Colorado Springs, CO: Nav Press, 1988), 113

But, not everyone agrees. *Christianity Today* asks, "Is mass evangelism dead?" and "Are city-wide crusades a thing of the past?"[22] In their survey of a variety of scholars and ministers,[23] sixty-two percent say, "No, mass evangelism is not dead," and thirty-eight percent say, "Yes, mass evangelism is dead." In the article, those who believe mass-evangelism is still viable today offer four reasons. First, Luis Palau's organization continues to see fruit at large evangelistic festivals. The ministers interviewed for the article opine, "It appears that some people are still interested in this method of learning about the gospel."[24] Second, they point out that, "You wouldn't be asking this question if you were focusing on the two-thirds world, where mass evangelism is still huge."[25] Third, they state, "In a world that is more celebrity-conscious and less serious by the day, the ambiguous opportunity presented by fame will continue to draw crowds for better and for

---

[22] Harold B. Smith et al., eds., "Is Mass Evangelism Dead?" *Christianity Today* (July 2007): 54. *ATLA Religion Database*, EBSCOhost (19 June 2016).

[23] The scholars and ministers interviewed for the article include: Leith Anderson, Edith L. Blumhofer, Nigel M. de S. Cameron, Chuck Colson, J. Samuel Escobar, John W. Kennedy, Douglas LeBlanc, Paul L. Maier, Grant McClung, David McKenna, H. W. Norton, Roger Olson, Ben Patterson, Jim Reapsome, Stephen A. Seamands, Ron Sider, Uwe Siemon-Netto, Howard A. Snyder, Agnieszka Tennant, and Elmer L. Towns.

[24] Blumhofer et al., n.p.

[25] Blumhofer et al., n.p.

worse."[26] Fourth, they assert, "There will always be the need and opportunity for large public events in which the Good News is proclaimed."[27]

In the same article in *Christianity Today*, those who felt that mass-evangelistic events are no longer viable, give the following three reasons. First, "In youth culture worldwide, the typical 'evangelistic crusade' may now be in the process of being replaced by concerts and other forms of gatherings that have an evangelistic byproduct." Second, "Billy Graham appears to be the last of a noble but dying breed." Third, "While millions of 'decisions' may have been registered, any strategy that has a 1 percent success rate has to be deemed a failure."[28] However, even those who feel that evangelistic events are of limited effectiveness acknowledge, "In the majority world, it appears that large-scale evangelism is still finding a place."[29] Michael Cassidy believes,

> Operated in relatively small towns or cities, where community prevails, and where churches and clergy are well united, mass evangelism has the power of dynamite. But imported simplistically or at random into large heterogeneous cities, and confined exclusively to a series of public rallies, it is probably counter-productive, relatively ineffective and not worth the costs and energy involved. But for the right place, at the right time, with the right men and methods, with comprehensive church-centered follow-up, and with the blessing of the Holy Spirit, mass evangelism is still a viable form of effective ministry whose potentialities outweigh its many obvious limitations.[30]

---

[26]Blumhofer et al., n.p.

[27]Blumhofer et al., n.p.

[28]Blumhofer et al., n.p.

[29]Blumhofer et al., n.p.

[30]Michael Cassidy, "Limitations of Mass Evangelism and Its Potentialities," *International Review of Mission* 65, no. 258 (1976): 215. *ATLA Religion Database with ATLASerials*, EBSCOhost (1 September 2017).

The Setting of the Project

The survey took place at an international evangelistic meeting in northeast Brazil. Brazil contains an estimated population of 205,823,665 people. Roman Catholics comprise 64.6%, 22.2% claim to be Protestant, while 2.2% follow a Spiritist religion, and 8% claim no religion.[31] But, like any nation that has a high percentage of people who claim to be Christian, many people only attend church occasionally and many are not actively serving the Lord. Although parts of Brazil have large churches, there remains a great need for evangelism throughout northeast Brazil in the states of Ceará, Piauí, Bahia, Rio Grande do Norte, Paraíba, Pernamuco, Alagoas, and Sergipe. The evangelistic ministry of Rubens Cunha is systematically visiting mid-size cities throughout this region of Brazil and conducting evangelistic campaigns. For this research project, the researcher partnered together with Evangelist Cunha to conduct an evangelistic campaign in Northeast Brazil. The research project took place at an event in Caicó, Brazil in the state of Rio Grande do Norte, a city with a population of 66,246[32] and a total of nine evangelical churches.[33]

---

[31]"Brazil," *CIA World Factbook*, 1 September 2017, n.p., "https://www.cia.gov/library /publications/the-world-factbook/geos/br.html (1 September 2017).

[32]"Historia, " *Municipo de Caico*, (20 January 2014), n.p.. http://caico.rn.gov.br/pagina.php?codigo=3. (19 November 2018).

[33]Daniel King, "Pre-Crusade Survey of Local Church Pastors," Caicó, Brazil, 25 May 2018.

Statement of the Problem

The problem was that the researcher did not know who is coming to his events and he did not know why they attend. The primary goal of an evangelistic campaign is to lead the lost to Christ; the secondary one is to encourage the local church to be involved in evangelism. The researcher's ministry spends large sums of money in order to conduct each evangelistic event, and he wanted to know if this money is being spent wisely. If everyone who comes to an event is already a Christian and attends church on a regular basis, then the evangelist has failed in his primary purpose of reaching the unsaved. But, how can the researcher know if the attendees are Christians or non-Christians? That is the problem this project tried to solve.

Research Questions

The aim was to conduct a sample survey of a single mass evangelistic campaign in Brazil in order to seek answers to the following questions: Who attends a large evangelistic event? Is everyone who attends an evangelistic campaign already a Christian? What percentage of the crowd are unbelievers? Are the attendees religious or secular in their background? If they are religious, what church do they identify with? Why did people decide to attend? How did people hear about the event? Which part of the advertising was successful? What attracted people to come to the event? Do they come for the music, the preaching, or the spectacle? Or do they arrive because they are bored and there is nothing else to do? Do they attend out of curiosity or because they want to receive a miracle or because a friend invited them? What beliefs do people bring to the event? Do they look to the preacher as a shaman or a miracle worker or as a foreign curiosity? What are the demographics, economic level, and educational level of the people who attend? Are they children, youth, or adults? Are the local churches involved in the outreach? Do the pastors of the local churches think the event was worthwhile? What impact did the event have on local churches? Do the unbelievers who attend understand the message about Jesus that is presented? Do people remember the information that is imparted through the sermon? Do people respond to the message? Are people really getting saved at the event?[34] The answers to these questions helped the researcher to determine whether the majority of those attending the event were already Christian or non-Christian, and will assist in establishing better strategies for conducting campaigns of mass evangelism.

Definitions of Terms

The term "evangelist" comes from the Greek word *euangelistes*, derived from the root word *euangelion* translated as "gospel." Both Greek words are related to *angelos* which means "angel or messenger."[35] This type of messenger is one who brings tidings of a great victory or good news. In ancient Greece when a battle was won, a messenger (evangelist) would be sent to all the surrounding cities to announce the victory. The word

---

[34]This is a spiritual question that cannot be answered by a researcher since only God knows the hearts of men. However, the researcher can record how many raised their hands in response to the question, "Do you trust Jesus to save you from your sins?" The researcher can also record the number of decision cards filled out by counselors.

[35]Gerhard Friedrich, "*euangelion*," *Theological Dictionary of the New Testament*, vol. 2, ed. Gerhard Kittel (Grand Rapids, MI: Eerdmans, 1987), 710.

"evangelist" appears three times in the New Testament.[36] Philip is called an evangelist (Acts 21:8); Paul mentions evangelists in his list of ministry offices, along with apostles, prophets, pastors, and teachers (Eph 4:11); and Paul tells Timothy to do the *"work of an evangelist"* (2 Tim 4:5).

The word "gospel" means good news, and the evangelist is one who preaches the good news. The word "gospel" is an exact Anglo-Saxon equivalent of the Greek *euangelion* from the Anglo-Saxon words *god* meaning "good" and *spell* or *spiel* meaning "speech."[37] The Greek word *euangelion* is used seventy-four times in the New Testament and the verb form *euangelizomai* is used an additional fifty-two times.[38] Jesus is the first evangelist of the New Testament, since He went about "preaching the good news [*euangelion*] of the kingdom" (Matt 4:23). Throughout the writings of Paul, who used the term *euangelion* sixty times, the heart of the Gospel message is that God

---

[36]The fact that the word evangelist is only used three times is not meant to demean the office of the evangelist. The title of *bishop* is only used five times (See L. Coenen, "Bishop," *The New International Dictionary of New Testament Theology*, vol. 1, ed. Colin Brown [Grand Rapids, MI: Zondervan, 1971], 191), and amazingly (given the current prominence in the body of Christ on the local church pastor) the word *pastor* (shepherd) is only used once to refer to the ecclesiastical office of a pastor (See E. Beyreuther, "Shepherd," *The New International Dictionary of New Testament Theology*, vol. 3, ed. Colin Brown [Grand Rapids, MI: Zondervan, 1971], 568). Jesus is the "good shepherd" (John 10:11, Heb 13:20; 1 Pet 2:25) and there is a rich Old Testament tradition of referring to the leaders of God's people as shepherds (Jer 3:15), but in the New Testament, the apostle (mentioned 131 times) was far more prominent. (See C. Brown, "Apostle," *The New International Dictionary of New Testament Theology*, vol. 1, ed. Colin Brown [Grand Rapids, MI: Zondervan, 1971], 128.)

[37]U. Becker, "Gospel, Evangelize, Evangelist," *The New International Dictionary of New Testament Theology*, vol. 2, ed. Colin Brown (Grand Rapids, MI: Zondervan, 1971), 114.

[38]Becker, 110.

provided for the salvation of humankind through the birth, death, and resurrection of Jesus.

Evangelism is the proclamation of good news about the death and resurrection of Jesus Christ and the salvation that is available to everyone who calls on His name. Evangelism is rooted in the Great Commission, Jesus' command to His disciples to "go into all the world and preach the Gospel to every creature" (Mark 16:15). The goal of evangelism is to bring people to a point of decision where they accept Christ.

Over the centuries, the Church has obeyed the command of Jesus to evangelize with a variety of different methods, including one-on-one evangelism,[39] literature evangelism, children's evangelism,[40] church planting,[41] and mass evangelism. According to Ed Matthews, "Mass evangelism is the attempt to proclaim the Good News to a large number of people simultaneously . . . "[42] For the sake of this paper, mass evangelism is defined as "the preaching of the Good News of Jesus Christ's birth, life, death, and

---

[39]See Jin-Gu Park, "A Study on the Person to Person Evangelism Training of Laity," (D.Min. proj., Oral Roberts University, 1995).

[40]See Robert James King, "The Impact of a Children's Crusade on the Conversion Process in Mexico." (D.Min. proj., Oral Roberts University, 2002).

[41]See Randall Scott Loescher, "Recruiting, Assessing, Training and Deploying Church Planters in Open Bible Churches' Central Region," (D.Min. proj., Oral Roberts University, 2001).

[42]Ed Matthews, "Mass Evangelism: Problems and Potentials," *Journal of Applied Missiology* 4, no.1 (April 1993): n.p., http://web.ovu.edu/missions/jam/massive1.htm (1 June 2016).

resurrection to a large crowd of people for the purpose of convincing individuals to make a decision to call on Jesus for salvation from sin."[43]

Limitations of Study

First, there was no guarantee that the knowledge gained from this study would be useful in other contexts. Since the circumstances, religion, and culture of every nation are different, the conclusions from a sample of one evangelistic event in Brazil do not necessarily apply to evangelistic events that take place in other locations, and in other cultures. Second, even though there are many different methods of evangelism, the focus of this research was limited to mass evangelism. This project is limited to a study of preaching the Gospel to one large crowd of people. Third, even though evangelists are frequently asked, "What do you do about follow-up?" the focus of this research project is upon the proclamation of the Gospel, not discipleship. The follow-up process that turns converts into disciples, while important, was outside the scope of this project.

Assumptions

First, in this study it was assumed that the Bible is the inspired Word of God. Second, it was believed that engaging in evangelism is a vital part of being a Christian. Third, it was presumed that mass evangelism is a legitimate form of evangelism that is both biblical and useful for building the church. Fourth, it was expected that it is possible

---

[43] Although television and radio ministry have been called "mass evangelism," in this project, "mass evangelism" will refer to preaching to a mass of people in a face-to-face setting. Television, radio, and Internet evangelism will be referred to as "media evangelism."

to gain meaningful information from a sample of attendees at an evangelistic event. Fifth, it was anticipated that participants in the sample will answer the survey questions honestly. Sixth, it was thought that the survey instrument can collect meaningful data that can be accurately evaluated.

Conclusion

In this chapter, a biblical rational for evangelism was developed, the background and significance for doing a project on mass evangelism was examined, the setting of the project was described, the precise nature of the problem and research questions that were studied were delineated, terms were defined, and the limitations of the study were explained. In the next chapter, a theological, biblical, and historical case will be made for the validity of mass evangelism. Keep reading.

CHAPTER 2

HISTORICAL REFLECTION

Is mass evangelism effective? Should mass evangelism be done? What role has mass evangelism played in the past history of the church and what part should it play in the future of the church? The focus of this research project is an evangelistic campaign in the nation of Brazil. Is there a theological and historical basis for a crusade in Brazil to take place?

To answer these questions, this chapter turns first to the story of Jonah in the Old Testament and then it looks at the history of Philip the Evangelist who preached to multitudes of people in Samaria. Then the chapter examines what God has accomplished through the practice of mass evangelism across the past two thousand years of church history. It will be shown that mass evangelism is a practice that dates back to the earliest days of the church and that continues to bear fruit in modern times. Particular attention will be paid to mass evangelists like John Wesley, George Whitefield, Jonathan Edwards, Francis Asbury, Charles Finney, D. L Moody, Billy Sunday, Billy Graham, and Luis Palau. The unique contribution of Pentecostal mass evangelists will be explored by looking at the ministries of John Alexander Dowie, Aimee Semple McPherson, Oral Roberts, T. L. Osborn, and Reinhard Bonnke. Finally, this chapter will examine the cultural context of mass evangelism in the nation of Brazil and detail the author's experiences in the arena of mass evangelism. All this accumulated evidence will suggest that the crusade in Brazil has a solid biblical and historical basis for taking place.

Biblical Narrative

What does the Bible say about mass evangelism? The Bible provides two great examples for the modern-day mass evangelist, the first is the prophet Jonah in the Old Testament and the second is the evangelist Philip in the New Testament. What can today's evangelist learn from them?

Mass Evangelism in the Old Testament—Jonah

The greatest example of an evangelist in the Old Testament is the prophet Jonah. Although all the prophets of the Old Testament were known for speaking the word of God, and several of the prophets spoke the word of God to foreign nations, the story of Jonah's message to the wicked city of Nineveh and the city's subsequent repentance stands unique in the history of Israel. The book of Jonah reveals the importance of the role of the evangelist in preaching about repentance. When God wanted the people of Nineveh to repent, He sent a preacher named Jonah; when God wants people in Brazil to repent, He sends an evangelist.

Nineveh was the capital of the kingdom of Assyria, a large empire during the time of the Israelite kings. The ruins of Nineveh lay across the river from the modern-day city of Mosul, in northern Iraq. Four times, the book of Jonah calls Nineveh "a great city" (1:2; 3:2; 3:3; 4:11), and indeed it was the greatest city of its day. The total area of Nineveh was about seven square kilometers and there were fifteen large gates in its walls.

Archaeologists say it contained between one hundred thousand and one hundred fifty thousand people, making it one of the largest cities of its time. The city of Nineveh was sinful[1] like Las Vegas, violent like inner-city Chicago, and militarily aggressive like Baghdad under Saddam Hussein. God's command to Jonah to go and preach in Nineveh was equivalent to God telling a modern-day preacher to go preach in Mosul, which was recently under the control of ISIS. Jonah was worried his head would be chopped off. The repentance of the king of Nineveh is like Abu Bakr al Baghdadi (the head of ISIS) repenting, publically turning from Islam, and announcing that he is now serving the Christian God. The repentance of Nineveh was a true miracle.

What lessons can an evangelist who is preaching in Brazil learn from the book of Jonah? First, the book teaches the reader that God is a God of compassion. In Jonah, God sends a "great storm" (1:4), then He sends a "great fish" (1:17). Jonah finally visits a "great city" (3:3). But, the real theme of the book is a great God who has compassion on everyone who repents. Sometimes the evangelist feels like he or she has to preach hard against sin, but when preaching, it is important to remember the compassion of God for

---

[1]The city of Nineveh was a sinful city, known for debauchery and violence. The Assyrians impaled enemies on stakes at the entrance to their towns. They collected heads and hung them as decorations from trees in the king's garden. They tortured people by cutting off their nose or ears, blinding them, or amputating their arms. They piled up skulls as a warning to anyone who would oppose their rule. They skinned their victims and used the skin as a decoration on their city walls. It is probable that theft and murder was common in the city. E. R. Clendenen, "Jonah, Book of," in *Holman Illustrated Bible Dictionary*, ed. C. Brand, C. Draper, A. England, S. Bond, & T. C. Butler (Nashville, TN: Holman Bible Publishers, 2003), n.p., Logos Bible Software Version 5.2 2014).

those who are lost. God is compassionate even when the church might preach condemning messages. Some perceive Jonah as a "doom and gloom" preacher, but Jonah's message was not the right message, nor was it preached from the right attitude, even though God used it to impact the entire city. The entire point of the book is God's compassion, not His judgment. It would be better to use this book as a text explaining God's grace than as a text to justify the preaching of judgment.

Also, the book of Jonah teaches the reader about the importance of repentance. In response to Jonah's preaching, the entire city repents. They fast and put on sackcloth and ashes. From the least to the greatest, from the king to the animals, they all repent of their wrongdoing. Repentance is a miracle that is needed in the world today. Being swallowed by a great fish and surviving is a big miracle. Indeed, it is one of the most well-known miracles in the Bible. Most pastors preach about Jonah as the protagonist of an amazing story about a man swallowed by a whale, but the greatest miracle in the book of Jonah is the repentance of an entire city. In today's culture, people would never wear sackcloth and ashes, but genuine repentance still produces a change in a person's heart and actions. For example, someone who repents today might make restitution to those he has wronged. Also, someone who repents might make a radical change in the way he or she acts. An alcoholic might stop drinking. A sex addict might make a commitment to stay away from sexual encounters. A person who uses bad language might clean up his vocabulary. Repentance is more than saying a prayer; it involves a change in one's actions.

Jonah is a missionary evangelist but his story is more of an example of what not to do as an evangelist. At the beginning of the story, Jonah runs away from the people God has called him to preach to. Later, Jonah preaches a message of destruction and condemnation to the people of Nineveh. He never imagined that God would actually forgive the evil Ninevites.[2] When Jonah refuses to go preach in Nineveh and God retrieves him and mercifully delivers him, Jonah is thankful. Yet when Jonah preaches in Nineveh and the people repent and are mercifully spared, Jonah is angry and resentful. It should have been easier for one who had received mercy to extend mercy to others. In like manner, the evangelist should extend mercy, forgiveness, and grace when he or she preaches. Every evangelist is simply a former sinner saved by grace. It is good to remember this fact from time to time. Finally, Jonah becomes resentful when God does forgive them. In contrast to Jonah, the evangelist today should joyfully go where God sends him, preach a message of forgiveness, and rejoice when people are saved.

Mass Evangelism in the New Testament—Philip

Philip is the only biblical character who is specifically called an evangelist, which means his life provides an example for the modern-day evangelist. The first view of

---

[2] Those who receive mercy should also give mercy (See 2 Sam. 22:26; Matt 5:7). The Assyrians had been flexing their muscles and intimidating all their neighbors. Jonah probably knew people who had been killed or sold into slavery by the Assyrians. This is why he is so resentful when God chooses to forgive the Ninevites. But he forgets that God has shown mercy to him. In the first half of the book, God is merciful toward Jonah despite his disobedience, and in the second half of the book, God is merciful to the entire city of Nineveh. Jonah is happy to receive mercy, but angry when mercy is given to another group who clearly deserves to be punished. Jonah's motto might be, "Mercy for me, but not for thee."

Philip is in Acts 6:1-7, where Philip is appointed to be a deacon. In Acts 8, Philip ministers to the multitudes in Samaria and witnesses one-on-one to the Ethiopian eunuch. He is mentioned a final time in Acts 21:8-9 when Paul visits him in Caesarea.[3] What can an evangelist preaching in Brazil learn from Philip's example?

It is important for those who are called to be evangelists to have a servant's heart.[4] (Acts 6:1-7). At the beginning, Philip was not an evangelist. He was chosen to be one of seven deacons and he volunteered to help serve food to widows. The best way to be used by God is by finding a place to serve.

The evangelist must go (Acts 8:5). Notice, Philip did not stay in Jerusalem, he went. Evangelists should be willing to go where it is dangerous or uncomfortable (Acts 8:5). Philip went to Samaria where it was potentially dangerous and definitely uncomfortable, but he went anyway. In Samaria the inhabitants had a centuries-long

---

[3] It is on this visit that Luke likely heard Philip's story.

[4] Philip's ministry begins with an attitude of servanthood. In the same way, the modern-day evangelist should begin his or her ministry with the attitude of being a servant. Philip was not an Apostle; he was simply an ordinary believer, a Hellenist who was chosen as one of seven deacons assigned to care for the Hellenistic widows by serving food (Acts 6:5). Since he was a Hellenistic Jew, Philip served as a bridge between the two communities. He had a good reputation, was full of the Holy Spirit, and full of wisdom (Acts 6:3). He was ordained into a ministry of helps when the Apostles laid hands on him and prayed over him (Acts 6:6). By serving faithfully, Philip freed up the Apostles to spend time studying God's word and preaching. By serving, he was following in the footsteps of Jesus, who said, "I did not come to be served but to serve" (Mark 10:45) and "the greatest in the kingdom is the servant of all" (Matt 23:11). Later, because he had served faithfully; God promoted him to become the first evangelist.

animosity towards the Jews. Traditionally, they had no contact with one another. They hated each other, yet Philip went there to preach.[5]

The work of an evangelist is to preach[6] about Jesus (Acts 8:5). Philip preached Christ to the lost people of Samaria. The writer of Acts does not give us an outline of Philip's message to the Samaritans, but it is likely that when Philip preached "the Christ"

---

[5]The Samaritans were descendants of Jews who intermarried with foreign women during the time of the captivity. Jews were known for despising Samaritans. They avoided speaking or interacting with them. Jews thought Samaritan people were unclean, and they feared that they themselves would become unclean by speaking with them. Yet, Philip broke tradition and went to those who were different from the Jews. By doing this, he followed the example of his master, Jesus, who had ministered to the Samaritan woman at the well (John 4). When the Samaritans accepted the Gospel, it was a great breakthrough because it proved that Christ is for the whole world. The Samaritans were excluded from having a relationship with God under the Old Covenant according to Ezra 4:3, "You have no part with us." But under the New Covenant, a door miraculously opens for them to become included. No wonder there was joy in their city. Richard Belward Rackham writes, "The Samaritans were worse than aliens. They were heretics, schismatics, more to be hated than infidels." Rackham, *The Acts of the Apostles: An Exposition* (Longdon: Metheun, 1901), 112.

[6]The word in Acts 8:5 "preached" or "proclaimed" (*kerusso*) is in the imperfect active tense that implies continuous action (A. T. Robertson, *Word Pictures in the New Testament* (*Ac 8:5*) (Nashville, TN: Broadman Press, 1933), n.p., Logos Bible Software Version 5.2 2014). Philip did not just preach once. He began preaching, and he preached, and he kept preaching. What did Philip the evangelist preach about? He preached Christ to the lost people of Samaria. Because of his preaching, many miracles began to occur.

he preached a version of the *kerygma*[7] that is recorded in Peter's sermon in Acts 2. The message of the early Apostles was that Jesus Christ was born in fulfillment of Old Testament prophecies about the Messiah, was accredited by signs and wonders, taught about the coming of the kingdom of God, died on a cross, was buried, rose again, and is now seated at the right hand of God in heaven. The *kerygma* also includes a call to repentance, the promise that "everyone who calls on the name of the Lord shall be saved" (Acts 2:21; Rom. 10:13), and an invitation to be baptized in water. The message of the evangelist today should be similar.

The Gospel is for everyone, regardless of race, nation, gender, or background (Acts 8:5). When Philip preached to the Samaritans it was a revolutionary act in his day. When the Samaritans accepted the Gospel, it was a great breakthrough because it proved that Christ is for the whole world, not just the Jews. The evangelist should be willing to take Christ to the whole world.

The preaching of God's word attracts multitudes (Acts 8:6). When God's word is preached, one can expect large crowds of people. Some will accept Jesus, some will ridicule and mock, but when the Gospel is preached there is definitely not silence. Mass evangelism is not meant to remain silent or hidden. When people start accepting Jesus, a

---

[7]The Greek word *kerygma* means "preaching." C.H. Dodd used the word to refer to the core of Christian apostolic preaching. He says, "Preaching…is the public proclamation of Christianity to the non-Christian world." According to him, the four speeches found in Acts 2-4 represent the *kerygma* (the content of the preaching) of the Jerusalem church in its earliest days. See C.H. Dodd, *The Apostolic Preaching and Its Developments*, (New York, NY: Harper and Row, 1964), https://postbarthian.com/2012/10/15/the-apostolic-preaching-and-its-developments-by-c-h-dodd/ (29 March 2019).

ruckus ensues. Some have questioned the value of mass campaign evangelism in today's society, but Philip's story provides a valuable example for today's evangelist. Mass evangelism is not the only way people come to Jesus, but Philip's example shows it is a valid way to minister to people. Philip preaches to masses of people in the city of Samaria and many people are saved and baptized. The story of what happens in Samaria provides a theological justification for the use of mass evangelism by the church today.[8]

The preaching of God's word should be accompanied by miracles (Acts 8:6-7).[9] Philip demonstrates that when the Gospel is preached, it is normal for miracles to occur.

---

[8]Both Nineveh and Samaria could be considered "unreached fields." Before Philip went to Samaria, there were no churches there (although Jesus did preach in Samaria in John 4). This may indicate that the evangelist is primarily called to unreached places where there are few believers or no churches.

[9]The word *semeion,* usually translated as "miraculous signs," is mentioned thirteen times in Acts. See: Ajith Fernando, *Acts*, The NIV Application Commentary (Grand Rapids, MI: Zondervan, 1998), 272. Jesus said, "These signs will follow those who believe: In My name they will cast out demons . . . they will lay hands on the sick, and they will recover" (Mark 16:17-18). When Jesus sent the disciples out to preach, "They went out and preached everywhere, the Lord working with them and confirming the word through the accompanying signs" (Mark 16:20). Paul said, "For our gospel did not come to you in word only, but also in power . . ." (1 Thess 1:5). A powerless Gospel is no Gospel at all. The church does not need a new definition of the Gospel, but a new demonstration of the Gospel. The message needs miracles; declaration requires demonstration. In terms a sixth grade student would understand, the church needs both "show-and-tell."

Some have said miracles were only for the Apostles,[10] but Philip was not an apostle—he was an evangelist. His example shows that God's power worked for the second generation of believers and indicates it should work in every generation of believers.

The Gospel sets people free from demons (Acts 8:7). Jesus took authority over demonic forces and He gave this authority to His disciples (Matt 10:1; Luke 9:1). He commanded them to "cast out demons" (Matt 10:8). When God's word is preached with power, the devils that are in people get stirred up and begin to act up. The evangelist should not be scared or bothered by demonic manifestations. He should simply take authority over them in the name of Jesus and keep preaching. People are set free when the Gospel is proclaimed.

---

[10]Some churches teach that miracles have ceased. This theological position is known as cessationism. Cessationists believe the main purpose for miracles in the lives of the Apostles was to authenticate the written word of God. They believe healing gifts were only given to the original Apostles and as the Apostles died at the end of the First Century; the gifts of healing mentioned in 1 Cor. 12:9 slowly died out and became obsolete. They believe that once the Canon of Scripture was completed, there was no longer any need for miracles. They believe the written word of God is sufficient to meet all the spiritual needs of the body of Christ. Thus, they believe that in modern times the healing gift of the evangelist has ceased. (See Richard B. Graffin, Jr. "A Cessationist View," in *Are Miraculous Gifts for Today?* ed. Wayne A. Grudem (Grand Rapids, MI: Zondervan, 1996), 42). In contrast, Pentecostal/Charismatic churches believe that miracles continue to authenticate the preaching of God's word today, and it is common for Pentecostal/Charismatic evangelists to pray for the sick. See Douglas A. Oss, "A Pentecostal/Charismatic View," in *Are Miraculous Gifts for Today?* ed. Wayne A. Grudem (Grand Rapids, MI: Zondervan, 1996), 280).

Great joy follows the evangelist (Acts 8:8).[11] When Philip evangelized, the people of Samaria celebrated because so many sick and paralyzed people were healed. They were happy because the demon-possessed were set free. They rejoiced because their sins were forgiven as they responded to the Gospel. Great joy follows the preaching of God's word.

When evangelists preach, people are baptized (Acts 8:12).[12] After evangelists lead people to Jesus, they need the help of other ministry gifts to disciple people (Acts 8:14). First, Philip the evangelist preached and multitudes were saved and healed. Then, when the church in Jerusalem heard what God was doing, they sent Peter and John to

---

[11]Throughout Luke/Acts, joy ensued when people accept the Gospel. Luke emphasizes joy as a response to good news, starting when the angels appeared to the shepherds (Luke 2:10). The gospel is accepted by the Samaritans with great joy (Acts 8:8). The Ethiopian is filled with joy after his baptism (Acts 8:39). Later in Pisidian Antioch, the Gentiles were "glad" when they believed (Acts 13:48), and the Gentiles "rejoiced" when they received a letter from the Jerusalem council (Acts 15:31).

[12]Baptism is a sign of salvation. It is not necessary for salvation, but it is a public testimony that conversion has occurred. For a discussion of the Pentecostal view of baptism see: Andrew Ray Williams, "Water Baptism in Pentecostal Perspective: A Bibliographic Evaluation," *Spiritus: ORU Journal of Theology* 4, no. 1 (2019): Article 9, (April 22, 2019). Is salvation an event or a process? The answer is "yes," salvation is both an event and a process. (For a discussion of Pentecostal soteriology see Wolfgang Vondey, "Soteriology at the Altar: Pentecostal Contributions to Salvation as Praxis," Transformation 34 (3) (n.d.): 223–38. doi:10.1177/0265378816675831.). The Samaritans heard the message, believed, and were baptized in water. Later, Peter and John laid hands on them to receive the Holy Spirit. The direction one is facing is more important than the place one is at. The worst sinner who has turned toward Jesus is better off than the legalistic Pharisee who thinks he is holy, but has secretly turned away from God because of pride.

authenticate the move of God and to disciple the new believers. After Philip completed his job as an evangelist, the job of the Apostles began. The most common question the evangelist is asked is: How do you follow up on new believers? The truth is no evangelist can do everything alone. The evangelist is not the only one involved in the process of turning a convert into a disciple. Standing beside the evangelists are the other five-fold ministry gifts: the pastor, the prophet, the teacher, and the apostle (Eph. 4:11).

When evangelists preach, sinners are attracted to the Gospel (Acts 8:9-13). The power of God is greater than any counterfeit magic. Simon the magician astonished the people of Samaria with his magic but when Philip showed up it was obvious that Simon's power paled in comparison to God's power. Simon stopped being astonishing and was astonished himself. There are many different belief systems and religions in the world today, but God's power stands supreme. Simon was a charlatan, but when he saw the miracles, he believed the Gospel and was baptized. In the same way, many people of all religious backgrounds are attracted to the Gospel today.

Evangelists should not seek personal glory (Acts 8:18-19). Simon was not interested in using the power of God to help people; he was more interested in using it to build his own prestige. In some ministry circles, evangelists are looked down upon. This is because of numerous scandals that have resulted from evangelists who have abused their position. It is time to restore integrity to the evangelistic ministry.

Evangelists are not driven by money (Acts 8:20-24). When Peter was offered money for the gift of the Holy Spirit, he was enraged.[13] The story of Peter's response to Simon serves as a reminder that the gifts of the Holy Spirit can never be sold, only received.

The real Gospel exposes false motives (Acts 8:20). Simon did not want the Holy Spirit so he could help people; he wanted Him for his own personal gain. When the Gospel is preached, false motives are unable to remain hidden for long.

Evangelists realize that some who respond to the Gospel will fall away. The Bible says that Simon believed and was baptized (Acts 8:13). This is the same language the book of Acts uses for others who were saved. Later, Peter curses him and says, "You have no part in us" (Acts 8:21).[14]

---

[13]This brings to mind the story of Elisha's servant Gehazi who tried to make money off of Naaman. In a similar manner, Martin Luther fought the sale of indulgences. Today, some evangelists have tried to merchandise the anointing instead of staying focused on leading the lost to Christ. Jesus did not die on the cross so that preachers could become wealthy.

[14]Was Simon really saved? If so, how did he lose his salvation? How do people today lose their salvation? Sometimes evangelists are criticized because not everyone who gets saved in their meetings end up attending a local church. The evangelist is often asked, "Why do some of those who get saved in your meetings fall away?" It is a shocking statistic that 380 of the 500 people who heard the last words of Jesus did not follow His command to wait for the Holy Spirit in the upper room. The fact that some might pray a prayer of salvation at a crusade and later continue to live in sin is no reason to stop praying with people for salvation.

Evangelists must go where God sends them (Acts 8:26). Philip was in the middle of leading a successful revival in Samaria when an angel of the Lord told him to head south along the desert road to Gaza. As Philip walked along the road, he fulfilled Jesus' command to "go out into the highways and hedges" (Matthew 22:9).[15]

Evangelists should be sensitive to God's voice (Acts 8:26). Philip is led, first by the angel of the Lord, and then by the Spirit. Both times, he obeys. Luke uses this to show that Philip's mission was Spirit-led and Spirit-inspired. So it should be with the evangelist today. When God speaks, it is important to listen and obey.

When evangelists obey, doors are opened to share the Gospel (Acts 8:27-29). Some people have hard hearts toward God and some are open and ready to receive. As the evangelist stays sensitive to the Spirit's leading and follows His leading, the evangelist will discover those who are ready to respond to the Gospel.

---

[15]God does not want His people to stay inside the four walls of the church. He wants His followers to take the Good News out on the roads. Many preachers today would love to minister to the surfers in Hawaii or in an upscale neighborhood in California in the midst of luxury, but God is looking for someone who is willing to go to the desert. God often sends evangelists to spiritual deserts. A hot, dry road through the middle of the desert is not the most comfortable place to be called, but it is important to go where God tells one to go. There is ministry waiting to be accomplished in the spiritual deserts of the world.

Evangelists are desperately needed (Acts 8:30-31). The Ethiopian eunuch needed someone to explain the Scriptures.[16] As seen in a few verses previously in Acts 8:5, when evangelists preach, every Scripture leads to Jesus (Acts 8:32-35). Jesus is the central point of the Bible. No matter where one starts reading in the Bible, the scripture leads to Jesus. The difference between a real evangelist and another preacher who just uses the title is how much they talk about Jesus. Preachers talk about many different subjects these days. Some preach on prosperity; others on holiness; still others on how to be successful in business. Often, preachers sound like they are reading excerpts from Reader's Digest more than they sound like they are preaching the real Gospel. But for the successful evangelist, it does not matter where he begins, he always ends with Jesus. For the genuine evangelist it does not matter what subject he's talking about or where he begins to read in the Bible, ultimately, his or her sermon will be about Jesus Christ. The evangelist may begin by talking about how to have a happy, fulfilling marriage. But by the end of the message, the true evangelist will come to the place where he invites people to give their lives to Jesus so they can have a successful marriage. The evangelist may talk about finding peace in desperate times, but ultimately his sermon will lead back to Jesus, the Prince of Peace.

---

[16]Today there are many people who have questions about God and the meaning of life. Who will answer these questions? The need is urgent. If the evangelist does not go, then who will tell them about Jesus? How can they understand unless someone explains? As Paul writes, "For whoever calls on the name of the Lord shall be saved. How then shall they call on Him in whom they have not believed? And how shall they believe in Him of whom they have not heard? And how shall they hear without a preacher? And how shall they preach unless they are sent? As it is written: How beautiful are the feet of those who preach the gospel of peace, Who bring glad tidings of good things!" (Rom 10:13-15).

When Jesus is preached, people get saved! (Acts 8:35-37). When the Ethiopian heard the Good News he asked, "Is there anything to prevent me from being baptized?"[17] When the evangelist preaches the Gospel, he or she can expect people to desire to come to God.

The Gospel brings great joy! (Acts 8:39). In Samaria, the whole city was filled with joy after Philip preached. The Ethiopian is also filled with joy after being baptized. The Gospel truly is good news.

When a person gets saved, he or she often becomes a witness to others about Jesus. After being baptized, the Ethiopian continued his trip home. One can imagine him eagerly sharing the good news about Jesus with everyone in his country. As the treasurer in charge of the kingdom's wealth he was a man of considerable influence. Today, the Christians in Ethiopia trace their spiritual heritage back to this spiritual patriarch. Even when ministering to one person, the evangelist has the potential to impact an entire community or nation.

---

[17] The Ethiopian eunuch had come from far away to worship the Lord but when he arrived at the temple, he was not allowed to enter because he was a foreigner and a eunuch (Deut 23:1-2). The man must have been quite disappointed. He had traveled a long distance and spent a great deal of money to come to Jerusalem only to be turned away. He still desires to worship God, so he purchases a scroll of the prophet Isaiah at great expense. As the Ethiopian rides home, he reads from Isaiah 53, the great Messianic prophecy about Jesus dying on the cross, but does not understand what he is reading. God sends Philip the Evangelist to explain the passage to the man. Starting at that very place, Philip tells him the good news about Jesus. It is possible that they continued reading until they came to Isaiah 56:3-7 which promises a day will come when even eunuchs and foreigners will be able to worship God. When Philip informed the Ethiopian that the coming of Jesus Christ inaugurated a new day when there is a place for eunuchs and foreigners, the Ethiopian asks, "Is there any reason why I should not be baptized?" Philip replies, "No!" Immediately, the Ethiopian gives an order for the chariot to be stopped and Philip baptizes him in water (Acts 8:38).

The Spirit sends evangelists wherever they are most needed (Acts 8:39). Evangelists often travel from place to place (Acts 8:40).[18] Philip, the only person in the New Testament who is specifically called an evangelist, was an itinerant preacher, going from place to place sharing the good news. Today, evangelists often travel in a similar manner. Philip's example sets a biblical precedent for today's evangelist.

Evangelists should have godly families, above reproach (Acts 21:8-9).[19] Acts 8 contains many examples for today's evangelist to learn from. Philip the Evangelist was involved in both mass evangelism and one-on-one evangelism. Just as Philip took the Gospel to the end of his world, the evangelist today should be ready to take the Gospel to the "ends of the earth." Just as the people of Samaria and the Ethiopian eunuch needed

---

[18]Philip begins his ministry in Jerusalem. When persecution breaks out, he moves to Samaria and preaches there. In obedience to the angel of the Lord, he ministers on the desert road. After being caught away by the Spirit, he is found at Azotus and he preaches in all the cities (Acts 8:40) until he finally arrives at Caesarea and settles down there (Acts 8:40, 21:8). Evangelists are the shock troops of the kingdom. Their function is similar to the Navy Seals or Army paratroopers, who are the first to advance into enemy territory to prepare the way for the main battle group. The evangelist moves in, does his or her job, and then moves on to his or her next assignment. In colloquial terms, they "blow in, blow up, and blow out."

[19]One of the great challenges for evangelists today is in the familial area. The life of an evangelist is often difficult because of extensive traveling and a busy schedule. Paul asks in 1 Timothy 3:5, "If anyone does not know how to manage his own family, how can he take care of God's church?" Unfortunately, the author of this project knows of several evangelists whose ministries have been damaged because of divorce and rebellious children. It is significant that the Bible tells us that Philip had four virgin daughters who all prophesied. Philip raised his daughters to be holy and pure. Each of the four daughters kept her virginity in the midst of a city full of immorality and wickedness. The daughters were also involved in ministry with Philip. His daughters were a wonderful testimony to Philip's commitment to be a godly father. Philip's family provides a picture of what an evangelist's family life should model. First, the evangelist should be faithful to his wife. Second, the evangelist's children should live godly lives. Third, the evangelist's children should also be involved in the ministry.

Jesus, many people today need Jesus. The modern evangelist who is preaching in Brazil would do well to imitate Philip's ministry as it is recorded in Acts 8.

Historical Narrative

Mass evangelism is not a new innovation. A study of church history suggests that mass evangelism has been an important component of many different moves of God. In this next section, the historical methods of evangelism throughout church history will be examined with a particular focus on how mass evangelism has been conducted over the centuries. These historical precedents provide a justification for conducting a mass evangelism event in the present day.

Early Mass Evangelism

The use of mass evangelism can be traced back to the earliest days of the church. The first Christians faced an almost insurmountable evangelistic problem. A pagan and sinful culture surrounded them on all sides. The sophisticated philosophers of Rome were not interested in a Jewish man named Jesus who was executed as a common criminal, nor did they care to hear the claims of a ragtag group of religious fanatics who were an offshoot from the Jewish religion. Yet, in many ways the disciples began to evangelize at the perfect time in history for three reasons. First, Greek was the *lingua franca*, the common language that was used everywhere for commerce and education.[20] Because of this common language, the early evangelists were able to preach in Greek everywhere

---

[20]Michael Green, *Evangelism in the Early Church* (Grand Rapids, MI: Eerdmans, 2003), 33.

they went. Second, the Romans imposed peace, *Pax Romana*, upon the entire Empire so it was safe to travel. Third, the Romans built roads throughout the empire so it was easy to travel. It was in this atmosphere that the disciples began to proclaim the Gospel. Many different methods of evangelism were used by the early church and one of these methods was mass evangelism.

The second generation of the church was also evangelistic and they practiced mass evangelism as the opportunity presented itself. Irenaeus (AD 130-200) was a bishop in Lyons, located in what is now France. He was known for preaching in the market place in the city of Lugdunum and in the surrounding towns and villages.[21] Cyprian (AD 200-258), the Bishop of Carthage, preached in the marketplace during a time of persecution at the risk of being arrested by the authorities.[22]

Eusebius reports on correspondence between Jesus and Abgar of Edessa. The historic Jesus did not really write the letters, but the document is an important second-century AD record of the content of the disciple's preaching. In the letters, Jesus promises to send a disciple to Edessa and he sends Thaddaeus who heals Abgar of a disease and asks for the opportunity to preach to a crowd of local citizens. Thaddaeus says,

> Since I have been sent to proclaim the word publically . . . tomorrow assemble for me all thy citizens, and I will preach the word of God, concerning the coming of Jesus, how he was born; and concerning his mission, for what purpose he was sent by the Father; and concerning the power of his works . . . and how he humbled himself, and died and debased his divinity, and was crucified, and descended into

---

[21]Green, 304.

[22]Green, 304.

Hades, and burst the bars which from eternity had not been broken, and raised from the dead, for he descended alone, but rose with many, and thus ascended to his Father."[23]

Eusebius wrote about the early second century AD,

> Then starting out upon long journeys they performed the office of evangelists, being filled with the desire to preach Christ to those who had not yet heard the word of faith, and to deliver to them the divine Gospels. And when they had laid the foundations of the faith in foreign places, they appointed others as pastors, and entrusted them with the nurture of those that had recently been brought in, while they themselves went on again to other countries, with the grace and the co-operation of God. For a great many wonderful works were done through them by the power of the divine Spirit, so that at the first hearing whole multitudes of men eagerly embraced the religion of the Creator of the universe.[24]

Notice that these evangelists were traveling from place to place preaching the Gospel to crowds of people; they gave away copies of the Bible, and they saw mass conversions.

In a fictitious, but philosophical, narrative, *Recognitions of Clement,* there is a story about a believer named Barnabas who preached on the streets in Rome. He was verbally attacked by educated philosophers with "grappling hooks of syllogisms." He responds to them,

> We have it in charge to declare to you the words and the wondrous works of Him who hath sent us, and to confirm the truth of what we speak, not by artfully devised arguments, but by witnesses produced from amongst yourselves. For I recognize many standing in the midst of you whom I remember to have heard along with us the things which we have heard, and to have seen what we have seen. But be it in your option to receive or to spurn the tidings which we bring to you. For we cannot keep back what we know to be for your advantage, because, if we be silent, woe is to us; but to you, if you receive not what we speak, destruction.[25]

---

[23]Eusebius, *The Church History of Eusebius*, 1:13, 19, (*NPNF* 1.102).

[24]Eusebius, *The Church History of Eusebius*, 3:37, 2-4 (*NPNF* 3:169).

[25]Clement, *Recognitions of Clement (ANF* 8:79*).*

Notice his appeal to witnesses who have been touched by the power of God. Celsus, an outspoken critic of Christianity made this accusation about Christians in AD 177:

> Their aim is to convince only worthless and contemptible people, idiots, slaves, poor women, and children. They behave like mountebanks and beggars; they would not dare to address an audience of intelligent men . . . but if they see a group of young people or slaves or rough folk, there they push themselves in and seek to win the admiration of the crowd . . . [26]

This criticism shows that the early Christians were known for preaching to crowds of people.

Another early church father, Origen (AD 184-253), gave a report about the preaching habits of early believers: "Christians do not neglect, as far as in them lies, to take measures to disseminate their doctrine throughout the whole world. Some of them, accordingly, have made it their business to itinerate not only through cities, but even villages and country houses, that they might make converts to God."[27]

One person who was impacted by Origen's ministry was Gregory Thaumaturgos (AD 210-260), who was born into a pagan family in Neocarsarea, located in modern Turkey. His parents sent him and his brother to school in Caesarea, where he studied under Origen, who converted them to Christianity. He returned home and became the leader of a church with seventeen members. He preached until his city was converted and only

---

[26] Origen, *Against Celsus* 3:49-55 (*ANF* 4:484-86).

[27] Origen, *Against Celsus* 3.9 (*ANF*: 4:468).

seventeen pagans remained. His name Thaumaturgos means "worker of miracles,"[28] so apparently, signs and wonders were common in his ministry.

In part because of mass evangelism, Christianity achieved spectacular growth during the three hundred years after Christ's resurrection. In three centuries, it grew geographically from Palestine to cover the entire Roman Empire. When the Christians endured persecution at the hands of the Romans, the sands of the coliseum became their pulpit as they were martyred for their faith.[29] One Christian who continued to preach as he was martyred was Polycarp (AD 69-156), the Bishop of Smyrna.[30]

Constantine was the first Roman emperor to be converted to Christianity. He issued the Edict of Milan in AD 313 that made Christianity the official religion of the Empire. Once Christianity became the favored religion in the empire, the nature of conversion changed greatly. Before Constantine, great sacrifice was required to become a Christian; after Constantine, becoming a Christian was a matter of convenience.[31]

---

[28]John M. Terry, *Evangelism: A Concise History* (Nashville, TN: Broadman & Holman Publisher, 1994), 35.

[29]Any mass evangelism done in the early days of the church was potentially dangerous. During his ministry, Paul is frequently arrested, beaten, or stoned when he preaches to the masses (See 2 Cor 11:23-27).

[30]*The Encyclical Epistle of the Church at Smyrna Concerning the Martyrdom of the Holy Polycarp* (ANF 1:39-44).

[31]Terry, 39.

The Post-Nicaean church (post AD 325) continued to advance across the Roman Empire primarily through the efforts of evangelistic bishops.[32] During the Middle Ages, the primary groups engaged in evangelism were the monastics. Some monks withdrew from society and lived solitary lived in the wilderness, but other monks were known for preaching the Gospel.[33] Francis of Assisi (1182-1226) was the son of a rich cloth merchant who left his rich lifestyle and devoted himself to helping the poor. He traveled from village to village feeding the poor, preaching the Gospel, and repairing church buildings. He attracted a group of disciples and Francis started a new order of friars. Francis sent his followers out two-by-two to preach the Gospel. Francis gave his monks strict rules to live by. They pledged to be obedient, to live in poverty, and to live in chastity. They dressed in rough cloth, wore no shoes, and preached a simple Gospel to the

---

[32]Ulfilas (AD 311-383), whose name means "little wolf," was a missionary to the Goths. Martin of Tours (AD 316-397) preached in the villages of Touraine, France, and was well-known as a miracle worker. The preaching of Ambrose of Milan (AD 340-397) impacted Augustine of Hippo (AD 387). John Chrysostom (AD 347-407) was such a great preacher that his name means "golden-mouthed." St. Patrick (late fifth century AD 461) went from village to village in Ireland preaching the Gospel and baptizing new believers. See Terry, 40.

[33]One evangelist monk was Columba (AD 521-597) who started a monastery with twelve monks on the Island of Iona near Scotland, and from there, evangelized the Picts in northern Scotland. Augustine of Canterbury (early sixth century to AD 604) was sent as a missionary to Britain by Pope Gregory the Great (Terry, 48). Another monk who became a famous evangelist was Boniface (AD 680-754), who chopped down a sacred oak tree dedicated to Thor and built a chapel from the wood. He went on to preach the Gospel throughout Bavaria and Thuringia. Everywhere he went, he tore down heathen shrines and built churches. Eventually, as an old man, he was martyred by a group of pagans; but it is estimated that he baptized over one hundred thousand Germans (Terry 50). Bernard of Clairvau (1091-1165) was a powerful preacher during the Middle Ages who preached justification of faith and forgiveness of sins. See Robert G. Tuttle, *The Story of Evangelism*, (Nashville, TN: Abingdon, 2006), 203.

people. By 1264, there were around two hundred thousand Franciscans who lived in eight thousand cloisters.[34] One famous Franciscan was Berthold von Regensburg (d. 1272). He regularly preached to large crowds of people because the churches were too small to hold all the people who came to hear him preach. His message was a call to repentance.[35]

During the Middle Ages, the churches held services in Latin, but in the years before the Reformation, there arose preachers who preached in the language of the people.[36] The task of the mass evangelist during the Middle Ages was fraught with danger because he risked martyrdom when he confronted the ecclesial and governmental authorities of his day. Yet, it was the preaching of these men who called the masses to repentance in their own languages that showed the desperate need for a Reformation in the church.

---

[34]Paulus Scharpff, *History of Evangelism*, trans. Helga Bender Henry (Grand Rapids, MI: Eerdmans, 1966), 6.

[35]Scharpff, 7.

[36]Peter Waldo (1140-1205) ministered in Southern France and formed a group called "the Poor Men of Lyons." He sent them out two-by-two to preach repentance on the streets, in houses, and in caves (see Terry, 59). Johann Tauler (1300-1361) was known for weeping while preaching. He led many people to Christ along the Rhine River and his sermons influenced Martin Luther. John Wycliffe (1329-1384), a professor of theology at Oxford University, translated the Bible from Latin into English so that the common people could read the Scripture. He sent out a group of "Poor Priests" who functioned as traveling evangelists (see Scharpff, 7). John Hus (1369-1415) ministered in the city of Prague. Large crowds came to hear him preach; but he was excommunicated from the Catholic Church in 1410, and eventually was burned at the stake for his teaching. Girolamo Savonarola (1452-1498) was a Catholic evangelist in Florence, Italy, who called large crowds of people to repentance (see Scharpff, 9).

The Reformation's Influence on Mass Evangelism

The focus of the Reformation was not mass evangelism, but reformation of the existing church. However, the teachings of Luther and Calvin laid the foundation for the evangelical church to focus on mass evangelism in later centuries. Thus, their theological contribution is worth looking at. Martin Luther's (1483-1546) doctrine of "justification by faith" became the foundational truth preached by the evangelist. On occasion, he did minister to large crowds. For example, in Zwickau, he preached to an estimated twenty thousand people from an upstairs window.[37]

John Calvin (1509-1564) taught that, "the work of evangelism is God's work, not ours, but God will use us as his instruments."[38] Calvin sent out eighty-eight evangelists from Geneva to France between 1555 and 1562. Because of their preaching, the French Calvinists (known as the Huguenots) grew to number over one hundred thousand followers by 1559.[39] In a letter to a group of Reformers suffering persecution in France, Calvin wrote, "Let every one strive to attract and win over to Jesus Christ those whom he can."[40] Calvin turned Geneva into a model Christian city. It served as a refuge for many Protestants fleeing persecution. When they returned to their homes, they carried Calvin's

---

[37]Scharpff, 11.

[38]Joel R. Beeke, "Calvin's Evangelism," *Mid-America Journal of Theology* 15, (2004): 69, *ATLA Religion Database with ATLASerials*, EBSCOhost (6 November 2017).

[39]Terry, 79.

[40]Bonnet, *Letters of Calvin,* 3:134, quoted in Joel R. Berke, 2004. "Calvin's Evangelism." *Mid-America Journal of Theology* 15 (2004): 73, *ATLA Religion Database with ATLASerials*, EBSCOhost (6 November 2017).

teachings with them. One example is John Knox (1514-1572), who became a fiery reformer in Scotland. Under Nikolaus von Zinzendorf (1700-1760), the Moravians developed a zeal for evangelism and they sent out over two hundred missionaries to Africa, North America, and around Europe.[41]

The three biggest theological innovations of the Reformation were Luther's emphasis on justification by faith, the restoration of the primacy of Scripture and the teaching on the "priesthood of every believer."[42] These revelations both equip and empower every Christian to study Scripture for oneself and to do evangelism. Jesus commanded every believer to share the Gospel, but under the Roman Catholic Church, there developed a separation between the clergy and laity. However, the Reformation restored the laity to their rightful place of ministry. It took time for this seed to bear fruit, but the teaching of Luther and Calvin became the foundation for the edifice that Wesley and Whitefield would eventually build. It is to their lives that the modern-day evangelist owes the deepest debt.

Mass Evangelism in the 1700s-1800s

John Wesley

The modern era of mass-evangelism began on March 29, 1739. On that day, George Whitefield invited his friend and mentor from the Holiness Club, John Wesley, to preach with him out in the open fields of England. Wesley records the day in his journal, "I

---

[41]"Nokolaus von Zinzendorf," *Christianity Today*, n.d., n.p., http://www. christianity today. com/history/people/denominationalfounders/nikolaus-von-zinzendorf.html. (19 March 2018).

[42]Terry, 76-77.

could scarcely reconcile myself at first to this strange way of preaching in the fields, of which [Whitefield] set me an example on Sunday; I had been all my life (till very lately) so tenacious of every point relating to decency and order that I should have thought the saving of souls almost a sin if it had not been done in a church."[43] When some churches denied Wesley the opportunity to speak, he took the message outside the church into the fields and thousands heard the Gospel message. From that time on, Wesley preached in the open more than he preached indoors. Basil Miller reports, "In the last five months of 1739, he preached five hundred times, and only five of these sermons were delivered in a church."[44] On August 22, 1773, Wesley preached to a crowd at Gwenap Pit in Cornwall which he estimated to be about 32,000 people.[45] Wesley was often criticized for his field preaching by clergy. He wrote in defense of the practice,

> I wonder at those who still talk so loud of the indecency of field-preaching. The highest indecency is in St. Paul's Church, when a considerable part of the congregation are asleep, or talking, or looking about, not minding a word the preacher says. On the other hand, there is the highest decency in a churchyard or field, when the whole congregation behave and look as if they saw the Judge of all and heard Him speaking from heaven.[46]

---

[43] John Wesley, "Wesley Begins Field-Preaching," *Journal of John Wesley*, vol. 15 (March 1739), n.p., *Christian Classics Ethereal Library*, https://www.ccel.org/ccel/wesley/ journal.vi.iii.i.html (18 March 2018).

[44] Basil Miller, *Ten Famous Evangelists* (Grand Rapids, MI: Zondervan, 1949), 19.

[45] Bennett, David. *The Altar Call: Its Origins and Present Usage* (Lanham, MD: University Press of America, 2000), 2.

[46] Wesley,.vi.vii.xv.

Wesley continued to preach outdoors until his death. Wesley is estimated to have traveled over four thousand miles every year. The distance he rode on horseback is said to equal ten trips around the globe. He often preached twenty sermons every week, over forty thousand sermons in his lifetime. Wesley also appointed other preachers to preach the Gospel. By the time he died, the Methodist church claimed 135,000 members and 541 itinerant preachers.[47] His fervent passion for preaching God's Word and his organizational skills are the reason the Methodist church continues to this day.

Wesley did not give altar calls in the modern sense. On occasion, he would hold post-service meetings for those who were concerned about the condition of their souls. He also invited those who were interested in joining the Methodist society to tell him about it the next morning.[48] People often responded to his messages with a deep awareness of sin and a desire to be saved. Wesley's response was to encourage them to spend time in prayer until they found salvation.[49]

George Whitfield

Like Wesley, George Whitefield (1714-1770) was also a pioneer of mass evangelism. He often preached in the open air to as many as twenty thousand people at a time and he called himself, "The Gospel Rover." He preached energetically, without

---

[47] H. K. Carroll, *A Religious Encyclopedia, or, Dictionary of Biblical, Historical, Doctrinal, and Practical Theology,* vol. 3, ed. Philip Schaff (Edinburgh, T. & T. Clark, 1884), 2494

[48] Bennett, 4.

[49] Bennett, 9.

notes, and his voice was clear and powerful. He carefully explained Gospel concepts to those with no religious background. In 1739, Whitefield preached at Kingswood, a town next to a coal mine. As the coal miners left work, they stopped to listen to him. As he preached, white streaks appeared on the miner's cheeks as tears poured from their eyes.[50]

Whitefield crossed the ocean between Great Britain and America thirteen times, and he became one of the best-known preachers on both sides of the Atlantic. In his lifetime, he preached over eighteen thousand times to an estimated ten million people. It is believed that more than ten percent of New England's population got saved in Whitefield's meetings. Over fifty thousand people became members of churches in New England churches because of his preaching.[51]

Whitefield preached before the sound system was invented, but his strong voice could still be heard by tens of thousands of people. Benjamin Franklin (American revolutionary, scientist, and inventor), did an experiment to discover how many people could hear Whitefield preach and found that over thirty thousand were able to hear the preacher.[52]

---

[50]Joseph Belcher, *George Whitefield: A Biography with Special Reference to his Labors in America* (New York: American Tract Society, 1857,) 73-74.

[51]Cassidy, 203.

[52]"Benjamin Franklin on Rev. George Whitefield," *National Humanities Center*, 1739: n.p., http://nationalhumanitiescenter.org/pds/becomingamer /ideas/text2/ franklinwhitefield.pdf (18 March 2018).

Whitefield often preached on the New Birth, the origin of sin and God's plan for dealing with it, and on the imitation of Christ's righteousness to repentant sinners.[53] Instead of giving altar calls, Whitefield "urged those who were under conviction to go home, fall on their knees before God and plead with Him to give them the grace of salvation."[54]

Jonathan Edwards

Another significant figure in the history of American evangelism is Jonathan Edwards. In America, the young Whitefield met Jonathan Edwards (1703-1758), who sparked the First Great Awakening. Edward's sermons were long and dry. He spoke in a low serious voice without any hand gestures or sudden movement of his body. In the early years of his ministry, he often read directly from a full manuscript. When he preached about hell, he was graphic in his depictions of the fire and horror that waited for the sinner there. Many of his listeners responded by crying out in repentance. Edwards believed it is important to preach the law of God in order to awaken sinners before presenting the Gospel. Edward's classic fire and brimstone sermon is titled, "Sinners in

---

[53]Bennett, 13.

[54]J. I. Packer, in a paper on Whitfield presented to the Whitefield Fraternal, May 1994, at the College Church in Wheaton; quoted by William A. Giovannetti, "A Strategy for Linking Crusade Evangelism with Church Planting," (DMIN proj., Fuller Theological Seminary, 1996), 46.

the Hands of an Angry God." He delivered the sermon for the first time on July 8, 1741, in Enfield, Connecticut.[55]

For most of Edward's ministry, he preached to his congregation of about six hundred in North Hampton. However, during the height of the First Great Awakening, Edwards preached outside, mainly because the churches were not big enough to contain the crowds that came to hear him speak. Edwards did not specifically give an altar call or pray with sinners for salvation, but at the end of his sermon he did call people to come to Christ and asked them to meet him privately to receive spiritual counsel.[56]

Francis Asbury

As the American frontier expanded, much evangelism was done by "circuit riders" who would ride from town to town preaching the Gospel. The most famous of these circuit riders was Francis Asbury. Wesley sent Francis Asbury (1745-1816) to America to preach the Gospel. He became the first Methodist bishop in America and a hard working evangelist who remained a bachelor his whole life. When Asbury arrived in America as a young man in October 1771, the population was widely scattered and mostly rural. So, Asbury jumped on a horse and became a circuit rider, a clergyman who traveled on horseback from church to church. Because of his tireless effort, he can be

---

[55]Jonathan Edwards, *Sinners in the Hands of an Angry God* (Boston, S. Kneeland and T. Green, 1741), 1.

[56]R. Allen Street, *The Effective Invitation* (Grand Rapids, MI: Kregel, 2004), 89.

credited with almost singlehandedly establishing the Methodist church on American soil.[57]

Asbury evangelized the frontier. On the American frontier, no formal churches had been built yet. So, Asbury preached from improvised pulpits in people's homes, in the woods, in fields, on river banks, in stables, in courthouses, in tobacco sheds, and in public squares, wherever he could gather a crowd that would listen to him. He preached at times to crowds of 1,000,[58] 1,200[59], 1,600,[60] 3,000[61], and up to 6,000.[62] As Asbury traveled, he appointed other men to be circuit riders. They followed his example in traveling from place to place to share the Gospel. He rode an average of six thousand miles every year. During his forty-five years of ministry in the United States, it is estimated that Asbury traveled by horseback and carriage over three hundred thousand miles and delivered around 16,500 sermons.

Bennet states that Asbury invited people who desired to get saved to come forward to a mourner's bench or seat that was left open in front of the pulpit. Asbury

---

[57]Darius L. Salter, *America's Bishop: The Life of Francis Asbury* (Nappanee, IN: Francis Asbury Press, 2003), 9.

[58]Francis Asbury, *The Journal of Francis Asbury*, vol. 2 (New York, NY: Methodist Episcopal Church, 1821), 16, 33, 192, 232, 388, 396. https://archive.org/details/journalrevfranc03asbugoog.

[59]Asbury, 113.

[60]Asbury, 260.

[61]Asbury, 13.

[62]Asbury, 355.

encouraged his preachers to always leave at least one seat open in front of the pulpit for mourners.[63] Terry concludes that Asbury's ministry thrived in part because of his theology. The Presbyterian church taught that grace is limited to the elect and the concept of predestination, but the Methodists preached that God's grace is available to everyone and that every individual has free will to either accept salvation or to reject it.[64] When Asbury arrived in America, there were about six hundred Methodists in the country. By the time he died, the Methodist faith had spread all over the new country and claimed over 214,000 members.

The Cane Ridge Revival

Another famous event in American history that could be classified as "mass evangelism" was the Cane Ridge Revival. The Cane Ridge Revival occurred August 6-13, 1801, at Cane Ridge, Kentucky. It attracted as many as twenty-five thousand people, over ten percent of the population of the state of Kentucky. It was characterized by lively preaching and it invoked strong emotions in many people. One of the key organizers was Barton Stone, but dozens of preachers participated, including Presbyterians, Baptists, and Methodists. Stone was a Presbyterian preacher who was invited to Kentucky by the

---

[63]Bennett, 29.

[64]Terry, 128.

frontiersman, Daniel Boone.[65] Peter Cartright, a Methodist preacher, wrote that at the Cain Ridge Camp Meeting

> . . . the mighty power of God was displayed in a very extraordinary manner; many were moved to tears, and bitter and loud crying for mercy. The meeting was protracted for weeks. Ministers of almost all denominations flocked in from far and near. The meeting was kept up by night and day. Thousands heard of the mighty work, and came on foot, on horseback, in carriages and wagons. It was supposed that there were in attendance at times during the meeting from twenty to twenty-five thousand people. Hundreds fell prostrate under the power of God, as men slain in battle. Stands were erected in the woods from which preachers of different churches proclaimed repentance toward God and faith in our Lord Jesus Christ, and it was supposed by eye and ear witnesses, that between one and two thousand souls were happily and powerfully converted by God during the meeting. It was not unusual for one, two, three, and four to seven preachers to be addressing the listening thousands at the same time from the different stands erected for the purpose. The heavenly fire spread in almost every direction.[66]

The move of God at Cane Ridge sparked other camp meetings and revivals along the American frontier. Farmers and frontiersmen would load the whole family in a horse drawn wagon and come from near and far for gatherings that lasted for a week or more. Camp meetings became a common occurrence on the American frontier. They provided an opportunity for the rough and tumble, largely uneducated, frontiersmen and their families to gather for a time of fellowship and religious exhortation.[67]

At the camp meetings, an enclosed altar area was set aside for seekers to examine their lives and to repent. These altar areas often contained a few rough wooden benches

---

[65]Nathan Boehm, "Daniel Boone Associated with Revival," *Word Nuggets*, 23 April 2010, n.p., https://wordnuggets.wordpress.com/2010/04/23/daniel-boone-associated-with-revival/ (18 March 2018).

[66]Peter Cartwright, *Autobiography of Peter Cartwright* (Nashville, TN: Abingdon, 1956), 33-34.

[67]Terry, 137.

where "the mourners" could cry out to God. The preachers called people to come forward to the altar to pray. There they were greeted by counselors who prayed with them, often at great length, until they had an encounter with God, which was often marked by tears and deep groans.[68]

Many people on the American frontier got saved at camp meetings. Francis Asbury noted that camp meetings were like "fishing with a large net."[69] Peter Cartwright was perhaps one of the first to ask people to raise their hands to respond to Christ. At one meeting around 1822, he asked those who did not believe in Christ to raise their hands. No one did. Then he asked those who "expected to get to get to heaven through [Christ's] merits" to raise their hands. Thousands of people raised their hands and over two hundred "professed religion" and 170 joined the Methodist church.[70]

Charles Finney

Further innovations that have influenced the modern day evangelist, particularly in the development of the altar call, come from the ministry of Charles Finney. The second Great Awakening in American history was sparked by Charles Grandison Finney (1792-1875), who was trained as a lawyer. In the fall of 1821, he was converted at the

---

[68]Jason Cherry, *The Culture of Conversionism and the History of the Altar Call* (Athens, AL: JEC, 2016), 52-53.

[69]Francis Asubury, *Journal of Francis Asbury*, vol. 3 (1821), 251.

[70]Peter Cartwright, *The Autobiography of Peter Cartwright: The Backwoods Preacher* (Cincinnati: L. Swormstedt & A. Poe, 1859), 23-24.

age of 29.[71] On that day, he decided he need to settle the question of his salvation so he walked into the woods near his home in Adams, New York. He promised himself, "I will accept it today, or I will die in the attempt."[72] He had an encounter with God and he experienced a strong emotion. Describing that day, he wrote, "No words can describe the wonderful joy that was shed abroad in my heart. I wept aloud with joy and love. The waves came over me and over me, one after another, until I cried out, 'I shall die if these waves continue to pass over me. Lord, I cannot bear any more.'" The next morning, Finney was scheduled to argue a case for a client, but he told the man, "I have a retainer from the Lord Jesus Christ to plead his cause and I cannot plead yours."[73]

Finney developed a variety of "New Measures" for promoting revivals that were both effective and controversial. Many of his innovations are commonly used by mass evangelists today. Finney targeted the urban cities of America; he required the local churches to work together, he organized prayer groups in advance of the revival, he advertised by using handbills and newspapers; he trained counselors to pray with those who came forward to the anxious bench; he sent out teams door-to-door to invite people to the revival; and he used professional musicians.[74]

Finney called sinners forward to the "anxious seat" or "anxious bench." This was a bench at the front of the church where those who were thinking about becoming

---

[71]Charles Finney, *Memoirs* (New York: Fleming H. Revell, 1876), 20.

[72]Finney, *Memoirs,* 14.

[73]Finney, *Memoirs,* 24.

[74]Terry, 145-146.

Christians could sit and receive prayer. Believers gathered around the sinners and prayed with them as they cried out for salvation. Finney did not invent the "anxious seat," but he did use it extensively in his ministry. Finney witnessed more than five hundred thousand people get saved under his ministry. In 1832, the Presbyterian churches alone recorded around thirty-four thousand people who joined their ranks after confessing their faith in one of Finney's meetings.[75] Finney's book on revival became a blueprint for other evangelists to follow.

D. L. Moody

The merging of business methods with the practice of evangelism is due to the organizational expertise of D. L. Moody. Dwight Lyman Moody (1837-1899), known as D. L. Moody, became the most famous evangelist of the late nineteenth century. He was well-known in Chicago for his work among poor youth and the YMCA. He was launched to national fame when he visited Great Britain for a preaching tour from 1873 to 1875. The news of his revival meetings in England, along with his soloist Ira Sanky, created great excitement in America's newspapers. Soon, the two of them received invitations to hold large city-wide evangelistic campaigns across America. For twenty-five years, he traveled all over the United States holding campaigns and inviting people to follow Jesus. At one event in Brooklyn, he preached to twenty thousand people at a time and they only admitted non-church members.

Moody was excellent at illustrating biblical truths with simple and interesting stories. He was not well educated (he only finished the fifth grade), but he preached the

---

[75]Cassidy, 203.

Gospel message with a simplicity that the common man found compelling. He was asked why he told so many stories and he explained, "I use these stories [to] touch the heart and while it is soft, send right in the arrow of truth."[76]

Moody was a businessman and he turned evangelism into a business, not for the sake of money, but for the sake of souls. He applied the principles of big business to his evangelistic campaigns with great success. First, he focused on large cities. Moody said, "Water runs downhill and the highest hills in America are the great cities. If we can stir them we shall stir the whole country."[77] Second, his campaigns were highly organized. Local church and business leaders were organized into committees to prepare publicity, prayer, finances, music, and counseling for Moody's campaigns.[78] A large temporary "tabernacle" was often built to hold the crowds, and three meetings were held each day of the campaign, except for Saturday. Third, Moody used music effectively to attract people to the meetings. His musical sidekick was Ira Sankey, who traveled with him for many years. Sometimes, the meetings were advertised with the tagline, "Mr. Moody will preach the Gospel and Mr. Sankey will sing the Gospel."[79]

On Sunday, October 8, 1871, Moody was preaching to a large crowd in Chicago. His theme was from Matthew 27:22, "What shall I do then with Jesus which is called

---

[76]Lyle W. Dorsett, *A Passion for Souls: The Life of D. L. Moody* (Chicago, IL: Moody, 1997), 185.

[77]D. L. Moody quote from a display at the Billy Graham Library, Wheaton, IL. (20 February 2015).

[78]Terry, 153.

[79]Terry, 154.

Christ?" When he finished his sermon, he told the people, "I wish you would take this text home with you and turn it over in your minds during the week, and next Sabbath we will come to Calvary and the Cross, and we will decide what to do with Jesus of Nazareth." As Sankey rose to lead the congregation in a hymn, fire bells interrupted the service. It was the beginning of the Great Chicago Fire that destroyed eighteen thousand buildings and left one hundred thousand people homeless.[80] That night, over a thousand people were killed in the fire, including some people who had been in Moody's service. For the rest of his life, Moody remembered that event and it became the motivation for the altar calls he gave in every service. Moody wrote, "I want to tell you of one lesson that I learned that night which I have never forgotten, and that is, when I preach, to press Christ upon the people then and there and try to bring them to a decision on the spot. I would rather have that right hand cut off than to give an audience a week now to decide what to do with Jesus."[81]

Finney called people forward to sit in the "anxious bench" at the front of the auditorium, but Moody set up "inquirer's rooms" to the side of the auditorium.[82] He asked those who were interested in salvation to go into the inquirer's room where counselors were prepared to pray with them. Moody used "decision cards" in the later years of his

---

[80]Dorsett, 151.

[81]Stephen Flick, "D. L. Moody's Lost Opportunity," n.d, n.p., https://christianheritagefellowship.com/d-l-moodys-lost-opportunity/ (18 March 2018).

[82]William Mcloughlin Jr., *Modern Revivalism: Charles Grandison Finney to Billy Graham* (Eugene, OR: Wipf & Stock, 2005), 244.

ministry. Before the service, the cards were given to the workers who were instructed to capture the names and addresses of the inquirers.

During his forty years of ministry, Moody led over a million people to Jesus, founded three Christian schools, launched a Christian publishing business, and inspired thousands of preachers to be soul winners. He left behind Moody Bible Institute and Moody Church in Chicago, Illinois. After Moody's death, Reuben Archer Torrey (1856-1928) took over his ministry and continued to hold large campaigns in the United States and in other parts of the world, including Australia.[83]

Mass Evangelism in the Twentieth Century

Billy Sunday

The next significant mass evangelist was Billy Sunday (1862-1935), a famous baseball player who became a preacher. In 1886, he was walking down the street in Chicago when he saw a wagon full of woman singing. Someone invited him to a revival meeting, and that night he was born again.

Sunday often built large wooden tabernacles for his meetings, and his team recruited an army of volunteers to help plan and publicize his events. His events often lasted six to ten weeks and cost between $30,000-$200,000.[84] Sunday was like a preaching machine. Photographs of him preaching show him with his jacket off, his tie

---

[83] Adam Wade Greenway, *"The Integration of Apologetics and Evangelism in the Ministry of Ruben Archer Torrey,"* (PhD Diss., Southwestern Baptist Theological Seminary, 2007), 42.

[84] Terry, 163.

loosened, and his foot propped up on the podium. He used simple but rough vocabulary words. He brought his athletic past to the platform and was known for grabbing chairs and shaking them at the devil, standing on top of the pulpit, and even doing handsprings. He often preached messages on salvation through Christ, old-time religion, the evils of drinking, and American patriotism.[85]

Sunday asked people to "hit the sawdust trail" in order to be saved. His team built temporary tabernacles for his meetings and they covered the dirt floor with sawdust in order to keep down the dust. "Hitting the sawdust trail" meant to walk down the center aisle to the front. Sunday waited there with his hand outstretched to shake the hands of the converts. His assistant handed the convert a little booklet that explained that by coming forward the person had become a child of God and had received eternal life.[86] Sunday used follow-up cards to record the names of those who came forward during the altar call[87] and distributed them to the local churches after the campaign was over.

Sunday received large "love" offerings on the final day of his campaigns. He lived an extravagant lifestyle and was criticized for it. His wild, flamboyant style of evangelism was criticized by many religious pastors. There arose many evangelists who imitated Sunday until the nation was overrun with preachers competing for offerings. This caused general disrepute to fall upon evangelists, which culminated in a novel by

---

[85]Terry, 161.

[86]Terry, 162.

[87]Cassidy, 203.

Sinclair Lewis in 1926 about Elmer Gantry, a fictional evangelist and con-man who chased money and women.[88]

Billy Graham

After Sunday's death, there were not any nationally known evangelists holding large events until the rise of Billy Graham (1918-2018), who is widely acknowledged as the greatest evangelist of the twentieth century. His impact on the practice of mass evangelism is profound and can scarcely be exaggerated.[89] Graham was known for a simple trust in God's word.[90] Of great significance was Graham's restoration of integrity

---

[88]Sinclair Lewis, *Elmer Gantry* (New York, NY: Signet Classics, 2007), n.p.

[89]The Gallop organization has rated Graham as "One of the Ten Most Admired Men in the World" fifty-one times. Graham was featured in *Time Magazine, US News and World Report, Life Magazine, Newsweek, People, The Saturday Evening Post,* and many other magazines. He had a personal relationship with many of America's presidents; George W. Bush gives him credit for leading him to the Lord. See (John Pollock, *The Billy Graham Story* (Grand Rapids, MI: Zondervan, 2003), 283. He met many world leaders and celebrities.

[90]Evangelist Chuck Templeton was an early friend of Billy Graham's. Templeton was handsome, talented, charismatic, and many people (including Graham) said he was a better preacher than Graham. But Templeton went to Princeton and studied liberal theology and biblical criticism and eventually became an agnostic and resigned from the ministry. See Charles B Templeton, *Farewell to God: My Reasons for Rejecting the Christian Faith* (Toronto, Ontario: McClelland & Stewart, 1996). Graham found himself deeply bothered by Templeton's skepticism about the Bible. He started to question the Bible's trustworthiness and he knew that doubt would destroy his effectiveness. He says, "I began to study the subject intensely. I also thought of Christ's own attitude toward the scriptures, and how he never once intimated they might be false. Then one night I got my Bible and I went out in the moonlight and put it on a stump and knelt down. I said, 'Oh God, I cannot prove everything. I cannot answer all the questions, but by faith I accept this book as the word of God.' From that moment on, I have never doubted God's word. When I quote the Bible I believe I am quoting the very word of God and there is an extra power in it. One month later we began the Los Angeles crusade." (Billy Graham quote from a display at the Billy Graham Museum, Wheaton, IL (20 February 2015). See also

to the office of the evangelist.[91] He became famous in America during a crusade in Los Angeles, California[92] and became known worldwide during a crusade in London, England.[93] Over the course of his ministry, Billy Graham preached the good news of

---

Billy Graham, *Just As I Am: The Autobiography of Billy Graham* (San Francisco, CA: HarperCollins Worldwide, 1997), 139.

[91]During an evangelistic campaign in Modesto, California, in 1948, Graham called his team together to pray and discuss criticism directed at the evangelists. From this discussion came a set of principles to guide their future ministry. These principles included absolute financial and moral integrity; cooperation with all the churches whenever possible; avoidance of emotionalism, sensationalism, and negative preaching; and systematic follow-up of new believers. See Graham, *Just As I Am*, 128.

[92]Before 1949, Graham had already conducted several citywide evangelistic campaigns, but he was still relatively unknown. Then Graham was invited to conduct a revival in Los Angeles. The meetings became front-page news all over America and Graham became well-known almost overnight. The meetings caught the attention of newspaper magnet William Randolph Hurst, who reportedly told his newspapers to "Puff Graham." Other national newspapers followed suit and within a few weeks, Graham was known across America. In 1950, Graham started the "Hour of Decision" weekly radio program. The program often aired live coverage of Graham's crusades. Five years later, the program would be carried by 850 stations and would generate thousands of letters with testimonies of changed lives. The Billy Graham Evangelistic Association was incorporated in order to provide a legal covering for the start of the radio program. Soon, an evangelistic film was being produced and in 1951, a television program was launched. (See Pollock, 58-61).

[93]In 1954, Billy Graham went to London for a crusade. At first, Graham faced great opposition by the press, but he soon won them over. Every night for three months, London's Harringay Arena was packed to overflowing. The final meeting of the crusade was held in Wembley Stadium, where a record-breaking 122,000 people attended. Time Magazine wrote, "By almost any standard of measurement, Billy Graham's month-long London crusade ended as still another record-smashing triumph for the tireless evangelist. In all, Billy preached to 955,368 people, more than in any previous 30-day period in his life, and inspired 42,487 to come forward to make their 'decision for Christ.'" Despite early rumors that the crusade, which cost $840,000 to mount, might become his first major campaign to lose money, it had an estimated $42,000 surplus. The last week, when Graham sailed home to rest up for his next crusade (in Berlin, starting Oct. 16), he left behind him an army of 22,000 Christian laymen who had helped with the crusade and were now ready to continue their work for evangelism in local churches. Still another

Christ to an estimated 215 million people face-to-face in over 185 countries on all six continents. His largest crusade was in Seoul, South Korea, in 1973, with 1.1 million people. His largest meeting in North America was in Central Park, New York City in 1991, with a gathering of 250,000. The Billy Graham Evangelistic Association is now led by Graham's son Franklin Graham, who says, "The opportunity for evangelism is greater than it has ever been. More people who need to meet Jesus Christ are alive today than any other time in history. Every soul is precious in the sight of God."[94] Will Graham, the grandson of Billy Graham, is now conducting evangelistic campaigns in America and around the world.

Luis Palau

Another significant figure who has influenced the practice of mass evangelism is Luis Palau. Graham served as a role model for Luis Palau (1934-present), who was born in Argentina and has often been called "the Billy Graham of South America."[95] Palau

---

permanent result of the crusade was the formation in London of six thousand new Bible-study groups, which Graham called "bridges between the church and God." (See "Billy's Victory in London," *Time* 88, no. 3, 15 July 1966, n.p., *Academic Search Complete,* EBSCOhost (5 September 2017). If Los Angeles launched Graham to national prominence in America, the London crusade brought him to world-wide attention.

[94]Billy Graham quote from a display at the Billy Graham Museum, Wheaton, IL. (February 20, 2015).

[95]Palau was greatly influenced by Billy Graham's ministry. As a teenager, he often listened to Graham's preaching on the radio. In 1961, Luis and Pat Palau volunteered at Graham's crusade in Fresno, California, where they learned how to mobilize people for a crusade. Later, Palau served Graham as a translator at some of his crusades Latin American crusades. In 1978, Billy Graham gave a large sum of money ($100,000) to help launch Palau's ministry. See Koo, 56.

graduated from Multnomah Bible College in Portland, Oregon, in 1961. While there, he met and married Pat Scofield, a fellow student, on August 5, 1961.[96] Palau's first city-wide crusade took place in Bogota, Colombia, in 1966. Within the next few years, his opportunities exploded, and soon he became the most well known Hispanic evangelist.[97] Palau's history of ministering throughout Central and South America provides a model for an evangelist doing crusades in Brazil. Although Brazil speaks Portuguese and much of the rest of Central and South America speaks Spanish, there are many parallels in the

---

[96]Luis Palau and David Sanford, *Calling America and the Nations to Christ* (Nashville, TN: Thomas Nelson, 1994), 71.

[97]In 1969, Palau did fourteen campaigns just in Mexico. In 1970, his team did crusades in the capital of El Salvador and a crusade in Mexico City that drew 106,000 people over ten days, with 6,675 people accepting the Lord. In 1971, he did a crusade in a large bull ring in Lima, Peru, that drew 103,000 people over two weeks and resulted in almost 5,000 decisions for Christ. In Guatemala, Palau preached to 130,000 people in twenty-two days, with more than 3,000 trusting Christ for salvation. In 1972, the Palau team did a crusade in San Jose, Costa Rica, that resulted in 3,200 salvations. In 1973, Palau did a crusade in Santa Domingo, Dominican Republic that drew 70,000 people and witnessed 2,400 people getting their lives right with God. A crusade took place in Quito, Ecuador, in 1974, which resulted in 3,120 registered decisions. One technique that Palau used to great effect in his Latin American crusades was counseling people on live television. In the weeks prior to his crusade, he would buy several hours of television time each night and sit in the studio and pray for people as they called in. In 1982, a massive crowd of 700,000 people came to hear Palau preach in Guatemala City. In 1984, 25.7 percent of the 90,000 people at a crusade in Arequipa, Peru, responded to the Gospel. In Lima, 3,147 people made decisions for Christ. For many years, Palau focused his evangelism in Latin America, but in 1981 he did his first crusade in the United States. However, it was not until the early 1990s that he began to focus his evangelism efforts in North America. In 1992, he preached to 72,000 people in Phoenix, Arizona. In 2004, Palau preached in the country of his birth in Mar del Plata, Argentina, to more than 300,000 people; and in 2008 he preached to 850,000 people in Buenos Aires, Argentina. See Koo, 261-271.

history and culture of these nations. In particular, Palau has proved effective at preaching the Gospel in countries where the Roman Catholic Church is strong.

The History of Evangelism in the Pentecostal/Charismatic Context

The practice of mass evangelism has evolved over the centuries, but the biggest innovation in the past century is due to the rise of the Pentecostal movement. The evangelistic event that will take place in Caicò, Brazil will include a variety of practices that are distinct to the Pentecostal movement including praying for the sick and the casting out of demons. This section will examine the unique contributions of Pentecostal evangelists to the practice of mass-evangelism by looking at the lives of some of the more prominent Pentecostal healing evangelists like John Alexander Dowie, Aimee Semple McPherson, Oral Roberts, T. L. Osborn, and Reinhard Bonnke.[98]

With the explosion of Pentecostalism after the Azuza Street Revival in 1906, a new kind of evangelist arose. The healing evangelists were concerned with more than the saving of souls; they also believed that Jesus can heal the body. They noticed that in the

---

[98]There are dozens of bibliographies about the lives of Moody and Graham but relatively few bibliographies are available about Pentecostal evangelists. The Billy Graham Museum at Wheaton endeavors to cover the history of American evangelism but the only Pentecostal it mentions is one small plaque about Aimee Semple McPherson. Pentecostals have contributed significantly to world evangelism and are currently the fastest growing segment of Christianity. See Vinson Synan, *The Century of the Holy Spirit* (Nashville, TN: Thomas Nelson, 2001), 372. Yet they are ignored by many evangelical histories of evangelism. For information on healing evangelism see, David Edwin Harrell Jr, *All Things Are Possible: the Healing and Charismatic Revivals in Modern America* (Bloomington, IN: Indiana Univ. Press, 1975) and Roberts Liardon, *God's Generals: Why They Succeeded and Why Some Fail* (New Kensington, PA: Whitaker House, 1996).

New Testament, the ministry of Jesus, Peter, Paul, and Philip were all authenticated by signs and wonders. They taught that Jesus Christ is the same yesterday, today, and forever (Hebrews 13:8). They believed that if Jesus healed people when He walked on this earth, that He would heal people today.[99] They preached a "full-Gospel," good news for the body, the soul, and for the spirit. They believed that salvation has benefits in eternity and here on this earth.[100]

John Alexander Dowie

A forerunner of the Pentecostal movement and one of the first healing evangelists was John Alexander Dowie (1847-1907), who was born in Edinburgh, Scotland. In 1860, his family immigrated to Australia. During his time there, he was healed instantaneously of dyspepsia. Because of this miracle, he felt God was calling him into the ministry. As a young pastor in Newtown, Australia, he experienced a tragedy that caused him to hate disease for the rest of his life. Over forty members of his congregation died in an epidemic. He said, "My heart was sick and faint as I saw my people lay dying in this epidemic and did not know how to tell them to get healing, the healing I myself had

---

[99] For more on healing evangelism see T. L. Osborn, *Healing the Sick: A Living Classic* (Tulsa, OK: Harrison House, 1992); *The Gospel According to T .L. and Daisy* (Tulsa, OK: Osborn Publishers, 1985); and T. L. Osborn, *The Message that Works* (Tulsa, OK: Osborn Publishers, 1997). Also see Oral Roberts, *God Still Heals Today (*Tulsa: Oral Roberts. 1984) and Oral Roberts, *If You Need Healing, Do These Things* (Tulsa: Oral Roberts, 1969).

[100] For more on Pentecostal theology, see Wolfgang Vondey, *Pentecostal Theology: Living the Full Gospel*, Systematic Pentecostal and Charismatic Theology Series (London: Bloomsbury T&T Clark, 2017), 37.

received. I did not know how to preach divine healing as a doctrine or how to practice it as a ministry."[101] He began to study God's word concerning divine healing, and the next little girl he prayed for was healed. Because of this experience, he preached divine healing for the rest of his life. In 1888, he came to America as a missionary. His reputation as a healer had preceded him and people lined up in the lobby of his hotel to receive prayer. As miracles began to happen, he received invitations to minister in churches across the United States. His theology was based on two presuppositions. First, "Jesus Christ is the same yesterday, today, and forever" (Heb. 13:8). Second, "Disease, like Sin, is God's enemy, and the devil's work, and can never be God's will."[102]

In 1890, he established his headquarters in Chicago. He built a tabernacle at the south entrance to the World's Fair, across the street from Buffalo Bill Cody's Wild West Show. Above the Tabernacle was a twenty-foot sign advertising God's healing power. Two key people were healed during this time, which catapulted his ministry into a national spotlight. One was the niece of Buffalo Bill Cody and the other was the cousin of Abraham Lincoln. Eventually, he built the largest wooden arena of his time, which seated eight thousand people. On December 31, 1899, he established what he claimed would be a utopian Christian community. He purchased over eleven square miles of land and named his city Zion. The city was supposed to be completely free from sin and

---

[101]John Alexander Dowie, *The Gospel of Divine Healing and How I Came to Preach It* (Chicago: Zion Publishing, 1874), 9-14.

[102]John Alexander Dowie, "Talks with Ministers on Divine Healing," 2-3; "God's Way of Healing," in *Leaves of Healing*, vol. II (Zion City, IL; Zion Printing and Publishing, October 18, 1895), 23-27.

sickness. Thousands of Christians were attracted to the idea of living in such an ideal city and many moved there. Unfortunately, Dowie experienced a stroke that severely limited his ability to lead the community. He also struggled with people from within his ministry who wanted to take over, and he started preaching some strange doctrine in his later years.[103] Despite his flaws, he was a significant contributor to what would be known as the "healing movement" in America.[104] Dowie's theology of healing influenced other healing evangelists like John G. Lake (1870–1935)[105] and F. F. Bosworth (1877–

---

[103]In his later years, Dowie told his followers that he was Elijah, and he started wearing the garments of a biblical high priest.

[104]Paul G. Chappell, "The Divine Healing Movement in America," (Ph.D. diss., Drew University, 1983), 284-330.

[105]Lake learned to hate illness and death because several members of his family experienced crippling disease which threatened to kill them. Lake took them to see John Alexander Dowie and when they were prayed for, they were healed. This ignited faith in Lake's heart for God's healing power. Even though Lake was extremely talented in business and capable of making what was considered a fortune in his days, he decided to give up his job in order to become a missionary to Africa. He gave away all his money and possessions and committed to live a life totally dependent upon God. Through a series of miracles, God provided everything he needed to move his family to Africa. While there, he saw tremendous miracles and founded the Apostolic Faith Mission, but tragically, his wife died while he was there. When he returned to the United States, he set up healing homes in Spokane, Washington. They reported over one hundred thousand healings in a six-year period. Later, Lake moved to Portland, Oregon to start another church. One of his converts during these days was Gordon Lindsay, who went on to found Christ for the Nations. See Roberts Liardon, *John G Lake: The Complete Collection of his Life Teachings* (Tulsa, OK: Albury, 1999), 220.

1958).[106] But his loud and aggressive attacks on those who disagreed with his theology created an antagonism towards the healing message with some evangelical believers.[107]

---

[106]F. F. Bosworth (1877-1958) was saved at a Methodist revival meeting at the age of sixteen. He was born in Utica, Nebraska and grew up in Fitzgerald, Georgia. Bosworth caught a cold and for eight years he suffered from lung problems. Doctors told him he would not live for long. But, at a Methodist Revival, a female evangelist named Mattie Perry prayed for him to be healed and he was instantly healed. His family moved to John Alexander Dowie's city Zion, Illinois, and he became the director of the Zion City concert band. In Zion, he became a close friend of John G. Lake. He was filled with the Holy Spirit when Charles Parham came to Zion to preach. He visited the Azusa Street Revival. He pastored the First Assembly of God church in Dallas, Texas for eight years. In 1912, he invited Maria Woodworth-Etter to hold six months of meetings at his church. He resigned from the Assemblies of God and joined the Christian Missionary Alliance because he came to believe that although tongues are a gift of the Holy Spirit they are not necessarily the "initial evidence" of being filled with the Spirit. He launched out into the healing ministry at the age of thirty, along with his brother Burt (B.B.). Bosworth is known for teaching on healing, but his primary gifting was as an evangelist. He was one of the first to recognize that healing is a powerful tool for reaching the lost. In Ottawa, Canada in the 1930s, he conducted a campaign that filled a 11,000 seat auditorium. So many miracles were reported at this campaign that people brought the sick in cars, ambulances, and even hearses. At a revival at Chicago Gospel Tabernacle, he received a great deal of publicity in the Chicago Daily News when a large number of deaf students from a school for the deaf were healed which forced the closure of the school. It is estimated that one million decisions for Christ were made in his meetings. Bosworth is best known for writing *Christ the Healer*, which became a classic book on God's healing power. For more on Bosworth see "Christ the Healer," *Healing and Revival.com*, n.d., n.p., http://healingandrevival.com/BioBosworth.htm (3 April 2019). Bosworth greatly influenced T. L. Osborn.

[107]Dowie preached in Chicago during the same time frame as Moody. Both of them were actively involved in ministering to the thousands of people who attended the Chicago World Fair in 1893. But, they were not friends. Dowie attacked Moody viciously from his pulpit and Moody responded in kind, although with a softer tone. Dowie's flaws discredited his message and Moody's antagonism towards the Pentecostal move of the Holy Spirit continues to influence the school that bears his name to this day.

Aimee Semple McPherson

A Pentecostal woman with a gift for evangelism was Aimee Semple McPherson (1890-1944), who founded the Four-Square Church.[108] Sister Aimee became famous at a time when most churches did not allow a woman to speak from the pulpit. She was known for her flamboyant style, her flowing white dresses, and her creative way of sharing the Gospel.[109] McPherson condensed her theology into four memorable points that she called "The Four-Square Gospel." She preached: Jesus is the Savior, Jesus is the Healer, Jesus is the Baptizer with the Holy Spirit, and Jesus is the Soon-Coming King. Her theology continues to influence Pentecostal evangelists today.

Oral Roberts

Oral Roberts (1918-2009) was a tent evangelist, pioneer of Christian television, and founder of Oral Roberts University. "Something good is going to happen to you!" is the message which Oral Roberts has proclaimed to millions. He coined phrases such as

---

[108]"Our Story. The History and Future of the Foursquare Church," *Foursquare.org.*, n.d., n.p., https://www.foursquare.org/about/aimee_semple_mcpherson (19 March 2018).

[109]Every Sunday night, McPherson preached an illustrated sermon at her church. For example, when she preached on Noah's Ark, she invited the Los Angeles Zoo to bring their animals to her auditorium. When she preached on the fire of God, she parked a fire truck on her platform. She was the first woman to ever preach a message over the radio. During the middle of the Great Depression, her feeding ministry provided food for over 1.5 million people. One year, she preached 336 times in one hundred and fifty days, traveled over fifteen thousand miles to forty-six American cities, and appeared on forty-five different radio stations. For more on McPherson see Synan, 131-138.

"Expect a miracle,"[110] "God is a good God,"[111] and he developed the concept of "Seed-faith."[112]

Roberts was struck with tuberculosis when he was a teenager. As he lay dying on his bed, God spoke to him, "Son, I am going to heal you and you are to take my healing power to your generation. You are to build me a university and build it on My authority and the Holy Spirit."[113] Soon after that, his brother in-law took him to an evangelistic tent meeting. The evangelist laid his hands on Roberts' head and spoke to the disease, "You foul tormenting disease, I command you in the name of Jesus Christ of Nazareth, come out of this boy! Loose him and let him go free." Instantly, Oral was healed.[114]

On Christmas day in 1938, he married his wife Evelyn. She was a major source of his strength as she supported his dreams. For several years, Roberts pastored a small church in Enid, Oklahoma, but he became discontent because he was not seeing anyone being healed. One day, God spoke to him through 3 John 2, "Beloved, I wish above all things that thou mayest prosper and be in health . . ." Roberts realized that God wants his

---

[110]See Oral Roberts, *Expect a New Miracle Every Day* (Tulsa, OK: Oral Roberts Evangelistic Association, 1963).

[111]See Oral Roberts, *God is a Good God* (Tulsa, OK: Bobbs-Merrill Company, 1960).

[112]See Oral Roberts, *The Miracle of Seed-Faith* (Tulsa, OK: Oral Roberts Evangelistic Association, 1982).

[113] Oral Roberts, *Expect a Miracle: My Life and Ministry* (Nashville, TN: Thomas Nelson, 1995), vii.

[114]Roberts, *Expect a Miracle: My Life and Ministry*, 33.

people to be blessed abundantly and to live in absolute health. This divine revelation exploded in his spirit and created tremendous faith to believe for miracles.[115]

At his first crusade, Roberts prayed for three things. First, he asked God to bring one thousand people to the service. Second, he asked that the entire $160 rent would be paid by the offering. Finally, he asked for one person to be healed dramatically so that everyone who saw it would know that it was a miracle from God. All three prayers were answered.[116]

He started holding tent crusades, and his ministry received national attention when a gunman fired a bullet at his head during a service. The miracles that were occurring caught the attention of pastors. Soon Roberts began to receive invitations to hold crusades in cites around the United States.[117]

Roberts was one of the first Christian evangelists to realize the potential of television. He broadcast his healing crusades across the nation, and his message of God's goodness captured the imagination of thousands. The dramatic signs and wonders of his ministry changed the prevalent theology of his day as ministers realized that God still heals today.

---

[115]Roberts, *Expect a Miracle: My Life and Ministry*, 71-73.

[116]Roberts, *Expect a Miracle: My Life and Ministry*, 78.

[117]Roberts, *Expect a Miracle: My Life and Ministry*, 90

God told Oral Roberts to start a university. He said, "Raise up your students to hear my voice, to go where my light is dim, where my voice is heard small, where my healing power is not known . . . even to the uttermost bounds of the earth. Their work shall exceed yours and in that I am well pleased."[118] Even though Oral had no land, no money, no faculty, and no students, he launched out in faith to build what would eventually become a 250 million dollar campus, which has graduated thousands of students who are dedicated to "go into every person's world" with the Gospel of Jesus Christ. Roberts also started a hospital.[119] The roots of Oral Roberts University are found in the mass evangelism tent crusades of Oral Roberts. It is a school "forged in the fires of healing evangelism."[120] Roberts was an innovative evangelist and his example continues to motivate the students of Oral Roberts University to take God's light around the world.

---

[118]Roberts, *Expect a Miracle: My Life and Ministry*, 162.

[119]Roberts combined medicine and the healing power of God in a state of the art medical facility named the City of Faith. Even though this project received a lot of negative publicity from the media, Roberts managed to build the tallest building in Oklahoma. The hospital was forced to close because not enough patients came, but Robert's idea about the "merging of prayer and medicine" is now a common practice in hospitals across America. See Roberts, *Expect a Miracle: My Life and Ministry*, 301.

[120]Oral Roberts University Presidential Search Committee: Appendix A: History of Oral Roberts University, n.p., n.d., http://www.oru.edu/pdfs/pres-seach-committee/appendix_a.pdf, 1 (1 April 2019).

T. L. Osborn

T. L Osborn (1923-2013)[121] was the first to conduct large open-air healing meetings since the days of the early church. After he saw four visions of Jesus,[122] praying

---

[121] Osborn was saved at the age of fourteen while kneeling next to a limestone rock in an oak grove next to a cow pasture. At the age of sixteen, Osborn joined Pastor Earnest Dillard in ministering in revivals around the United States. At a church in Almo, California, he met Daisy Washburn, who was attending the meetings with her youth group. They fell in love with one another and got married on April 5, 1949, at the respective ages of age of 17 and 18. For the next couple of years, they traveled around California holding revival meetings and for a short time became pastors of a church in Portland, Oregon. They went to India as missionaries at the ages of 20 and 21 in 1945. While they were in India, they were disappointed at the lack of converts. Osborn found it difficult to communicate the Gospel to the Hindu and Muslim people of India. Although they were supposed to stay in India for several years, they went home disappointed after only ten months. See Synan, 332.

[122] When they returned to the States, Osborn began to fast and pray in order to discover the reason why their ministry was so ineffective. Because they were unable to convince Hindus and Muslims about Jesus Christ, the Osborns realized that "people must have proof of the gospel and evidence that Jesus is alive." Osborn tried to attend a meeting conducted by a healing evangelist named Charles Price, but Price died right before the camp meeting. Osborn cried out to God, "Lord, who will now pack the nation's auditoriums and proclaim the gospel in power and miracle demonstrations, so that the people will believe God's word?" In response to his prayer, Osborn reports that he received four visions of Jesus. In July of 1947, he heard a woman evangelist named Hattie Hammond preach a sermon titled "If You Ever See Jesus, You Can Never Be the Same Again." Osborn cried and prayed all night asking for an encounter with the living Savior. The next morning, he reports, "the Lord Jesus walked into my bedroom at 6:00 am." Osborn's second vision of Jesus occurred at a William Branham (1909-1965) meeting in Portland, Oregon. At the meeting, Osborn witnessed hundreds of people being healed instantaneously. Osborn says, "I was captivated by the deliverance of a little deaf girl over whom he prayed." Branham commanded the deaf spirit to come out of the girl and instantly she was able to hear. For Osborn, this was a vision of Jesus working in a person. Osborn's third vision of Jesus was in the pages of the New Testament. After seeing the miracles that occurred at Branham's meeting, Osborn and Daisy read through the New Testament together as if it was there first time reading it. The verse that impacted them was Hebrews 13:8, "Jesus Christ is the same yesterday, today, and forever." The final vision of Jesus in Osborn's ministry occurred when Osborn saw Jesus work a miracle through his own ministry. In the fall of 1948, the Osborns held a healing revival at their church in Oregon and all the people they prayed for reported being healed.

a mass prayer for the sick became a defining ingredient in Osborn's preaching.[123] He found that when he preached a simple message about Jesus and then prayed for the sick, people would be healed. He invited them to the platform to share their testimony and when the crowd heard about the miracles, they would return to their neighborhoods and invite their friends and family to come to the crusade. The Osborns proclaimed the Gospel to millions in seventy-three nations through massive crusades which numbered

---

The Osborns became convinced that preaching about a miracle-working Jesus was the answer to world evangelism. Soon thereafter, they left the United States once again and went to Jamaica. See "Edith Dhana Prakash, *A Critical Investigation of Tommy Lee Osborn's Work in India: Its Impact and Implications"*, (PhD Diss., Regent University, 2013), 58-61.

[123]In Jamaica, Osborn tried to lay hands on each individual who needed healing but he was quickly overwhelmed because of the number of people who wanted prayer. At that time, William Branham had a system of giving out numbered cards to people who needed healing prayer, but in a typical service he was only able to pray for a small percentage of those who had cards. So many people wanted prayer that Branham became physically exhausted trying to pray for all the people. In Jamaica, Osborn tried to give out numbered cards like Branham, but he soon had to stop because he found that the policemen who were assigned to give out the healing cards were selling them to the people instead of giving them away. Because of the large crowd, Osborn knew he would not be able to lay hands on each individual. Osborn recalled a conversation he had with F. F. Bosworth who had asked Osborn, "If I give an altar call and fifty people respond and I lead them in a prayer of salvation, how many of them are saved?" Osborn replied, "All of the them." Bosworth continued, "So, if I give a call for healing and fifty people respond and I lead them in a prayer for healing, how many of them can God heal?" Osborn asked, "Why not all of them?" Because of this conversation, the idea to pray a single mass prayer for healing was born.

from twenty thousand to three hundred thousand.[124] They published books, docu-miracle crusade films, Bible studies, and audio tapes in 132 languages. They gave away scores of vehicles equipped with films, projectors, and sound systems to help national pastors evangelize their people. They supported over thirty thousand native missionaries and planted hundreds of churches.

According to Osborn, the essence of the mission of Christianity lies in four issues. First, that people shall know that "the bible is as valid today as it ever was." Second, that "the mission of every believer is to win the lost to Christ." Third, that "every soul won can become Christ's representative." Fourth, "that miracles, signs and wonders will continue to be what distinguished Christianity from being just another religion."[125] T. L and Daisy have probably preached to more people face to face in non-Christian nations and seen more healing miracles than any other couple in history. Their example continues to inspire a new generation of healing evangelists today.

---

[124]The Osborns' life passion was: "To express and propagate the Gospel of Jesus Christ to all people throughout the world." Their maxim was "No one deserves to hear the Gospel repeatedly until everyone has heard it once." Their motto was "One Way – Jesus; One Job – Evangelism." Their guiding principle: "Every Christian believer – a witness for Christ." "About Osborn Ministries International" *Osborn.org*, n.d., n.p., https://osborn.org/ about/osborn-ministries-international (1 April 2019).

[125]Tommy Lee and Daisy Osborn, in *Faith Library in 23 Volumes: 20th Century Legacy of Apostolic Evangelism*, vol. 1 (Tulsa: OSFO International), 413.

Reinhard Bonnke

Another evangelist who has shaped Pentecostal evangelism is Reinhard Bonnke (1940-present).[126] Bonnke and his wife Anni spent seven years as missionaries in the country of Lesotho, reaching out to people in the traditional way; but Bonnke became frustrated at the low number of salvations. In a mighty step of faith, in 1974, he launched his evangelistic organization, which is now known as "Christ for All Nations." The ministry held its first crusade in the national stadium in the country of Botswana. Out of the many churches in the city, only one small fellowship decided to help with the crusade. Bonnke was disappointed when only one hundred people came the first night. Yet, as he preached a powerful message, a man jumped up and shouted, "I've just been healed!" Other healings began to happen, and news spread across the city that God was doing miracles. By the last night of that first crusade, the entire stadium was packed. Thousands were saved and healed, and twelve years later, when Reinhard returned to do another crusade in the city, the leader of a large denomination announced that eighty percent of his pastors had been saved in that first crusade. While Bonnke was in Lesotho, God

---

[126]Bonnke was born in Germany on the eve of World War II. After the war, his father pastored a small Pentecostal church in Krempe, Germany. From an early age, Bonnke knew God was calling him to be a missionary to the continent of Africa. At the age of eleven, he was filled with the Holy Spirit. He attended a Bible school in Swansea, Wales, that had its roots in the Welsh revival. On his way home from Bible school, he miraculously had an encounter with George Jeffreys, a famous evangelist who had founded the Elim Pentecostal Churches. He married Anni Sülzle in 1964. His denomination required every missionary to pastor for two years, so right after they married, they planted a church in Flensburg, Germany. After two years, they moved to South Africa to serve with the Apostolic Faith Mission. He was sent to the Kingdom of Lesotho. It was known as the "boneyard for failed missionaries," but Bonnke achieved great success. He wrote a series of Bible lessons and distributed them to every house in Lesotho using a team of one hundred "bicycle-evangelists."

showed him a vision of a "blood-washed Africa," an Africa washed in the blood of Jesus. Bonnke began to proclaim, "All of Africa shall be saved, from Cape Town to Cairo."[127]

Bonnke's first tent seated eight hundred people, but later a huge tent was purchased to accommodate the massive crowds of people who began coming to Bonnke's crusades. This tent seated thirty-four thousand people and covered three football fields, but the tent was too small. Soon, crowds of up to one hundred and fifty thousand people were attending each meeting. As the size of the crowds multiplied, Bonnke started to hold his crusades outside on fields. He formed two crusade teams, one for east Africa and one for west Africa, so that the ministry could accelerate.

He has now given away 103 million books in over 123 languages. He often holds "Fire Conferences" to train church leaders for world evangelism. People flock to his crusades because of the miracles which result from the preaching of God's word. Bonnke often says that he is "plundering hell to populate heaven,"[128] and the reports from one crusade prove that he is accomplishing exactly that.[129] Bonnke prays for the sick to be healed, he casts out demons, and he prays for people to be filled with the Holy Spirit. His ministry has documented over 75 million decisions for Christ. His story demonstrates that

---

[127]Bonnke, *Living a Life of Fire* (Orlando: E-R Productions, 2011), 259.

[128]Bonnke, *Living a Life of Fire*, 244.

[129]On November 12, 2000, 1.2 million people came to a single crusade meeting that Bonnke held in Lagos, Nigeria. Over thirty thousand pastors and church leaders attended the "Fire Conference." In this historic, six day crusade, over six million people heard the gospel message. Blind eyes were opened, breast tumors disappeared, the lame walked, mutes began to speak, and many other miracles were reported. Six million booklets were passed out and over two thousand churches participated in following up on all the converts who were saved.

a Pentecostal evangelist who believes that God moves on the earth today can be powerfully effective at advancing the kingdom of God.

Cultural Narrative

Evangelism in the Brazilian Culture

The nation of Brazil is the fifth largest country in the world, and it covers half of South America. Its population of over two hundred million people is deeply religious: 64.6% of the nation is Roman Catholic and 22.2% is Protestant.[130] In addition, there are a variety of Afro-Brazilian religions like Umbanda, Candomblé, and Macumba.[131] How has the Gospel spread throughout Brazil?

The history of evangelism in Brazil has largely been a competition between the Roman Catholic Church and the Protestant church. When the Catholic explorers first arrived, they compelled the natives to convert at the point of a sword. Brazil was settled in 1500 by Alveres Cabral along with a Catholic Portuguese Armada who conquered the native people using a cross and a sword as "their symbol of faith and empire."[132] Evangelism and colonialism went hand in hand. The Roman Catholic Church became the dominate religion of Brazil, but often struggled with syncretism as the teaching of the

---

[130]"The World Factbook: Brazil," 13 November 2017, n.p., https://www.cia.gov/library/publications/the-world-factbook/geos/br.html (13 November 2017).

[131]Sherron Kay George, "Brazil: An 'Evangelized' Giant Calling for Liberating Evangelism," *International Bulletin of Missionary Research* 26, no. 3 (2002): 104, *ATLA Religion Database with ATLASerials,* EBSCOhost (6 November 2017).

[132]Jorge Cesar Mota, "Evangelism and Unity in Brazil," *The Ecumenical Review* 5, no. 2 (1953): 155, *ATLA Religion Database with ATLASerials,* EBSCOhost (6 November 2017).

church was intermingled with native religions and the religions of African slaves who were imported into the country.[133]

When the Reformation shook the church in Europe, the chaos spread to Brazil. The first Protestant missionaries were martyred[134] but over time, Protestants gained a foothold.[135] In the past century, the vibrant expression of the Pentecostal faith proved to be attractive to the people of Brazil and Pentecostalism grew rapidly, in large part because of their focus on evangelism. In 1911, two Swedish immigrants to the United States arrived in northern Brazil and emphasized the baptism of the Holy Spirit. Their work sparked the founding of the Brazilian Assemblies of God,[136] the first Pentecostal

---

[133]Zelia Soares, "Popular Piety and Evangelism in Brazil," *International Review of Mission 82,* no. 327 (1993): 403, *ATLA Religion Database with ATLASerials*, EBSCOhost (6 November 2017).

[134]In 1556, John Calvin sent two missionaries, M. Pierre Richer and M. Guillaume Charretier, to Brazil, but their work among the Indians did not produce any results. In 1557, Richer wrote to Calvin explaining that "the savages were incredibly barbaric" with the result that "we are frustrated in our hope of revealing Christ to them." The mission to Brazil ended in tragedy when the Portuguese attacked the Calvinists and strangled three of them. See Beeke, 80-81.

[135]The Methodist church was involved in Scripture distribution in 1825. The Methodists were also involved in ministering to the physical needs of the poor and disenfranchised. Presbyterian missionaries came from Scotland in 1859 and brought an intellectual focus and austere worship. The Baptists came in 1881, after the American Civil War. See Guillermo Cook, "The Protestant Predicament: From Base Ecclesial Community to Established Church: A Brazilian Case Study," *International Bulletin of Missionary Research* 8, no. 3 (1984): 99, *ATLA Religion Database with ATLASerials*, EBSCOhost (6 November 2017). The Episcopalians arrived in Brazil in 1890. (Jorge Mota, 156).

[136]Joanyr De Oliveira, *The Assemblies of God in Brazil: An Illustrated Historical Summary*, ed. Richard Hoover (Rio De Janeiro: Assemblies of God Publishing House, 1997), 22-23.

church in Brazil. Pentecostalism has been attractive to the poor of Brazil because of the Pentecostal church's "personal caring, the sense of personal worth, the spontaneous manifestations of joy in worship, and the missionary outreach that empowers Pentecostal believers to share their faith openly."[137] When asked why the Pentecostal church is growing in 1971, Manuel de Mello, the leader of the Brazilian *Igreja Evangelica* Pentecostal denomination, replied, "I think that the most important task of the Church is to evangelize."[138]

The public proclamation of the Gospel has been an important component of Pentecostal church growth in Brazil. Antônio de Campos Gonçalves lists a variety of evangelism methods that are effective in Brazil including public preaching.

> Today, not only on Sundays but also on weekdays, public preaching in the open air takes place all over the cities, drawing great crowds of more or less attentive people from every class, to whom the word of Salvation and of eternal life is preached, to whom Bible leaflets are given and who are invited to public services in the churches here, there and everywhere . . . a greater number of people hear the Gospel for the first time in the public squares than in the churches. In the latter, the believers, the parishioners, are in the majority, but those who attend in the public squares belong among passers-by who stop, listen, go on and are replaced by others, so that a single programme in a public square could well be heard by thousands, from the most diverse classes and social conditions.[139]

---

[137]George, 105.

[138]Manoel de Mello, "Participation Is Everything: Evangelism from Viewpoint of a Brazilian Pentecostal," *International Review of Mission* 60, no. 238 (1971): 246, *ATLA Religion Database with ATLASerials*, EBSCOhost (November 6, 2017).

[139]Antônio de Campos Gonçalves, "Evangelism in Brazil Today: Its Significance and Results," *International Review of Mission* 48, no. 191 (1959): 303, *ATLA Religion Database with ATLASerials*, EBSCOhost (November 6, 2017).

Although much evangelism has been done in Brazil, the nation does not have any evangelists who have attained a status or reach equivalent to that of the American Billy Graham. Most of the evangelism in Brazil has been done by church organizations and not through big crusades.

Differences Between the Brazilian Culture and American Culture

What are some of the differences between Brazilian culture and American culture that might effect how evangelism should be conducted in the Brazilian context? The answer might be found in the research done by Geert Hofstede who developed a six dimensional model for measuring the differences between national cultures.[140] The Gospel can work in any culture, but communicating the Gospel cross-culturally requires the Gospel communicator to be aware of his own cultural biases as well as the cultural characteristics of the culture to whom he is preaching. An evangelist and his message is received differently in different cultures thus it would be instructive to examine the differences between American culture and Brazilian culture.

---

[140]Geert Hofstede, "The Six-D Model of National Culture," *About Geert Hofstede*, n.d., n.p., https://geerthofstede.com/culture-geert-hofstede-gert-jan-hofstede/6d-model-of-national-culture/ (8 October 2018).

On Hofstede's Individual versus Collectivism scale[141], the United States ranks as a 38 and Brazil scores as a 91. This is the biggest difference between American and Brazilian cultures according to Hofstede's model. This difference could affect evangelism because an American evangelist typically pushes for each individual to make a decision to follow Christ, but in Brazil, the culture is overwhelmingly Catholic. It may be difficult to change a society that leans towards collectivism by emphasizing individual decisions.

On the Power Difference scale,[142] the United States scores a 69 and Brazil scores at 40. American culture is considered a small power difference country which means there is less inequality in America and Brazil is more of a large power difference culture. America has a strong middle class, but in Brazil there is a large gap between the rich and the poor. Reaching these different segments of society might take completely different

---

[141]Individualism is a society where the ties between the society are loose. Collectivism is a society where individuals are part of strong in-groups. In a collectivism society, the relationships comes first and the task comes second. But in an individualist society, the task comes first and the relationship may come afterwards. Geert Hofstede, "10 Minutes with Geert Hofstede on Indulgence versus Restraint," *YouTube* video, 9:33, posted March 2015, https://www.youtube.com/watch? v=zQj1VPNPHlI (March 29, 2019).

[142]If there is a large power distance inequality, this is considered a normal part of society. Superiors are superior beings. Power comes first and good and evil comes afterwards. Respect is the most important things a child can learn. These societies love centralization. If there is a small power distance in society inequality is to be fought against. In these societies, superiors are part of hierarchies. Power should be used legitimately and everyone is under the same rules of law. Independence is the most important lesson a child can learn. These societies love decentralization. Geert Hofstede,. "10 Minutes with Geert Hofstede on Power Distance," *YouTube* video, 11:27. Posted November 2014. https://www.youtube.com/watch?time_continue=3&v=DqAJclwfyCw (March 29, 2019).

evangelistic methods. In Brazil, giving away food and basic toiletries to those living in poverty might be an effective method for gaining an audience.

On the Uncertainty Avoidance scale,[143] the United States scores a 76 and Brazil scores 46. This scale reveals another large gap of thirty points between these two cultures. America is an uncertainty accepting society. People in the United States tend to be innovative and like fewer rules. But Brazil has a lower tolerance for uncertainty. This might make it potentially difficult for a Brazilian to quickly switch religions, especially when she does not know much about the religion that she is being invited to. In the context of Brazil, the evangelist should work to ensure that the potential convert knows there is a church community that is ready to welcome her. Clear communication is important in order to remove as much uncertainty from the conversion process as possible.

---

[143]In uncertainty avoiding societies uncertainty is a threat and must be fought. These societies are high stress and suffer from anxiety. They consider that what is different is dangerous. There is a need for rules and regulation. Innovations are adopted slowly. In uncertainty accepting societies uncertainty is noble and should be accepted as it comes. What is different is curious. These societies do not like rules very much. They want fewer rules, and tend to break rules. Innovation is accepted quickly. They are more tolerant of people who are different. Geert Hofstede, "10 Minutes with Geert Hofstede on Uncertainty Avoidance," *YouTube* video, 15;26. Posted March 2015. https://www.youtube.com/watch?time_continue=1&v=fZF6LyGne7Q (29 March 2019).

On the Indulgence versus Restraint scale,[144] the United States rates a 59 and Brazil rates a 68. America has some aspects of an indulgence society, but in many ways America is restrained in its attitudes and practices. Brazil is far more of an indulgence society, their culture is known for elaborate parties and celebration. For the evangelist in Brazil, this means that a festival might be more effective at reaching people than an apologetics conference. Since family and friends are extremely important in Brazil the evangelist must develop a strategy for evangelizing an entire family, not just an individual.

American culture has influenced mass evangelism. For example, American culture is driven by entertainment so American evangelists like Billy Sunday tend to be flamboyant. American culture says "bigger is better," so American evangelists may be drawn to mass evangelism so they can report "big numbers." American culture is materialistic, so American preachers (especially televangelists) have been accused of focusing too much on money. American culture likes organization, so Billy Graham carefully documented all the people who filled out decision cards in his meetings.[145] But, the practice of mass evangelism is not limited to Americans. Reinhard Bonnke is from

---

[144]In indulgent societies there is free gratification. They enjoy life and have fun. People tend to feel healthier and happier. They appreciate leisure and are optimistic and extroverted. They consider friends to be important. Brazil is a good example of an indulgent society. In restraint societies there is suppressed gratification of needs and they are regulated by strict social norms. The people feel less healthy and less happy. They feel that what happens to them is not their own doing. They are pessimistic and introverted. Geert Hofstede, "10 Minutes with Geert Hofstede on Indulgence versus Restraintism," *YouTube* video, 9:33. Posted March 2015. https://www.youtube.com/watch?time_continue=1&v=V0YgGdzmFtA (29 March 2019).

[145]Huston, 139-142.

Germany, Luis Palau is from Argentina, D. G. S. Dhinakaran was from India, Benson Idahosa was from Nigeria, and Aril Edvardsen was a great evangelist from Norway. In short, God has used mass evangelism in a variety of different countries and cultures. There is no reason to suppose that mass evangelism cannot be adapted to fit into the context of the Brazilian culture.

Personal Narrative

God called me to be an evangelist. This call goes back to when I was only five years old. My father pastored a small church in Cloudcroft, New Mexico. One Sunday, he invited a guest prophetess to minister at the church. God told her to prophesy over me that I am called to be an evangelist. I did not waste any time in fulfilling the call. I preached my first sermon (which I still have on cassette tape) at the age of six. When I was ten my parents became missionaries in Mexico and since they were my legal guardians, I had to go with them. To be part of my family was to be part of the ministry. Throughout my teen years, my family ministered extensively in Juarez, Mexico. Almost daily, we preached at churches and conducted evangelistic children's outreaches. In the barrios of Mexico, we conducted hundreds of mini-crusades with attendance of between two hundred people and one thousand people.

My understanding of mass evangelism has been shaped by my exposure to a variety of different ministries who engage in mass evangelism. My heroes when I was young were people like T. L. Osborn, Oral Roberts, and Billy Graham. I read their books and looked at the pictures of the crowds of people they preached to. I dreamed of doing the same thing someday. When we would drive past a soccer field in Mexico, I would grab my father's arm and tell him, "We could fill that field with people and preach to them." When I was still a teenager, I started my own ministry called "Clowns for Christ, International." My brother and I traveled across the United States doing evangelistic circus family nights at local churches.

In 1992, when I was fourteen years old, my father took me to a crusade in St. Petersburg, Russia conducted by Pastor Billy Joe Daugherty in the Olympic Stadium. When the Berlin Wall fell in 1989, the former USSR became a ripe harvest field.[146] Starting in November of 1991, every month for eighteen months, Daugherty did a crusade in St. Petersburg.[147] I watched him give an altar call and witnessed thousands of Russian people that were so hungry for God that they came running to the front of the stadium in order to get saved.

When I was fifteen years old, I was reading a book about how to be successful. The book recommended that young people set a goal of making one million dollars before the age of thirty. As I thought about making that a goal for my life, I realized that my priorities are different. I decided that money is not important to me—what is important is people. On that day, I wrote down this goal on a sheet of paper: "I, Daniel King, want to lead one million people to Jesus before I turn thirty years of age." Instead

---

[146]Sid Roth, "Sid Roth Welcomes Billy Joe Daugherty," *It's Supernatural.org.*, 4 September 2009, http://www.itssupernatural.org/sid-roth/sid-roth-welcomes-billy-joe-daugherty/ (10 September 2018).

[147]Claudia Kovar, "Victory in Eastern Europe / Daugherty Spreads Word to Albania," *Tulsa World.com.*, 14 July 1993, https://www.tulsaworld. com/archives /victory-in-eastern-europe-daugherty-spreads-world-to-albania/article_c68ede10-e9ed-50bb-ba8f-03dd1f1ec774.html (10 September 2018).

of trying to become a millionaire, I decided to reach a million people for God before I turned thirty.

In 1997, when I was eighteen, Luis Palau came to Juarez, Mexico for a festival. I was invited to participate in the children's festival dressed up as a clown. I witnessed thousand of people respond to the Gospel because of Palau's preaching.

My father is an alumnus of Oral Roberts University and he has always had a great respect for the evangelistic example of Oral Roberts. In fact, my father bought a tent in imitation of the tent ministry of Roberts. Since I was called to be an evangelist, I decided to attend ORU so that I could be exposed to his ideas of evangelism. Initially, I planned to major in Evangelism until I talked to the undergraduate evangelism professor at ORU and he told me that mass evangelism does not work. I switched my major to New Testament and decided to learn about mass evangelism from those who were doing it.

In 2002, I attended Billy Graham's crusade in Texas Stadium in Dallas Texas and heard him give an altar call in his trademark style. In 2003, when Franklin Graham did a festival in Tulsa, Oklahoma, I ministered at his children's festival as a clown. I went to San Jose, Costa Rica and Accra, Ghana with T.L. Osborn; to San Salvador, El Salvador with Mike Francen; to Ibadan, Nigeria with Richard Roberts; to Abuja, Nigeria with Reinhard Bonnke; and to Goma, Congo with Canadian Evangelist Peter Youngren where I met my wife Jessica who was working for him as a crusade director.

I met with Oral Roberts at his home in California and asked him questions about evangelism. On several occasions I asked T. L. Osborn about his methods of evangelism. I joined the Next Generation Alliance, a group of evangelists organized by the ministry of

Luis Palau. I asked Reinhard Bonnke and Peter Youngren for their advice for a young evangelist. My understanding of mass evangelism has been shaped by my exposure to the ministries and methods of these giants of the Christian faith.

When I graduated from ORU, I launched out into full-time evangelistic ministry. I started King Ministries International and traveled to various nations holding large evangelistic crusades and pastor training seminars. At these events, we witnessed amazing miracles and thousands of salvations. Before I turned thirty, I reached my goal of leading a million people in a salvation prayer. Now, eight years later, our ministry has preached the Gospel to over two million people face-to-face. My new goal is to lead a million people to Jesus every year. To date, I have visited seventy nations around the world and conducted over one hundred evangelistic events in my quest to save people from hell.

Mass evangelism has been used by God in both the Old and New Testaments and throughout church history. The history of mass evangelism gives this author hope that God will continue to use mass evangelism in the church going forward. But, what does the academic world have to say about mass evangelism? In the next chapter, this paper will examine some books and studies that have been done on the subject of mass evangelism.

CHAPTER 3

REVIEW OF RELATED LITERATURE

Introduction

The goal of chapter two was to examine the biblical, historical, cultural, and personal foundation for engaging in mass evangelism. This chapter will review similar research projects, examine the theorists and theoretical constructs for mass evangelism, and look at the methods of modern practitioners of mass evangelism. Much research has been done on person-to-person evangelism.[1] There is also a wealth of popular literature

---

[1] For example, at Oral Roberts University, Solomon Uche Ahibuogwu studied how to increase the knowledge of evangelism among international groups at Victory Christian Center, in Tulsa, Oklahoma. Uche Ahibuogwu, "Increasing the Knowledge of Evangelism among International Groups" (D.Min. proj., Oral Roberts University, 2013). Yong Koo Bang researched how to lead the unsaved parents of saved students to the Lord. Yong Koo Bang, "A Study of Child-parents Evangelism Methods for Students Living with Unbelieving Parents" (D.Min. proj., Oral Roberts University, 1999). Gloria I. Charry reviewed how to increase evangelism by training people to pray for the lost. Gloria I. Charry, "Increasing Evangelism through Training in Intercession" (D.Min. proj., Oral Roberts University, 2001). Desmond Herbert Rose examined the effectiveness of using James Kennedy's Evangelism Explosion in rural Missouri. See Desmond Herbert Rose, "Assessing Evangelism Explosion III in the Rural Context," (D.Min. proj., Oral Roberts University, 2000). Jang Geun Koak did his research in South Korea on how to train individual evangelists in effective person-to-person evangelism techniques. Jang Geun Koak, "Training for Effective Evangelism" (D.Min. proj., Oral Roberts University, 2002). Manichouba Singh Mairembam focused on helping the members of his church, Opening Doors Ministries of India, learn how to engage in personal evangelism for the purpose of sharing the Gospel with the non-Christian Meiteis of Manipur. Manichouba Singh Mairembam, "Increasing the Knowledge of Person to Person Evangelism among the Meiteis of Manipur" (D.Min. proj., Oral Roberts University, 2008). Lee Ho Noh

that has been written on personal evangelism.[2] In contrast, there is relatively little that has been written about mass evangelism. The disparity in the number of studies that have been done on mass evangelism and the number of studies that have been done on personal evangelism demonstrate the vital nature of this research project and the need for further studies to be done on mass evangelism.[3] After a review of the literature, it appears that personal evangelism is considered to be more effective than mass evangelism by

---

studied the problem of how to increase the knowledge of believers about evangelism at Yedam Church, a Methodist church in South Korea. Lee Ho Noh, "Increased Knowledge of Believers about Evangelism," (D.Min. proj., Oral Roberts University, 2007). Linda Lee Fannin worked to train young leaders in Hungary to engage in personal evangelism. See Linda Lee Fannin, "Changing Attitudes about Evangelism among Young Adult Leaders in Hungary," (D.Min. proj., Oral Roberts University, 2013). See R. Michael O'Mire developed a model for training laity in personal evangelism at Woodlawn Church in Royal Oak, Michigan. R. Michael O'Mire, "A Model for Empowering the Laity for Personal/relational Evangelism at Woodlawn Church," (D.Min. proj., Oral Roberts University, 1999). Jin-Gu Park did his research at Dae-gu Sang-il Church in South Korea on how to train believers to evangelize on a one-to-one basis. See Jin-Gu Park, "A Study on the Person to Person Evangelism Training of Laity," (D.Min. proj., Oral Roberts University, 1995). Kwang Sung Park made it his goal to train new converts to evangelize non-believers at Kansas Korean Full Gospel Church. See Kwang Sung Park, "Increasing the Awareness of Evangelism Opportunities among New Converts in Korean Immigrant Church," (D.Min. proj., Oral Roberts University, 2006). Seikhokam Touthang studied how to increase the knowledge of evangelism among Asian immigrants to other Asian immigrants in Tulsa. See Seikhokam Touthang, "Increasing the Knowledge of Asian Immigrants about Evangelism," (D.Min. proj., Oral Roberts University, 2005).The common thread among all these research projects is their focus on personal evangelism.

[2]See Bill Hybels and Mark Mittelberg, *Becoming a Contagious Christian* (Grand Rapids, MI: Zondervan, 1994); Rebecca Manley Pippert, *Out of Salt Shaker* (Downers Grove, IL: InterVarsity, 1999); and Jim Petersen, *Living Proof: Sharing the Gospel Naturally* (Colorado Springs, CO: NavPress, 1989).

[3]Oral Roberts University was founded by an evangelist who became famous for his tent crusades. The ratio of studies done at ORU on personal evangelism to the number of studies done on mass evangelism is currently 12:1. This ratio demonstrates a need for more studies to be done on the impact of mass evangelism.

many in the academic community and this perception has influenced the focus of the studies that have been done on evangelism. This chapter will examine the most salient books and studies that are available on this important topic.

Similar Research

Though studies on mass evangelism are fewer in quantity than studies on personal evangelism, there are some excellent studies on mass evangelism that are available. In the first section of this chapter, the best of these studies will be explored. The study by Terry Winter highlights the history of evangelism in America from 1730-1970; and the study by William Thomas paints a picture of a Billy Graham crusade that took place in Europe in 1975. Next, the impact of Luis Palau on Global Evangelism is examined beginning with a study by Hongnak Koo, and continues with a research project by Scott Bauer who considers a Luis Palau festival in California in 1994, and concludes with a research project by William Giovannetti who scrutinizes a Luis Palau festival that took place in Chicago in 1996. A final study by William Morrow evaluates how mass evangelism was used as a tool for planting churches in the Philippine Islands from 1960-1985.These studies provide a broad picture of how mass evangelism has been used over the past two hundred and fifty years. Four of the studies are about mass evangelism in North America, one documents the benefits and the drawbacks of mass evangelism in Europe, and one details how mass evangelism can be useful in the context of a developing nation in Asia. Taken together, these studies demonstrate that mass evangelism has worked in the past and indicate that mass evangelism will be part of what God does in the future. They also show that mass evangelism is a worldwide phenomenon that has worked in a variety of different cultures and countries.

Two Hundred and Fifty Years of Evangelism in America

Mass evangelism has played a significant role in the history of spiritually in the United States. Since before the Revolutionary War, evangelists who preach to the masses have shaped America. In a study titled, "Effective mass evangelism: a study of Jonathan Edwards, George Whitefield, Charles Finney, Dwight L. Moody, and Billy Graham," Terry Walter Royne Winter studies the evangelistic ministries of five of the great evangelists from church history.[4] Many of the bibliographical details he wrote about are included in chapter two of this research project. The purpose of Winter's dissertation was to study "five effective evangelists in order to gain practical insight into the subject of mass evangelism."[5]

After studying the lives of these five evangelists, he concluded that each evangelist had a definite conversion experience that was reflected in his push to get a response from his listeners; each had a sense of call to the ministry; each was a deeply committed Christian who placed his faith in God's word; each conducted their ministries with integrity; and each was gifted to preach and worked to develop his gift. All preached with authority and "moral intensity." Each of them issued definite invitations to elicit a response to the Gospel. The main differences between the evangelists were in the areas of

---

[4]Terry Walter Royne Winter, "Effective Mass Evangelism: A Study of Jonathan Edwards, George Whitefield, Charles Finney, Dwight L. Moody, and Billy Graham" (D. Pastoral Theology proj., Fuller Theological Seminary, 1968).

[5]Winter, 227.

methodology. As time progressed, each adapted the principles of evangelism to their own times. In Winter's analysis of their sermons, he concludes that each evangelist in his study appealed to Scripture, emphasized "the reality and power of sin and the need for forgiveness,"[6] preached on the death and resurrection of Christ as an atonement for sin, and explained the necessity of repentance and faith in the conversion process. None of them trivialized conversion. They all emphasized the importance of total commitment to Christ.

In his final thoughts, Winters concluded that there is a combination of human and divine elements in successful evangelism, and that there is a primacy of preaching that leads to conversion. He wrote, "The preaching of the gospel remains the method most effective in bringing people to a Christian conversion." He concluded that the Gospel is effective in all times (the Gospel is timeless) and for all peoples (the Gospel is universal). Even though there is a difference between content and terminology when comparing the sermons of various evangelists, the differences over a two hundred year period are relatively small.[7]

Winter's examination of historical evangelists is a helpful study for today's evangelist to read. Each of the five evangelists that he wrote about had different personalities and methods, yet they each had a huge impact on America. This shows that God can use anyone to shake a nation through mass evangelism. God is simply looking for someone who is willing to be used.

---

[6]Winter, 234.

[7]Winter, 235.

A Billy Graham Crusade in Europe in 1975

It is widely acknowledged that one of the greatest evangelists of the twentieth century was Billy Graham and no study on mass evangelism would be complete without looking at his impact. William Thomas wrote "An Assessment of Mass Meetings as a Method of Evangelism – Case Study of Eurofest'75 and the Billy Graham Crusade in Brussels."[8] Thomas served as a missionary in both Zaire and Europe. He was an American and a full-time evangelist with the European Baptist Federation. He received his doctorate from the Free University of Amsterdam. His study investigated the impact of a Billy Graham crusade in Brussels, Belgium. Attendance at Eurofest'75 over nine services totaled 101,805 and a total of 2,557 decision cards were filled out.[9]

Thomas wrote specifically with the European *Sitz im Leben* in mind, but he felt his work contains principles that can be applied in other contexts as well. Although this study is from the mid-seventies, it remains the most comprehensive study of a crusade and its long-term impact done to date. The central idea of Thomas' dissertation is that "mass evangelism, although only one method among others, is valid; but its validity for and success in a given time and place depend, in part, on an adequate understanding and

---

[8] William Thomas, *An Assessment of Mass Meetings as a Method of Evangelism – Case Study of Eurofest'75 and the Billy Graham Crusade in Brussels* (Amsterdam: Editions Rodopi N.V., 1977).

[9] Thomas, 206.

an application of the communication process," and an appreciation for the historical, ecclesiastical and social conditions that can potentially effect mass evangelism.[10]

Thomas adopted the working definition of evangelism from the Lausanne Covenant that evangelism is "the proclamation, by the power of the Holy Spirit, of the historical and biblical Christ as Savior and Lord, with a view to persuading people to come to Him personally by faith, and so be reconciled to God."[11] Then, he examined mass evangelism from a historical perspective and concluded, "Pietism and Methodism were the seed-bed from which modern crusades have sprung."[12] Thomas wrote at length on how communication theory and evangelism are linked.

Thomas conducted a survey of the population of Brussels and discovered that a large percentage of the region's population consider themselves to be Catholic but rarely go to church.[13] He analyzed the three stages of Eurofest'75 (preparation, penetration, and preservation) and compared the results to crusades that Graham has done in other locations. Thomas concluded that "Neither the Billy Graham Crusade nor Evangelism-in-Depth aroused much enthusiasm in Belgium."[14] He felt there was a lack of involvement from local churches. He suggested there are two reasons for this lack of participation; first, he observed that mass evangelism works best in the nations that have a Pietist-

---

[10]Thomas, 1.

[11]Thomas, 5.

[12]Thomas, 20.

[13]Thomas, 109-110.

[14]Thomas, 281.

Methodist background[15] and second, he felt that the Roman Catholic church should have been invited to participate at a greater level, although he acknowledges that in practice, this cooperation would have been difficult to achieve.[16] Because of the unique challenges of doing mass crusade evangelism, he suggested that Europe may see better results from smaller campaigns conducted by individual churches.[17]

Thomas' case study is an instructive example that informs the writing of this research project. He did an excellent job of analyzing Billy Graham's crusade in Brussels. He analyzes the spiritual climate of Europe, he interviews pastors to discover their opinion about the crusade, and he offers a clear-headed assessment of the benefits and the failures of the crusade. He detailed both the strengths and the weaknesses of crusade evangelism. He concluded that crusades can be effective, while lamenting that Graham's crusade in Brussels was not as effective as it could have been. In short, his dissertation is a brutally honest view of crusade evangelism. Both critics and proponents of mass evangelism can find material in this study to support their positions. Critics of mass evangelism would point to the relatively small results of the Brussels crusade as evidence that mass evangelism does not work in a modern developed nation with a post-Christian atmosphere. But, proponents of mass evangelism might acknowledge the disappointing results, while also criticizing the local churches for not participating enthusiastically enough in the event.

---

[15]Thomas, 217.

[16]Thomas, 147.

[17]Thomas, 284.

This research project examined a crusade in Brazil, a nation that is predominately Roman Catholic.[18] Many of the same challenges that Graham faced in Brussels with the Catholic church are also faced by the evangelical church in Brazil. Thomas postulated that crusades are most effective in nations that have a Pietist-Methodist background.[19] Since Brazil does not have that background, it may be more difficult to conduct a crusade there in comparison to nations that do have a Pietist-Methodist culture.

Luis Palua and His Contribution to Evangelism

There are a plethora of books and studies available about the ministry of Billy Graham. His life and example have left an indelible impact on the history of evangelism. But, he is not the only evangelist who has been used by God in the past fifty years, which is why this research project now turns to the innovative ministry of Luis Palau. Hongnak Koo completed his doctoral dissertation at Southwestern Baptist Theological Seminary in Fort Worth, Texas, on, "The Impact of Luis Palau on Global Evangelism: An Evaluation of His Evangelistic Theology and Strategy."[20] Koo examined the history, theology, and strategy of Luis Palau's ministry of mass evangelism. Much of Palau's history and Koo's research is covered in the second chapter of this project so this material will not be

---

[18] At the crusade in Caicó, Brazil, it was also difficult to cooperate with the Catholic church. The Catholic church actively opposed the crusade, and the evangelical churches were uninterested in trying to build a relationship with the Catholic church.

[19] Thomas, 21.

[20] Hongnak Koo, "The Impact of Luis Palau on Global Evangelism: An Evaluation of His Evangelistic Theology and Strategy" (PhD Diss., Southwestern Baptist Theological Seminary, 2008).

revisited here. Koo examined the theology of Palau, and he discovered that Palau believes the authority of the Bible is the foundation of evangelism. Palau believes salvation is the work of a sovereign God from beginning to end, but he also believes that God works through human agency. Palau believes in the urgency of evangelism. Palau believes the evangelist must have vision, compassion, holiness, and boldness; Palau believes the evangelistic campaign has a biblical and historical precedent. Palau believes evangelism is founded on Christian unity and cooperation and must be rooted in cultural relevancy and creativity. Palau believes there is a priority of evangelism over social reform efforts; and Palau is committed to discipleship.[21] Paula's example as a senior statesmen in the arena of world evangelism is worth following by today's evangelist.

According to Koo, Palau's messages come straight from the Bible; the content of his messages always present the simple gospel; Palau focuses on God's love, not His wrath; his messages are marked by relevancy to the life of his audience; Palau has "adopted a problem-solution approach. He normally lists many problems in the world, related to family, economics, politics, and so on, and presents Jesus Christ as the only answer to these problems."[22] Palau's pattern for his messages begins with humanity's problem by describing situations that are hopeless without Christ. Then he presents God's solution which is the hope of salvation through Christ. Finally, Palau gives an invitation and asks for a response of repentance for sins and faith in Christ. Palau is known for using simple language, forceful gestures and tones, and down-to-earth illustrations.[23]

---

[21]Koo, 77-124.

[22]Koo, 129.

Palau's simple and friendly style of presenting the good news of Jesus Christ along with his emphasis on grace is in sharp contrast to some street evangelists who shout through a mega-phone about the judgment and wrath of God. Palau's approach is an effective and proven method for obtaining results in a modern society that wants to hear good news, not bad news. Koo's study of Palau's life demonstrated that Palau shares many of the characteristics of the historical evangelists (Edwards, Whitefield, Finney, Moody, and Graham), whom Winter studied in his dissertation.

Koo's study about Palau is valuable because it documents the history of a ministry that has been used by God to bring thousands of people to Christ. Evangelists can learn many important lessons from Palau's life. Palau is not a North American evangelist, but he has been successful in reaching people in North America. He is also loved and respected across the Latin American world. Palau preaches a simple message that is full of good news about Jesus. His outreaches include churches from many different theological backgrounds. His commitment to train up a new generation of evangelists will continue to bear spiritual fruit for many years to come. His ministry as revealed in Koo's study, provides an example for future evangelists to aspire to and imitate.

---

[23]Koo, 138-141.

A Luis Palau Festival in California in 1994

Koo's dissertation gives a big picture analysis of Palau's ministry, but a couple of studies have also been done about specific events that Palau has conducted. In one of the few ORU research projects on mass evangelism, Scott G. Bauer writes, "Mission for a Multitude: A Strategy for Mobilizing 1000 People for Mass Evangelism."[24] In this study, Bauer, the son-in-law of Jack Hayford (a prominent Pentecostal Pastor and former president of the Four Square Denomination), examined how The Church On The Way in San Fernando Valley, California, used a Luis Palau festival to reach out to its community in 1994. Bauer's goal with his research project was to mobilize one thousand people for personal evangelism in conjunction with a mass evangelism event.

Bauer believed the best way to get a sinner to attend an evangelistic event is through a personal invitation. Because of this conclusion, he decided to intentionally train one thousand believers at Church On The Way in personal evangelism. To do this, he began by establishing a biblical basis for the priority of evangelism by inviting Evangelist Luis Palau to speak at the church for a crusade launch event and by scheduling a series of sermons on the importance of evangelism. Then he worked to equip the congregation for the task of personal evangelism by scheduling congregation-wide training sessions. Finally, he organized intercession teams to pray for the crusade.

---

[24]Scott G. Bauer, "Mission for a Multitude: A Strategy for Mobilizing 1000 People for Mass Evangelism" (D. Min. proj., Oral Roberts University, 1995).

The crusade was deemed to be a success.[25] The success of the crusade was judged by three metrics.[26] First, it produced a large number of decision-makers. Second, it increased the competence and confidence of those in the congregation who were trained in evangelism. Third, the crusade produced greater unity among the churches who participated.[27]

As a pastor, Bauer was concerned with discipleship of new believers, but he acknowledges that "disciple-making must begin with the 'finding' of the lost and their conversion to Christ."[28] In other words, "discipleship begins with a decision."[29] He pointed out that the main responsibility for follow up remains with local churches, not with the evangelist.[30] He concluded that Luis Palau's gifting as an evangelist helped to substantially increase the amount of evangelization that occurred in the San Fernando

---

[25] Two hundred churches participated. A total of 2,225 Christians committed to be involved in Friendship Evangelism by signing a card, on which they promised to pray for five lost people to be saved and to target those individuals for personal evangelism and to invite them to the crusade. Total attendance at the five-day crusade and related evangelism events was 54,025 people. See Bauer, 111. A total of 2,175 people made registered decisions for Christ at the crusade and related events. Of the 680 people at Church On The Way who filled out post-crusade surveys after participating in Friendship Evangelism at the crusade, 208 had at least one person make a decision for Christ, and in total, they witnessed 734 decisions. See Bauer, 133.

[26] Bauer, 126-127.

[27] Bauer, 133.

[28] Bauer, 38.

[29] Bauer, 10.

[30] Bauer, 93.

Valley during the time of the crusade.[31] He writes, "The Holy Spirit uses the gift of the evangelist to awaken the local church for both the equipping of evangelism and the release of evangelistic activity."[32]

Bauer wrote as a pastor who has an evangelistic heart. His study is important for those who want to know how crusades can benefit the local church. He carefully documented how The Church on the Way participated in the Palau crusade and he demonstrated that there can be a synergy between the local church and the evangelist. Bauer told how Palau and his team helped to train his congregation in techniques for reaching the lost and he documented exactly what results were produced because of the partnership. Far too many church pastors today are antagonistic towards the gift of the evangelist and they have a suspicion of the evangelist's motives when he comes to town. But, Bauer's study showed how an effective partnership between the local church and the evangelist can produce genuine church growth. Bauer showed that when Palau left town, the churches of San Fernando Valley were better off, both numerically and spiritually. In an effort to implement Bauer's research, the crusade that took place in Caicó, Brazil also worked to create synergy between the local churches and the evangelist. It was discovered that local involvement can contribute greatly to the success of the crusade.

---

[31]Bauer, 138.

[32]Bauer, 138.

A Luis Palau Crusade in Chicago in 1996

A third study about Luis Palau's ministry adds more texture to understanding his contribution to evangelism. In his study "A Strategy for Linking Crusade Evangelism with Church Planting," William A. Giovannetti examined the impact of a 1996 Luis Palau Festival in the City of Chicago and developed a strategy to link the urban evangelistic crusade with church planning.[33] He concluded that crusades are vehicles for reaping the harvest, and churches are instruments for keeping the harvest.[34] Generally speaking, Giovannetti was disappointed in the results of the crusade in Chicago[35] and despite his study, he never implemented his plan to plant a church in conjunction with a crusade. Giovannetti had some interesting ideas about church planting, but he misunderstood the nature of Palau's calling to the city of Chicago. Giovannetti's plans to plant a church in conjunction with a crusade are outside the scope of Palau's focus which is to work with existing churches, not to plant his own church.

The abstract nature of Giovannetti's plan without concrete implementation makes this project of limited value. In Caicó, Brazil, the team did not have a specific strategy for planting a church after the crusade. Instead, the goal was to strengthen and encourage the local churches that already existed. However, three months after the crusade, it was

---

[33]William A. Giovannetti, "A Strategy for Linking Crusade Evangelism with Church Planting" (D. Min. proj., Fuller Theological Seminary, 1996).

[34]Giovannetti, 55.

[35]The 1996 Say Yes! Chicago crusade involved 101 separate events over an eight week period; 1,800 churches participated. Total attendance was 139,795. A total of 9,606 decision makers were recorded, which included 3,916 salvations, and 3,545 rededications. The budget was around $4 million, which works out to $1,124 per profession of faith.

discovered that two churches were planted (one in the Carlindo Dantas Village and another in Sabuggi Village) as a direct result of people getting saved at the crusade. This unanticipated result validates another study in the Philippines that proves that church planting and mass evangelism can work together to produce true church growth particularly in developing nations.

Mass Evangelism in the Philippine Islands from 1960-1985

The preceding two studies were about mass evangelism in North American cities, but what impact does mass evangelism have in the developing world? William Brad Morrow answered this question in his enlightening study about the use of mass evangelism in the developing world titled, "Mass Evangelism and its Effect on Church Planting: A Filipino Case Study."[36] In this study, Morrow investigated the impact of mass evangelism upon church planting in the Philippine Islands. This study has direct relevance on this research project since it involves evangelism in the context of a developing nation.

Morrow's study is not exclusively about crusades; it is also about church planting. He quotes C. Peter Wagner, "The single most effective evangelistic method under heaven

---

[36]William Brad Morrow, "Mass Evangelism and its Effect on Church Planting: A Filipino Case Study" (PhD Diss., The Southern Baptist Theological Seminary, 2003).

is planting new churches."[37] Morrow's dissertation is focused on how crusade evangelism and church planting can be combined as a strategy.[38]

Morrow presented a Filipino case study of mass evangelism that examines how the Southern Baptist church combined mass evangelistic crusades with their church planting strategy in the Philippine islands from 1960-1985. From 1950-1960, evangelism consisted mostly of local evangelistic meetings held in the local churches. In 1960, the first large scale simultaneous New Life Campaign took place in Davao. It consisted of a series of protracted meetings that emphasized revival of believers and evangelism of unbelievers and resulted in 1,709 people making a profession of faith. The local churches were the primary location of the meetings and they were coordinated through the efforts of missionaries and nationals working together. The campaigns were considered a success, but follow-up was a challenge because there were not enough missionaries available to do all the discipling that was required.[39]

In 1963, Billy Graham came to the Philippines for a series of events called the New Life Movement, which resulted in 8,201 professions of faith. Local churches doubled, tripled, and even quadrupled in size. The next major crusade took place in 1968. The theme adopted by the Philippine Baptist Mission was "Christ the Only Hope." The campaign involved over two years of planning

---

[37]C. Peter Wagner, *Church Planting for a Greater Harvest* (Ventura, CA: Regal Books, 1990), 11, quoted in Morrow, 63.

[38]Morrow identifies three groups that have managed to combine mass evangelism with church planting. These are the Assemblies of God in the Philippines, the Rosario Plan in Argentina, and the Philippine Baptist Mission. See Morrow, 93.

[39]Morrow, 109.

and training. Local churches were trained and prepared for both the evangelistic thrust and the follow-up phase. Evangelists from the United States came to preach in most of the crusade locations. This nationwide effort had 181 participating churches and it produced 6,100 professions of faith. Two years later in 1970 the churches engaged in another New Life Asia-wide Crusade. This produced smaller results, with only 1,829 professions of faith. More simultaneous campaigns took place in 1974 and 1976. The biggest change came when American Baptist churches stopped subsidizing the Filipino churches in 1972. In the 1976 campaign, the local churches funded their own evangelistic efforts and provided most of the preachers. In 1977, Billy Graham returned to the Philippines for a crusade in Manila. At this event, 22,512 decisions were recorded; however, there was not much discernable growth in the local churches.[40] In the 1980s, there was a deliberate shift in strategy, as the churches decided to link mass evangelism and church planting efforts. The Mindanao Baptist Convention and the Philippine Baptist Mission set a goal to increase the number of churches on the island of Mindanao from 394 to 1085 over a five-year period. They accomplished this through church planting crusades. At one of these crusades in 1981, more than 350 local churches participated, about one hundred musicians and preachers from the United States came to help, and over 17,000 people made decisions for Christ. During a campaign in 1983, 7,500 people were saved, 1,200 baptized, and 44 new churches were planted. During the twenty-five

---

[40]Morrow, 126.

years covered by Morrow's case study, mass evangelism proved to be an effective long-term strategy for church growth in the Philippine Islands.[41]

For the purposes of this research project, Morrow's study was of tremendous value. This author's research took place at a crusade in the nation of Brazil, which is similar to the Philippines in many ways. Both are developing nations that have a Catholic background and a general hunger for a move of God. The amazing success of crusade evangelism in the Philippines over a thirty-year period demonstrate that in the context of a developing nation, crusade evangelism can be amazingly effective. Morrow's research also provided valuable insight into how to empower believers in developing nations to take responsibility for evangelizing their own nation. Morrow showed that in the 60s and early 70s that North American evangelists drove most of the evangelistic efforts but that in the mid-70s and early 80s, the local churches in the Philippines became the driving force behind evangelism. This shift from foreign finances and control to the use of indigenous finances and local vision made the church growth in the Philippines much

---

[41]Based on his case study, Morrow recommends the following steps for planting a new church. First, do research and planning. Second, develop a core group by establishing a Bible study. Third, conduct a simultaneous mass evangelism campaign. The participants in the small groups are trained to reach out to the lost and encouraged to invite the lost to the crusade. The preacher at the crusade can be a foreign evangelist or a national evangelist. A smaller local crusade may be more effective than a large stadium crusade since local believers may find it difficult to finance a large event. (For more on church planting crusades, see: David E. Godwin, *Church Planting Methods* (Desota, TX: Lifeshare Communications, 1984). Fourth, the Bible study groups and the people who get saved at the crusade combine to form a new church. The goal is for this indigenous church to be self-supporting, self-governing, and self-propagating. Finally, the church should repeat the church planting cycle. Morrow concludes by asserting that combining mass evangelism and church planting can "expedite the task of world evangelization., Morrow, 184.

healthier and longer lasting.⁴² Anyone who is doing evangelism in developing nations should read Morrow's case study in order to gain insight into how to effectively evangelize in the context of a developing nation.

Theorists and Theoretical Constructs

The purpose of this research project was to do an analytical study of a large evangelistic event in Brazil. The first section of this chapter examines examples of several research projects that have studied mass evangelism. In this second section, the theoretical basis for mass evangelism will be examined.

Many of the resources on mass evangelism study the history of mass evangelism but few resources are available that build a theoretical construct for mass evangelism. This is because mass evangelism is usually conducted by "doers" and theoretical constructs are usually built by those who study books. Theologians and mass evangelists do not always see eye to eye. Mass evangelists tend to preach a simple Gospel that is easily understood and theologians like to delve into the deepest truths of Scripture.

This section will examine the few resources that develop a theoretical construct for evangelists. The first study is a look at the role the evangelist plays in the modern church. The second study examines how Billy Graham's organization works to involve

---

⁴²The crusade in Caicó, Brazil was done as a partnership between the ministries of Evangelist Daniel King (from America) and Evangelist Rubens Cunha (from Brazil). Other participants in the outreach were from Canada, Paraguay, and Germany. The majority of the funding came from North America although the local churches did participate in a small portion of the expenses. The spending in Brazil was controlled by Brazilian crusade directors under the direction of an agreed upon budget. Once trust is established between people from different countries, this is an effective way to efficiently handle the expenses of an evangelistic event.

the local church in its endeavors. The third study builds a case for the use of mass evangelism in the world today.

What is the Place of the Evangelist in Today's Church?

In his DMin project on "The Gift of the Evangelist," Rice Broocks Jr. examined how to identify, train, and utilize the evangelist in the North American church.[43] Broocks pastors Bethel World Outreach Church in Nashville, Tennessee, and earned a doctorate in missiology from Fuller Theological Seminary in Pasadena, California. His book *God's Not Dead*[44] inspired a movie by the same name. His discipleship book *The Purple Book* has been used by a variety of churches to disciple new believers. In a time where the gift of the evangelist is often misunderstood and unappreciated, Broock's research serves as an excellent reminder of the importance of the evangelist in the world today.

The purpose of Broocks's research was to "identify marks of the gift of the evangelist in the Bible and the North American church."[45] He began by looking at the evangelist in Scripture. Based on Ephesians 4:11-12, he believes that the evangelist is a unique office called to equip the body of Christ for evangelism, to "prepare God's people for works of service." He pointed to Acts 21:8 as evidence that Philip the Evangelist is a biblical example of what activities the evangelist should engage in. He also examined Timothy's role in evangelism based on Paul's instructions to his spiritual son in 2

---

[43] Rice Broocks Jr., "The Gift of the Evangelist" (D. of Miss. proj., Fuller Theological Seminary, School of Intercultural Studies, 2010), 1.

[44] Rice Broocks Jr., *God's Not Dead* (Nashville, TN: W Publishing, 2013).

[45] Broocks Jr., "The Gift of the Evangelist," 5.

Timothy 4:5. Broocks writes, "In Ephesians 4:11 the evangelist is pictured as an equipper; in Acts the evangelist is seen as an extender of God's kingdom; and in 2 Timothy all believers are empowered to minister."[46]

Broocks believes the office of the evangelist has been severely overlooked in recent church literature. In a review of twenty-two different missional books, he found that only eight of them reference the evangelist, five of them describe the role of the evangelist, and none of them describe how the evangelist should be trained.[47] His research in this area demonstrates that within the modern missional movement there is a distinct lack of emphasis upon biblical evangelism. The buzzword "missional" has replaced the biblical term "evangelism," and this has created a weakness in the body of Christ.

Broocks started his research by asking a group of ministers questions about how the evangelist functions in their churches. After polishing his questions, he sent a survey to 280 ministers and recorded their responses. Through his research, Broocks distilled the marks of the evangelist down to a list of fourteen items. According to him, the evangelist is a preacher of the Gospel, a builder who helps lay foundations of true discipleship, an equipper who trains believers to reach non-believers, a catalyst who makes the church missional, a pioneer leading the community of faithful beyond the church walls, a strategist who devises plans and creates tools for ministry that are able to reach effectively into the culture and creatively present the gospel, a gatherer who seeks and

---

[46]Broocks Jr., "The Gift of the Evangelist," 27.

[47]Broocks Jr., "The Gift of the Evangelist," 44-45.

gathers the lost sheep, a planter who turns outreaches into new churches, a co-laborer who works best in the context of a team, a leader who is a multiplier that reproduces him- or herself in others, and a groundbreaker who opens new territory. He also believes the evangelist can potentially be a woman, connects with apostles and pastors, and values each and every convert, not just crowds.[48]

Broocks argues that the evangelist is more than an itinerant preacher or a holder of mass rallies. He believed the evangelist should be involved in leadership in the local church. He tested this principle at Bethel World Outreach Center in Nashville, Tennessee, the church where he is senior pastor. He worked to identify and develop people with evangelistic gifts within his church. Evangelists were identified through a combination of desire, witness of the Spirit, prophetic utterance, impartation from others, outward confirmation, leadership affirmation, and bearing fruit.[49] In training the evangelist, he discovered that the character, the motivation, and the message of the evangelist are all critical.[50] Because of his development of evangelists, his church was able to plant five satellite church campuses.

---

[48]Broocks, "The Gift of the Evangelist," 64.

[49]Broocks, "The Gift of the Evangelist," 101.

[50]Broocks, "The Gift of the Evangelist," 118-120.

Broocks reached five specific conclusions about the marks of the evangelist.[51] He also identified five responsibilities of the evangelist.[52] Broocks concluded with five observations about how the evangelist should work.[53] These observations by Broocks do a stellar job of restoring the office of the evangelist to the modern-day church. The body of Christ goes through cycles where one ministry office is more prominent than other ministry offices, and in the church today, the office that is most influential is the office of the pastor. Far too many churches today are run by pastors and have no room for the evangelist. But, the church needs all of the five-fold ministry gifts if she is going to be healthy.

Broocks' strength is his understanding of the role the evangelist can and should play in the local church. However, his study did not have much to say about the role of the evangelist in mass evangelism. Even though Broocks is to be commended for making

---

[51] First, Broocks believes there is not a gift of evangelism; everyone in the church is called to do evangelism. Second, there is a severe lack of evangelistic training. Third, the practical role of evangelism is missing in most churches. Fourth, the gift of the evangelist will work in any church; and fifth, there is a need to distinguish between the revivalist and the evangelist. See Broocks, "The Gift of the Evangelist," 138.

[52] First, Broocks says the evangelist leads the church beyond the walls of the church; second, the evangelist is the one who makes the church missional; third, the evangelist preaches the Gospel; fourth, the evangelist must ensure that new believers are properly grounded in God's Word; and finally, the evangelist is called to gather a harvest of souls. See Broocks, "The Gift of the Evangelist," 142.

[53] Broocks believes first the evangelist takes time to break new ground and gather new people; second, the evangelist will use every legitimate, righteous, and creative means to proclaim the gospel; third, the evangelist must follow the leading of the Holy Spirit; fourth, the evangelist will work with a team, including the pastor of the church; and finally, the evangelist will help identify and train new evangelists for the ministry. See Broocks, "The Gift of the Evangelist," 146.

a place for the evangelist in the local church, his dissertation lacks an understanding of the role the evangelist plays historically in mass movements. Broocks' ideal evangelist is still under the control of the local-church pastor, in contrast, many of the great mass evangelists of church history were not under one local church pastor but instead they brought many local church pastors together in order to impact an entire region with the Gospel. Although Broock has a lot of great insights about the evangelist, he has little to say about the practice of mass evangelism. For that, one has to go back once again to the ministry of Billy Graham.

Billy Graham's Method of Mobilizing the Body of Christ

The next resource that will be examined answered the question of how crusade evangelism can benefit the local church and detailed the overall philosophy of the Billy Graham organization toward mass evangelism. Sterling W. Huston wrote *Crusade Evangelism and the Local Church*.[54] Huston served as Billy Graham's Director of North American Ministries, and he earned his Doctor of Divinity from Roberts Wesleyan College in Rochester, New York. Almost every recent study of mass evangelism quotes from Huston's book.[55] It is both a defense of mass evangelism and a blueprint for how evangelists should work with local churches. Dan R. Crawford states that "The purpose

---

[54]Sterling W. Huston, *Crusade Evangelism and the Local Church* (Minneapolis, MN: Billy Graham Evangelistic Association, 1996).

[55]See Marrow 3, 53; Koo 148; and Bauer 65, 66, 67, 75, 76, 77, 79, 80.

of this book is to relate crusade evangelism to the local church."[56] Houston writes about evangelism's proclamation, purpose, principles, perspective, participation, preparation, promotion, preservation, product, person, and passion.[57] This book is important to read because Billy Graham is widely acknowledged as the greatest evangelist of the twentieth century and Sterling Huston was the crusade director who organized many of his most successful events. Graham's theology can be found in his extensive library of books, but Huston's book reveals Graham's methods. Huston's book revealed the "how to" side of getting churches and evangelists to work together. Huston is a theorist in the area of how to do effective crusades.

His first chapter is about evangelism's proclamation, the evangelist's ministry and message. Huston defines the evangelist as "an announcer of the good news of the Gospel."[58] The priority of the evangelist is not social issues, but to "call people to a commitment to Christ." The evangelist should preach with authority, simplicity, and urgency and should preach for a verdict.[59]

Next, Huston writes about evangelism's purpose, the primary objectives of crusade evangelism. The ultimate goal of the evangelist is to go beyond decisions to making disciples. Crusade evangelism seeks to evangelize the community and to

---

[56]Dan R. Crawford, "Crusade Evangelism and the Local Church," *Missiology* 15, no. 3 (1987): 375, *ATLA Religion Database with ATLASerials, EBSCOhost* (22 December 2017).

[57]Huston, 5.

[58]Huston, 17.

[59]Huston, 22.

strengthen the church. Crusades should be based on biblical principles, not just a superstar personality. Crusades should involve as many local churches as possible in the initial planning.

Huston also writes concerning evangelism's principles, the keys to effective evangelism. It is important to recognize the role of the Holy Spirit and prayer in conducting a successful evangelistic event. Relationships are a key component of evangelism. It is vital to involve, organize, and train as many churches and individuals as possible. This can be accomplished by setting faith-sized goals for local church involvement and by sowing into relationships.

Then Huston examined evangelism's perspective, the partnership between crusade evangelism and the local church. There are many different ministries in the church and evangelism is one of those important ministries. Huston does not claim that mass evangelism is the only way for evangelism to take place, but he does say, "Crusades are a very effective way to evangelize . . . "[60]

Huston discussed participation and involving the local church in a crusade. Some churches are tempted to forgo participation in a crusade because of a desire to maintain doctrinal purity. However, cooperation with a crusade is not meant to imply total agreement with all doctrinal issues; it does, however, indicate a common desire to lead people to Jesus in one's community. Instead of building fences to keep other churches out, churches should allow the fire of the Holy Spirit to bring people together.

---

[60]Huston, 65.

According to Huston, the organizational process needs preparation in order to be successful. There are four phases of preparation for a crusade: organization, recruitment, training, and function (when volunteers fulfill the function they have been trained for). Local effort and local leadership are essential to making the crusade a success.[61]

In a chapter on promotion, Huston discusses the factors that influence crusade attendance. The first factor is publicity and advertising. The second factor is involvement. The third factor is a personal invitation.[62]

Huston also wrote about the program and communicating the message. Everything in the program should help lead people to respond to the invitation. The music, the testimonies, and the preaching should all work together to communicate the Gospel and to bring lost people to a point of decision. The mission never changes, the message of the evangelist never changes, the need for a Godly messenger never changes, the motivation for doing evangelism never changes, but the methods of the evangelist "must and will change."[63]

Then Huston turned to preservation, turning decisions into disciples. The primary responsibility for follow up lies in the hands of the local churches. Ultimately, it is the Holy Spirit who follows up on new believers. However, there are a variety of methods that Billy Graham's organization uses for follow-up, including personal counseling, Bible

---

[61]Huston, 94.

[62]Huston, 104-105.

[63]Huston, 120.

study groups, church follow-up, literature follow-up, Billy Graham's Decision magazine, discovery groups, telephone follow-up, and special targeted follow-up.[64]

The potential of the evangelistic crusade is to grow the church both quantitatively and qualitatively. Huston also wrote a chapter on the person whom God uses. The evangelist must have a personal relationship with Christ, a call from God, a healthy devotional life, must be a person of prayer, be Spirit-filled, have a compassionate social conscience, and possess a love for his or her brothers and sisters in ministry.[65]

In the final pages of the book, Huston examined the passion of the evangelist, the urgency to evangelize. A passion for souls is driven by one's love for Jesus Christ and by a sense of the lostness of mankind. The evangelist can maintain his or her passion for the lost by spending time in prayer, taking a spiritual inventory, and by staying close to a trusted Christian friend or a group of believers.[66]

Crusade Evangelism and the Local Church is an excellent resource both for the evangelist and for the pastor who is interested in participating in a crusade in his city. The book has extensive examples of how Billy Graham's ministry operates and it provides practical advice for conducting a successful crusade. Often, pastors and evangelists misunderstand one another. This book helps to alleviate that misunderstanding and encourages both of them to cooperate in fulfilling the Great Commission.

---

[64]Huston, 145.

[65]Huston, 174-180.

[66]Huston, 182-192.

Is There a Place for Mass Evangelism Today?

In the previous study, Huston detailed how an evangelistic crusade should be organized, but the underlying question remains, should evangelistic crusades be attempted at all? In *Going Public with the Gospel*, Lon Allison (a historian of mass evangelism who was the director of the Billy Graham Center at Wheaton College) and Mark Anderson (an evangelist with Youth With A Mission - Y.W.A.M.) defended the practice of mass evangelism.[67] Anderson got saved at a Billy Graham Mission in Minnesota, became a campaign coordinator for Evangelist Lowell Lundstrom, and has done many mass evangelism events, particularly in India.

Allison and Anderson wrote their book for two reasons. First, they believe "the proclamation of the gospel is a vital and primary means to lead the lost world to Christ."[68] They explained the publically spoken word has power to transform lives and is an important part of spiritual warfare. Second, they wrote the book to "propose some effective ways to proclaim Christ publicly in the present world."[69]

First, they built a case for the power of words. They point to the powerful words of both Adolf Hitler and Winston Churchill during World War II that worked to mobilize entire nations for the war effort. In a similar way, God uses His words to inspire and instruct and God speaks through His people. They write, "Public proclamation is a great

---

[67] Lon Allison and Mark Anderson, *Going Public with the Gospel* (Downer's Grove, IL: InterVarsity Press, 2003).

[68] Allison and Anderson, 13.

[69] Allison and Anderson, 14.

megaphone for the truth."[70] They established a biblical foundation for public proclamation and examine the church's history of public proclamation.

In the second section of the book, they examined the case of the missing evangelist. They argue that mass evangelism "has suffered neglect in the last couple of decades."[71] The office of the evangelist is needed in the body of Christ. In fulfilling his office, the evangelist should model an evangelistic lifestyle, train the church in evangelism, look for emerging evangelists, and proclaim Christ publically.[72]

In the third section of the book, they looked at how to preach Christ to today's generation. They identify five elements that should be in an evangelistic message: creation, our rebellion, God's love, our price, and eternal judgment and reward.[73] Then they encourage the evangelist to seek relevance by using an authentic preaching style, telling stories, using artistic methods like dramas and dance to share the Gospel, and by showing compassion. They finish by discussing the importance of preserving the fruit of evangelistic outreaches. Throughout the book, they share stories of successful evangelistic outreaches in India, Brazil, America, and Europe. Overall, *Going Public with the Gospel*, makes a solid case that in every age of Christianity church growth has involved the public proclamation of the Gospel and that mass evangelism can be used in a relevant and effective way today.

---

[70]Allison and Anderson, 37.

[71]Allison and Anderson, 71.

[72]Allison and Anderson, 74-75.

[73]Allison and Anderson, 101.

Going Public with the Gospel has direct application to this research project because the crusades of Mark Anderson were not huge crusades like the crusades of Billy Graham, instead they were relatively small events held in developing nations. Allison and Anderson build a solid case for the effectiveness and necessity of mass evangelism using historical evidence and personal antidotes. Plus their book provides a good theoretical basis for the practice of mass evangelism. The book's friendly, easy-to-read pace makes it an effective defense of the practice of mass evangelism which should be read by anyone who feels called to be an evangelist.

What Are the Benefits of Mass Evangelism?

The studies examined in this chapter list a number of benefits of mass evangelism. For example, Thomas lists fourteen potential benefits of mass evangelism in three different categories: personal, ecclesiastical, and social,[74] Morrow list seven benefits,[75] and Allison and Anderson mention twelve benefits of proclaiming Christ through mass evangelism.[76] Koo discusses six positive aspects of evangelistic campaigns according to Luis Palau.[77] Giovannetti argues that crusades are both theologically acceptable and pragmatically effective and lists several reasons to support his conclusion.[78] Through

---

[74]Thomas, 99-108.

[75]Morrow, 48-54.

[76]Allison and Anderson, 81-84.

[77]Koo, 80-82

[78]Giovannetti, 50.

his research, Bauer determined that crusade evangelism is one of many viable methods for reaching the lost.[79] The lists of benefits from each of these authors overlap in many instances. This author has synthesized the benefits of mass evangelism mentioned by the scholars examined in this chapter into the following areas.

First, large evangelistic events create unity in the community. Allison and Anderson believe mass evangelism creates unity among churches,[80] Thomas concurs when he says that crusades give a chance for cooperation among different churches.[81] Morrow concludes that crusades are an opportunity for churches to cooperate together in bringing the lost to Christ, create an opportunity to train church members in evangelism, and lead to unity among participating churches.[82] Right before Jesus was crucified, He prayed, "that [his disciples] all may be one…that the world may believe that You sent Me" (John 17:21), and mass evangelism is an opportunity to make this prayer come to pass. Often, a large evangelistic event draws churches and denominations together. Churches that rarely speak to one another find themselves working side-by-side to bring people to Jesus. This can create a remarkable synergy in the body of Christ. The relationships that are formed during a crusade often last long after the crusade is finished and greatly benefit the kingdom of God. Thomas points out that a crusade can be a time

---

[79]Bauer, 92.

[80]Allison and Anderson, 83.

[81]Thomas, 101.

[82]Morrow, 51-54.

of joy and fellowship among Christians[83] and this feeling can create lasting goodwill between the different parts of the body of Christ.

Second, large evangelistic events bring credibility to the church. According to Thomas, the crusade offers a cure for a religious inferiority complex[84] and he points out that crusades catch the attention of the government and the press.[85] Allison and Anderson believe that a crusade publically demonstrates the "bigness" of the church,[86] Palau says that when churches unify for a campaign, it enhances their self-image and helps to create spiritual awakening.[87] In many developing nations, the church is ignored by media and marginalized by society. However, during a large evangelistic event, the church is hard to ignore. Politicians see the large crowds and want to participate because of the potential for gaining new voters. Business owners see the value of catering to the needs of the Christian community. The media is willing to cover the story because it is impacting the entire community. Large evangelistic events make the church a force to be reckoned with.

Third, mass evangelism creates a God-consciousness in a city. Morrow, Palau, and the book by Allison and Anderson all agree that evangelistic campaigns create a

---

[83]Thomas, 108.

[84]Thomas, 100.

[85]Thomas, 103.

[86]Allison and Anderson, 83.

[87]Koo, 84.

widespread "God-consciousness."[88] Evangelists are God's brand ambassadors. Large evangelistic events take advantage of the miracle of marketing. Palau points out that this "God-consciousness" is accelerated by using all available mass media to publicize a campaign.[89] Thomas points out that a crusade attempts to reach a diverse audience through the power of marketing[90] and he mentions that crusades give the church the opportunity to reach people through mass media.[91] The evangelist is God's marketing department. One of the benefits of a crusade is the massive marketing campaign for Jesus. Even if a person does not get saved during the crusade, the marketing creates the awareness of Christ being the answer to life's problems. When someone gets in trouble they will think of Jesus.

Fourth, large evangelistic events revitalize the local church. Thomas explains that a crusade offers an opportunity for every Christian to get involved and a crusade makes it easy for believers to talk about Christ.[92] Koo emphasizes that an evangelism campaign is an opportunity to train believers for personal witnessing.[93] The preparation phase for a large evangelistic event requires lots of volunteers. The process of mobilizing, training, and empowering these volunteers creates energy and excitement in local churches. Large

---

[88]Morrow, 51; Koo, 83; Allison and Anderson, 82.

[89]Koo, 83.

[90]Thomas, 99.

[91]Thomas, 102.

[92]Thomas, 99-100.

[93]Koo, 233.

evangelistic events give individual church members the tools to witness. Doing a large evangelistic event often involves the printing of large numbers of flyers, invitations, tracts, and discipleship material. As these tools are placed in the hands of local believers, it gives them the ability and motivation to witness. The exciting nature of the event also provides a good excuse for believers to invite their unsaved friends to attend. Ideally a large evangelistic event involves personal evangelism on a mass scale. After the event is over, the volunteers return to their churches with new skills and fresh excitement about what God is doing. Many evangelists train each counselor to personally lead a person to Jesus. The counselor will continue to use this training in one-on-one encounters long after the crusade is over. According to Allison and Anderson this process of training the local church to evangelize actually disciples the church[94] and enhances the local church's sense of purpose,[95] They also believe that crusades allow the church to be obedient to the Great Commission,[96] and it creates contagious personal evangelists.[97]

Fifth, large evangelistic events benefit the local church and expand their vision. According the Thomas, there is potential for new life and new membership for local churches.[98] According to Houston, there are at least seven lasting benefits for the local

---

[94] Allison and Anderson, 82.

[95] Allison and Anderson, 81.

[96] Allison and Anderson, 81.

[97] Allison and Anderson, 84.

[98] Thomas, 102.

church that are the product of the crusade.[99] First is the training of the laity in evangelism. Second is the unity of the local churches across denominational lines. Third is an increased emphasis on witnessing in local believers. Fourth is the spiritual renewal that occurs in those who participate. Fifth are new additions to the church. Sixth is a new sensitivity in the local churches to community needs. Finally is a new appreciation for the power of prayer. One more benefit of a crusade according to Thomas is that mass evangelism can inspire people to be engaged in missions.[100]

Sixth, large evangelistic events are good for plowing new ground. Some crusades serve the purpose of "pre-evangelism." Even if there are few salvations, a crusade plows the ground for future evangelistic efforts. It introduces people to Christianity and raises awareness of who Jesus is. Later, the efforts of the local churches bring in the harvest. As Morrow demonstrates in his research about the Philippines,[101] this is especially true in developing nations where there is a majority of people who have not been exposed to the Gospel.

Seventh, large evangelistic events reach people that the church has difficulty reaching. The challenge with relying on church members to get people saved is that many churches are ingrown. Few believers know many non-Christians. The church family throws potluck suppers for one another, worships together, and spends time visiting the homes of other believers. Ask the typical Christian how many unbelieving friends they

---

[99]Huston, 163.

[100]Thomas, 103.

[101]Morrow, 4.

have and the answer is typically "not many." Koo explains that, "campaign evangelism proclaims the gospel to multitudes of people by all available means, giving unbelievers opportunities to hear the truth, believe in Jesus, and confess Him publicly."[102] In the context of a developing nation, crusades are accompanied by such a massive publicity campaign that thousands of unbelievers who have never met a Christian in their lives may attend out of curiosity. These people are difficult to reach through "friendship evangelism" because they are unlikely to have a Christian friend.

Eighth, large evangelistic events change the spiritual conditions in a region. According to Koo, during an evangelistic campaign, the prophetic voice of God helps to dispel the powers of darkness.[103] Allison and Anderson concur when they explain that a crusade dislodges the powers of darkness.[104] When a spiritual shift occurs, conditions can change in the natural realm too. This is why Thomas points out that a crusade can have a social and moral impact.[105]

Ninth, large evangelistic events allow God to move in a big way. Thomas points out that because of population explosion, a method is needed to reach people in mass.[106] He also believes that mass evangelism gives opportunity for a public confession of

---

[102]Koo, 81.

[103]Koo, 84.

[104]Allison and Anderson, 83.

[105]Thomas, 104.

[106]Thomas, 102-103.

faith.[107] Morrow also celebrates the fact that a crusade is an opportunity for sowing and reaping on a mass scale.[108]

Tenth, large evangelistic events create an atmosphere for miracles. In Acts 8, when Philip the evangelist preached in Samaria, there were multitudes and there were miracles. At a large evangelistic event, there is often an atmosphere for miracles. These miracles draw people to Jesus. The public testimony of people who have received miracles creates an atmosphere of faith in an entire city. According to Allison and Anderson, mass evangelism glorifies God.[109]

Eleventh, large evangelistic events change lives for eternity. The number of salvations at crusades have been grossly overestimated by some evangelists and grossly underestimated by opponents of mass evangelism. The reality is that many people do get saved at large evangelistic events. If ten percent of a crowd of fifty thousand people give their lives to Jesus this represents five thousand new believers. Many average size churches do not pray with five thousand people for salvation in twenty years. One cannot reach everyone through crusades, but the mass evangelist can reach some. Churches work many years to plant seeds into a community, and according to Thomas, crusades are an opportunity to harvest where many have sown.[110] Offering a similar sentiment, Morrow asserts that crusades offer the opportunity to "draw the net," to reap the benefits of

---

[107]Thomas, 100.

[108]Morrow, 60.

[109]Allison and Anderson, 84.

[110]Thomas, 103.

building relationships with unbelievers.[111] Allison and Anderson explain that crusades can pull the loose ends of the Gospel together.[112]

Practitioners and Practical Applications

In modern times, there are three paradigms that have been used in the arena of mass evangelism. These are crusades, healing crusades, and festivals. Billy Graham used the crusade paradigm successfully for over sixty years. The mass-healing crusade was introduced by T. L. Osborn as a way of demonstrating God's power in developing nations. In the past fifteen years, the festival model of mass evangelism was initiated by Luis Palau as a way of attracting people in an entertainment oriented society. This section will examine the similarities and differences between these three ways of doing mass evangelism.

Billy Graham Crusades

The Billy Graham method of doing crusades was originally invented by Charles Finney. In contrast to Jonathan Edwards, Finney believed that a revival does not require a divine move of God; instead, he believed it could be organized using the proper techniques. When Finney came to town, his team secured a location, organized churches, and invited local churches to supply a big choir.[113] As a former businessman, D. L. Moody added business-like principles to the process of preparing a meeting, including

---

[111]Morrow, 50.

[112]Allison and Anderson, 81.

[113]Winter, 100-103.

the use of extensive advertising.[114] This formula continued to be used by R. A. Torrey and Billy Sunday and was eventually adopted and updated for modern times by Billy Graham.

According to the Billy Graham Museum, a Billy Graham crusades involves extensive planning. The first step in a Billy Graham crusade is an invitation from a representative group of local church and community leaders. The second step for the Graham organization is to set up local committees that oversee the crusade activities and to account for all the money spent. Typically there are committees for prayer, ushers, choir, youth, finances, and follow up. The third step is to recruit volunteers and staff. Thousands of volunteers are trained to be counselors, choir members, ushers, and follow up workers. Members of Billy Graham's staff temporarily move to the city and set up a local office. The fourth step involves conducting pre-crusade events that include rallies, training seminars, and concerts. The fifth step is raising money to pay for the crusade. In affluent nations, all funds for the crusade grounds rental, printing, and staff are raised locally. In developing nations, the Billy Graham Evangelistic Association pays for some of the costs. After the crusade is over, a public audit of all the finances is published in a local newspaper. Graham's method of organizing crusades has proved to be an effective way of gathering large crowds together to hear the Gospel.[115]

Graham and his methods of evangelism have had a profound impact on the world. His organizational ability allowed him to gather large crowds. The large crowds attracted

---

[114]Winter, 154.

[115]Billy Graham Museum, Wheaton, IL, sign on the wall, (February 20, 2015).

the attention of the media and of politicians around the world. Graham's integrity and character enabled him to be an influence upon the culture for his entire life. Today, the name of Graham and the idea of mass evangelism are inseparable. His life will remain the gold standard for the crusade evangelist for many years to come.

Luis Palau Festivals

In the early years of his ministry, Palau did crusades similar to Billy Graham.[116] But later, he stopped calling his events crusades and instead called them festivals.[117] For example in 2003, he did a BeachFest during Spring Break in Fort Lauderdale, Florida,

---

[116]In 1961, Palau volunteered at Graham's crusade in Fresno, California, where he learned how to mobilize people for a crusade. See Palau and Sanford, 74..

[117]What's in a name? According to the Gospels, Jesus preached to "multitudes" (Matt 13:2). Jonathan Edwards called his meetings revivals or a "work of the Spirit of God." (*Distinguishing Marks of a Work of the Spirit of God,* 1741). John Wesley called his outdoor events "field-preaching." (John Wesley, *Journal of John Wesley* (1 April 1739). The Cain Ridge Revival sparked the spread of "camp meetings" because thousands of frontiersmen came with their wagons and their tents. See Paul K. Conkin, *Cain Ridge: America's Pentecost* (Madison, Wisconsin: University of Wisconsin Press, 1990). Finney called his events "revivals." (Charles Finney, *Lectures on Revivals of Religion* (Old Tappan, NJ: Fleming H. Revell, 1868), 8) D. L. Moody coined the term "campaigns" for his evangelistic events. This was terminology straight from the battlefields of the Civil War, in which Moody served as a chaplain to the troops in Chicago (Dorsett, 183). Torrey called his events "missions" (Greenway, 51). Billy Graham used the term "crusades." (Pollock, *The Billy Graham Story,* 53). This word has some negative connotations in the Muslim world because of the legacy of the crusades when Christians attempted to retake the Holy Lands with the sword (Tuttle, 189) Luis Palau calls his events "festivals" because he wants to create an atmosphere that attracts the lost (Koo,172). Some evangelists have used the term "invasion." (Two examples are Scott Hinkle and David Blanchard). Other evangelists have used the more neutral terms "concert" or "music fest." Regardless of what an evangelistic event is called, the idea is the same. The goal is to preach the Gospel to people who do not know Jesus.

that attracted a total attendance of 340,000 people.[118] Instead of having a choir made up of local church members, he invited contemporary Christian music groups to perform. He attracted people using extreme sports, a skate park, food venders, and children's activities like bouncy houses and face painting.

In 2007, Palau's son Kevin was inspired to reach out to their home city of Portland, Oregon. He built a relationship with the mayor of Portland (a prominent member of the LGBTQ community) and with other government officials. This led to a new initiative called "CityServe," a wholistic approach to evangelism where the evangelist works to serve the local community.[119]

The festival model for mass evangelism is different from Graham's crusade evangelism in several ways. First, a festival takes place in open areas like parks and beaches instead of inside stadiums or indoor arenas. Second, a festival invites contemporary Christian music artists instead of choirs. Third, a festival has a fun and family-friendly atmosphere instead of the feeling of a religious service. Fourth, a festival is sponsored by corporate sponsors and not just churches. Finally, festivals require fewer committees and may last only a couple of days instead of several weeks.[120]

---

[118]Luis Palau, "Photos," 20 February 2018, https://www.flickr.com/photos/luispalau/12622872025 (20 February 2018).

[119]Kevin Palau, *Unlikely: Setting Aside our Differences to Live out the Gospel* (New York: Howard, 2015), 7

[120]Koo, 173-174.

T. L. Osborn Healing Crusades

The missionary evangelist Tommy Lee Osborn pioneered the international healing crusade.[121] As a Pentecostal preacher, Osborn brought a unique Pentecostal perspective to crusade evangelism. His conviction that miracles happen today and that Jesus Christ still heals the sick add an element to crusade evangelism that is not present in the Graham or Palau methods of organizing a crusade.

In 1945, Osborn and his wife Daisy went as missionaries to the nation of India. After only ten months, they came home discouraged because they were unable to lead the Hindus and Muslims of India to Jesus through traditional missionary methods. They showed the people in India the Bible and in return the people showed them copies of the Koran and the Bhagavad Gita. When the Osborns were unable to prove which book was true, they gave up and returned home in defeat.

Osborn said he was changed after he had four encounters with Jesus. One morning at 6 o'clock, Jesus appeared to him. On another occasion, Osborn saw Jesus working through a preacher who was praying for the sick. Then, Osborn saw Jesus in the pages of the Bible. Finally, Osborn experienced Jesus working through his own prayers. Because of these revelations about Jesus, T. L. and Daisy returned to the mission field

---

[121]Osborn was part of the Voice of Healing movement that included other healing evangelists like William Branham, F. F. Bosworth, Gordon Lindsey, and Oral Roberts. They were all known for praying for the sick, but it was Osborn who adapted praying for the sick as a tool for reaching people in crusades on the mission field. For more on the Voice of Healing Movement, see Dennis Gordon Lindsey, "The History and Global Impact of Christ for the Nations Institute," (D.Min. Proj., Oral Roberts University, 2014), 12.

and eventually traveled to over ninety nations over a half-century of ministry and led millions of people to Jesus.[122]

Miracles became the proof to Osborn that Jesus is alive and the Bible is true. The banner on his crusade platform usually featured Hebrews 13:8, "Jesus Christ is the same yesterday, today, and forever." Praying a mass prayer for the sick was a defining ingredient in Osborn's preaching. Osborn often started his sermons by telling the story of a man or woman who had been healed in one of his services. Then he would tell a story about one of the miracles Jesus performed in the Bible. Then he prayed for the sick in a mass healing prayer. Osborn found that when he preached a simple message about Jesus and then prayed for the sick, people would be healed. Cripples walked, blind eyes were opened, and deaf ears were able to hear. He invited them to the platform to share their testimonies, and when the crowd heard about the miracles, they would return to their neighborhoods and invite their friends and family to come to the crusade. Osborn believes "that the most fundamental lesson possible to learn about missions and evangelism is that without miracles, Christianity is little more than another dead religion."[123]

In developing nations, miracles are an effective way to attract people. Graham's organizational expertise and Palau's method of using famous musicians, BMX bikes, and motorcycles are great bait for attracting people in the United States, but to a certain

---

[122]Prakash, 73.

[123]Tommy Lee Osborn and Daisy Osborn, "My Life Story," 11, in *Faith Library in 23 Volumes*, vol. 1 (Tulsa, OK: OSFO International, 1997), 84.

extent, the fewer miracles one has in a crusade, the more entertainment is needed to attract people. The strength of Osborn's healing evangelism lies in his reliance upon the supernatural.

Summary

In this chapter, various studies of mass evangelism have been evaluated. Each of the studies acknowledge the criticism of crusades, but they also demonstrate that mass evangelism is an important part of church history and make a case for its continued use today. After looking at the related literature, it is clear that crusades can be used by God to lead people to Jesus and to facilitate genuine disciple-making and church growth. The next chapter will move from the abstract to the concrete as it delineates how an actual crusade will be evaluated.

CHAPTER 4

METHODOLOGY

Introduction

What happens at an evangelistic event in a developing nation? Who attends the event? Why do they come? How do people hear about the event? Do local pastors think the event is successful? Does the evangelistic event produce any long-term effect? These questions are what this research project attempted to answer. In this chapter, the rationale for this study and the methods used to gather information about a mass evangelism campaign are examined. This chapter also includes a description of the measurement instruments utilized, the method of data collection, and an explanation of how the data was analyzed.

Rationale

The goal of this research was to provide a comprehensive look at a mass evangelism campaign taking place in Caicó, Brazil, located in the state of Rio Grande do Norte. It was expected that this research would provide a snapshot picture of the people who attended the event and would provide some insight into the long-term impact of the evangelistic campaign. The research done in this study will allow the researcher and other evangelists to conduct mass evangelism events more effectively in the future.

Rationale for the Project (For Topic)

Evangelism is the greatest assignment given to the church. The importance of evangelism is reflected in both the Old and the New Testaments. In the Old Testament, the prophet Jonah convinced the city of Nineveh to repent; in the New Testament, Jesus preached to multitudes, and Philip preached to crowds of people in Samaria. Throughout church history, mass evangelism was used by God to bring people to Jesus. The Great Commission instructs believers to go into all the world and preach the Gospel to every creature (Mark 16:15). This command includes the nation of Brazil. The desire to conduct the mass evangelism event that is being studied is rooted in the theological conviction that mass evangelism is an effective tool for presenting the Gospel to the unsaved, the historical evidence of how God has used mass evangelism in the past, a review of literature on the subject of mass evangelism, and in the researcher's personal experience in engaging in mass evangelism. The implementation of this research project allowed the researcher to assess who came to the event, why they came, and how they were impacted by the meeting.

Rationale for the Method or Design (For Methodology)

There are a variety of questions the researcher wanted to explore: Who comes to a mass evangelistic event? Why do they come? How do they hear about the event? What is their religious background? How do the people respond to the event? The best way to obtain these answers is to ask the people who are in attendance. An instrument for conducting a questionnaire survey was developed and was administered to a portion of the crowd at a mass evangelistic event. Several additional questionnaires were administered to local pastors and church members in order to provide insights into the general spiritual condition of the city, to measure how involved the local churches were in participating in the event, and to test the long-term impact of the event.

According to Kenneth Mayton, "A questionnaire is a means of eliciting the feelings, beliefs, experiences, perceptions, or attitudes of some sample of individuals."[1] A questionnaire survey is a good way to discover the demographic makeup of an audience and to get a "picture of various values, beliefs, and attitudes"[2] that are relevant to the research question of this project. Also, "Surveys are excellent tools to collect demographic and general behavioral information."[3] The collection of data about a crowd can be done in a relatively short amount of time by using a questionnaire survey.

Procedures

A mass evangelistic event[4] was held in northeast Brazil, in the city of Caicó, Rio Grande do Norte, the week of May 28-June 2, 2018. This event was organized by the ministry of Rubens Cunha, an evangelist and crusade organizer with many years of experience. A variety of marketing efforts were used to publicize the event, including

---

[1] Kenneth Mayton, "Research Resources," class handout from DMIN 786 Principles of Research, Oral Roberts University, 2016, 159.

[2] Nancy T. Ammerman et al., eds., *Studying Congregations* (Nashville, TN: Abingdon Press, 1998), 217.

[3] Ammerman et al., 218.

[4] This mass evangelism event will be organized utilizing a combination of methods developed by Billy Graham (crusades), Luis Palau (festivals), and by T. L. Osborn (healing crusades).

radio, television, flyers, banners, posters, and internet advertisements. Local churches were mobilized to promote the event, and believers were asked to serve at the event as ushers and counselors.

The actual crusade was a two-day event taking place on June 1-2, 2018. In the days prior to the event, several activities took place including a leadership conference to train local believers, a youth concert, and preaching in public schools. The event opened with songs and prayer. The researcher, Evangelist Daniel King, preached a message on healing and salvation to the gathered people, gave an altar call, and prayed for the sick. Immediately after the message was finished, the questionnaire survey was administered to a portion of the crowd. While the questionnaires were being completed, music continued to hold the attention of the crowd. The questionnaire was administered on both nights of the event in case there were any adjustments that needed to be made to the process of administering the questionnaire.

Sample Selection

A random sample of individuals at the event were surveyed. The goal was to sample at least ten percent of the crowd (for example, if ten thousand people are at the event, the goal was to question at least one thousand people). Generally, the larger the sample size, the more accurate the findings will be.[5] This sample size was judged to be large enough to be a representative sample of the entire crowd. An accurate estimate of the total number of people in the crowd was gathered by asking three people to count the

---

[5]Mayton, 73.

attendees by using clickers. The average of these three estimates provided the researcher with an approximate number of people in attendance at the event.

A team of one hundred trained interviewers were required to interview one thousand people. Each interviewer interviewed ten people over the course of an hour. It was expected that each interview would take six minutes to conduct. The researcher used local church pastors and trained counselors to conduct the interviews.

The pastors and counselors who administered the questionnaire were trained during the leadership conference that took place on the Wednesday night preceding the crusade. The researcher explained to them the importance of the research being conducted and described the appropriate procedures required to gather the information. At the training session, they practiced collecting a sample survey.

This random sample was not chosen haphazardly. Theoretically each member of the audience had an equal chance of being chosen to answer the questions.[6] To guarantee an equal opportunity for an individual to be questioned, the crusade grounds was divided up into one hundred squares of equal size, and each interviewer was assigned a specific area in which to conduct his or her interviews. If the interviewer was allowed to choose where they interview people, there could potentially be a lopsided sampling of the crowd. For example, if all the interviews took place at the front of the crowd, the answers gathered in the sample might be distinctly different than the answers given by those who are standing at the fringes of the crowd. Having a pre-assigned area for each interviewer facilitated the random nature of the interviews conducted.

---

[6]Ammerman, 219.

Construction of Questionnaire

The data was collected using the questionnaire that the researcher designed after examining several surveys that have been used by others in similar situations.[7] The questionnaire was administered in face-to-face interviews. The questionnaire was designed to be able to be answered in five to six minutes, which is a relatively short amount of time. The participants were asked to answer the questionnaire anonymously in order to ensure the validity of the test results. When many people are involved in a study the quality of each individual survey becomes a difficult issue. Thus, the researcher kept the survey simple in order to make the process as easy and convenient as possible.

The questionnaire survey was composed of a series of multiple-choice questions based on the Likert Scale (see Appendix A). Because of translation difficulties, open-ended questions and short-answer questions were avoided as much as possible; thus it was a "closed or restricted" questionnaire.[8] The questionnaire was translated into the local language of Portuguese.

The survey was conducted using Google Forms. An online Google Form was created by the researcher. Each questioner was able to access this form on a smart phone. They asked each participant the questions and recorded the answers on the online form. When each survey was completed, the questioner pressed, "enter" and Google Forms instantly compiled the information for the researcher. Since the Internet did not work for

---

[7]See Ammerman, 250-253; Huston, Appendix F; Thomas, 109.

[8]Mayton, 160.

some people, the researcher also had paper questionnaires and pens available. It was believed that using the online form would make the data collection and evaluation easier.

Additional Surveys

In addition to the sample survey administered to the audience, several additional surveys were administered. These additional surveys allowed the researcher to present a more full view of the results of the mass evangelism event. The additional surveys can be found in the appendix.

Appendix B: Pre-Crusade Pastor's Survey. Every pastor in the city was asked to fill out this survey in advance of the crusade. This survey helped the researcher access the spiritual conditions of the local churches and measured how many church members participated in promoting the crusade.

Appendix C: Post-Crusade Pastor's Survey. This survey helped the researcher to gauge the attitude of the pastors regarding the crusade. It was administered via Google Forms to the pastors immediately after the crusade was finished.

Appendix D: Survey of Pastors Three Months After the Crusade. The biggest criticism of crusade evangelism concerns the follow-up of new believers. This survey attempted to discover the long-term results of the crusade. This survey also revisited the attitude of the local pastors who participated in the crusade three month after the event.

Appendix E: Post-Crusade Church Members Survey. This survey was administered to several local churches on the Sunday evening following the crusade. The researcher visited these churches on the day after the event and the survey was administered at that time. These churches were deemed to be representative of all the participating churches. It assisted the researcher in discovering how many people in the local churches were involved in the crusade.

Data Analysis

After receiving the data from the questionnaires, the researcher compiled all the answers from the Google forms in order to organize, tabulate, and interpret the data. The data was examined for patterns of behavior and common themes. The percentages of respondents for each answer were calculated. The researcher calculated the mean,[9] the median,[10] and the mode[11] for each question in the questionnaire. The researcher also looked at the relationships among different variables. The answers from the pastor's pre-test, post-test, and three months later post-test were compared and contrasted.

Chapter Summary

In chapter 4, the rationale and the methods for the sample survey of attendees at a mass evangelism campaign were explained. The next chapter will consist of a presentation of the results from this researcher's survey of a mass evangelism campaign. Read on.

---

[9]The mean is the average.

[10]The median is the point below which half the answers fall.

[11]The mode is the answer that occurs most frequently.

CHAPTER 5

PRESENTATION OF RESULTS

Introduction

This project was designed to give a snapshot picture of an evangelistic crusade in northeast Brazil. The crusade took place on the evenings of June 1-2, 2018 in the city of Caicó, Brazil. The goal was to discover who came to the crusade, why they came, and what impact the crusade had on the city.

Caicó, Brazil is located in Northeast Brazil in the state of Rio Grande do Norte. According to a census in 2013, a total of 66,246 people live in the city.[1] The city has the highest rate of suicide in the state and the third-highest rate of suicide in the country of Brazil. Caicó is known as a stronghold of idolatry and the people fight mental depression and spiritual oppression.[2] The city is considered to be a stronghold of Catholicism. The patron saint of Caicó is St. Anne and every year a festival is held by the Roman Catholic Church to honor her memory. Caicó is also known for hosting the largest carnival in the state of Rio Grande do Norte.

---

[1] "History," http://caico.rn.gov.br/pagina.php?codigo=3 (September 11, 2018).

[2] Interview with local pastors, by author, 28 May 2018.

Nine evangelical churches participated in the crusade which represented almost all of the evangelical churches in the city.[3] The total membership of these nine churches equals 1,357 which is about 2% of the population of the city of Caicó.

The crusade was conducted as a partnership between the ministries of Rubens Cunha, a Brazilian evangelist, and Daniel King, the author of this paper. The costs of the crusade were split between the two ministries. Cunha has a team of crusade directors who organized the event and the researcher brought a team of people from North America to help with the ministry.

The planning for the crusade began six months in advance. A crusade director visited the city of Caicó and met with the local pastors. They indicated their eagerness to participate in the event. Permission was secured from local authorities to hold the event. Three months prior to the crusade, prayer cards were given to all the church members. Each believer was encouraged to write down the names of ten unsaved people on their prayer card and to begin to pray for them to be saved. When the event drew closer, the church members reached out to the ten people and invited each of them to attend the crusade. One month prior to the crusade, one thousand posters were distributed throughout the city. The local churches distributed seventy thousand crusade pamphlets and fifty thousand youth crusade invitations. In the eight days prior to the crusade, seven

---

[3]Two churches who did not participate are the Universal Church of God (*Igreja Universal do Reino de Deus*) and the World Church *(Igreja Mundial)*. These churches are classified in Brazil as neo-Pentecostal churches. They are known for offering miracles in exchange for offerings; and usually, they do not participate in outreaches with other churches. The Mormons and the Jehovah Witnesses also did not participate in the crusade. The Roman Catholic Church actively opposed the crusade.

sound cars were used to announce the crusade for six hours each day for a total of two hundred and fifty-six hours of sound car announcements. Seven hundred and fifty radio spots were run on three different radio stations over a fifteen-day period. WhatsApp, Instagram, and Facebook were also used to advertise the event.

The international team of ministers included six Americans, one Canadian, one Paraguayan, one German, and at least five Brazilians. The team arrived in the city on May 27, and immediately began ministering in local schools and neighborhoods.[4] A three-day training event was held for local believers on May 28, 29, and 30.[5] On Thursday, May 31, a preliminary youth concert was held at the crusade grounds.[6] On Friday and Saturday evenings, the crusade was conducted. Total attendance on Friday

---

[4] The team ministered in two schools and four neighborhoods. Total attendance at these events totaled 544 people. Originally, the team was scheduled to minister in more public schools, but at the last moment, the team was prevented from ministering in the schools because a Roman Catholic superintendent was concerned about the evangelical nature of the team's presentation. At the neighborhood events, packets of food were given away to hungry families.

[5] The attendance at the Soul Winning Training event on Monday night was 239 people; on Tuesday night 422 people were present; and on Wednesday night 485 believers came.

[6] Seven hundred ninety-two people attended the Youth Concert to listen to music artist Chris "Big C" Slager. No surveys were conducted because the researcher was not allowed to survey those under the age of 18.

night was 1,492 people.[7] Total attendance on Saturday night was estimated to be 4,300 people.[8] On Saturday morning, a children's festival was held at the crusade grounds,[9] a pastoral leadership seminar took place at a local church,[10] and a training session for children's leaders was organized.[11] A total of 641 people filled out decision cards at the crusade indicating they had decided to follow Jesus.

Originally, it was hoped that crusade attendance would be larger. There were two factors that limited the number of people who attended. First, in the week prior to the crusade there was a trucker's strike in Brazil that brought the country to a halt.[12] In an effort to enforce their strike, the truckers built barricades across many highways throughout Brazil. The lack of trucks available to take products to market caused produce to spoil in the fields, supermarket shelves to become empty, and gas stations to run out of

---

[7]Six people used clickers to count every person in the crowd. The six numbers were added together and divided by six to give an average number of 1,492 in attendance.

[8]Using clickers to count the crowd size proved to be extremely difficult when the crowd exceeded one thousand people. The attendance on Saturday night was estimated by measuring the size of the crusade grounds and guessing at the density of the people.

[9]Five hundred and four children were in attendance at the children's festival.

[10]Twenty-four pastors and church leaders came to the leadership seminar.

[11]Thirty-five youth leaders were trained.

[12]"Brazil Hopes Truck Strike Ends," *Yahoo News*, (29 May 2018), n.p., https://www.yahoo.com/news/brazil-hopes-end-truck-strike-eighth-day-141557061.html (4 September 2018).

fuel.[13] This unrest led to a general sense of political and economic uneasiness. The strike directly affected our crusade because the truck carrying a platform and sound system was unable to arrive in time. The crusade team was forced to quickly cobble together a platform and sound system from local resources which increased the cost of the event. Second, the crusade was actively opposed by the Roman Catholic Church. On Thursday night, the night of our youth festival, the Catholics decided to hold a parade to honor St. Anne. At the end of the procession, the local arch-bishop delivered a sermon and said, "Do everything you can to oppose the crusade. We should not accept their kind [the evangelicals] in our city. Do not go to the crusade and do everything you can to expel them from our city."[14]

Yet, despite the two problems that probably lowered total attendance, the organizers considered the crusade to be a success. People were saved; people were healed, and the local churches were strengthened. Overall, the crusade was a successful event that resulted in measureable results.

---

[13]"Brazil Takes Stock of a Week Long Strike and Its Not Pretty," *Bloomberg News*, (28 May 2018), n.p, , https://www.bloomberg.com/news/articles/2018-05-28/brazil-takes-stock-of-a-week-long-strike-and-it-s-not-pretty (4 September 2018).

[14]Another result of the Roman Catholic opposition was a closing of the public schools to the team. In ten years of doing crusades in Brazil, Evangelist Rubens Cunha has never had the local schools oppose a visit from his crusade team; but in Caicó the superintendent of the schools was a Roman Catholic, and he forbade the crusade team from visiting the schools to talk about the upcoming crusade. If the team had been able to visit the schools to invite the teenagers and distribute flyers, it probably would have resulted in a greater attendance at the crusade.

Data Presentation

Friday and Saturday Night Crusade Survey

A survey was administered to the crowd of crusade attendees on both Friday and Saturday nights. On Friday night, a total of 1,492 people attended and 178 responses were recorded. This represents 11.93%[15] of the crowd that was surveyed. On Saturday night, a total of 4,300 people attended and 483 responses were recorded. This represents 11.23%[16] of the crowd that was surveyed on Saturday evening. So, the goal of surveying 10% or more of the crowd was achieved on both evenings. All surveys were given in Portuguese but in this chapter they are translated into English.

Survey Question #1: Age of the Crowd

The first question on the survey was, "How old are you?" Those doing the questioning were instructed not to administer a survey to anyone under the age of 18.[17] The average age on Friday night was 38.36. The average age on Saturday night was 38.40. The median age on Friday night was 35. The median age on Saturday night was 38. The most frequent age on Friday night was 33, with 9 respondents. The most frequently occurring age on Saturday night was 18, which had 21 respondents.

---

[15] 178 x 100 / 1492 = 11.93%

[16] 483 x 100 / 4,300 = 11.23%

[17] Despite this instruction, seven underage surveys were collected on Friday night and fourteen were collected on Saturday night.

Table 1. Range of Ages of the Respondents to the Survey

Age Categories of the Respondents on Friday Night	#	Age Categories of the Respondents on Saturday Night	#
Ages 18-19	8	Ages 18-19	30
Ages 20-29	41	Ages 20-29	107
Ages 30-39	46	Ages 30-39	113
Ages 40-49	29	Ages 40-49	105
Ages 50-59	27	Ages 50-59	74
Ages 60-69	13	Ages 60-69	28
Ages 70-79	6	Ages 70-79	9
Ages 80-89	1	Ages 80-89	1

Survey Question #2: Gender of the Crowd

The second question was, "What is your gender?" On Friday night, 55 males made up 31% of the crowd, and 122 females made up 69% of the crowd. On Saturday night, 187 males made up 39% of the crowd and 294 females made up 61% of the crowd.

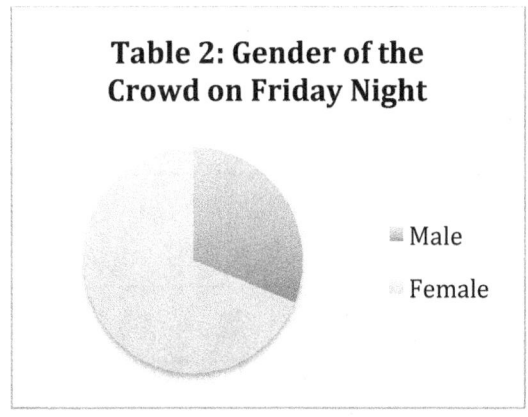

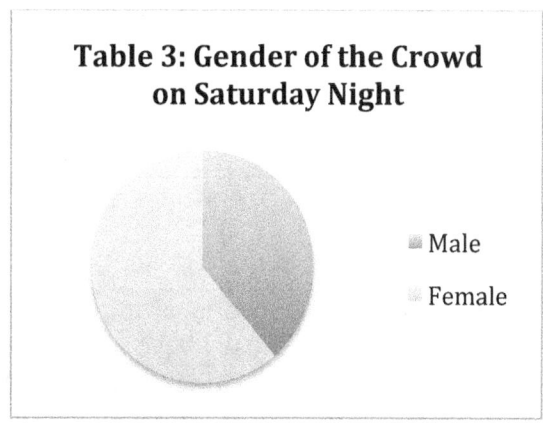

Survey Question #3: Prayer

The third question was, "Did you repeat the prayer with the preacher tonight?" On Friday night, 154 respondents replied "Yes" (87.5%) and 22 respondents replied "No" (12.5%). On Saturday night, 395 respondents replied "Yes" (82.6%) and 83 respondents replied "No" (17.4%).

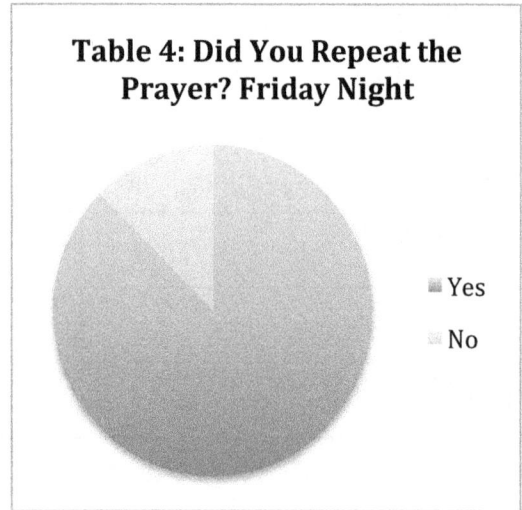
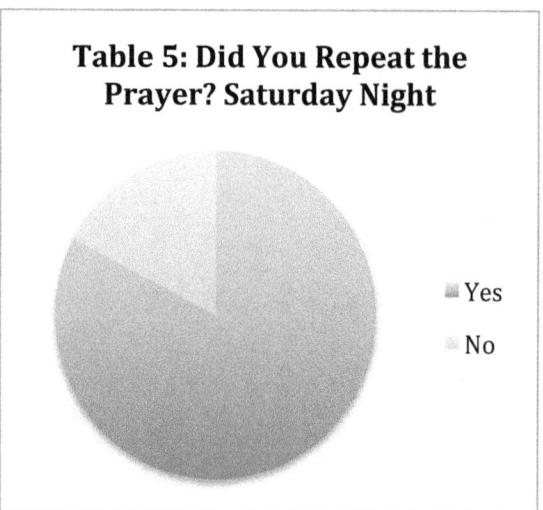

Survey Question #4: Why Did You Pray?

The fourth question of the survey was, "Why did you repeat the prayer with the preacher tonight?" This was an open-ended question and it produced a wide variety of responses. These responses have been broken down into several categories:

Table 6. Answers to Question 4: Why Did You Pray?

Nature of the Respondent's Answer	Number of Answers
The respondent mentions "faith" or "belief" in God. Example: "Because I had faith," "Because I have faith in Jesus," "Because I believe in God."	120
The respondent mentions a need for "healing" or the desire to receive a "miracle." Example: "Because I needed a miracle," "I needed to be healed," "Because my daughter needed to be healed."	98

The respondent prayed because he or she felt something that compelled them to pray. Example: "I felt good," "Because I felt the presence of the Lord," "I felt of God," "I felt I needed it," "Because I felt the Holy Spirit."	19
The respondent prayed because the preacher asked them to pray. Example: "Because he asked me to repeat," "Because he asked."	22
The respondent prayed because the prayer was beautiful. Example: "Because it was beautiful," "Because the prayer was beautiful."	9
The respondent prayed because he or she wanted to. Example: "Because I wanted to repeat," "Because I wanted to."	6
The respondent prayed because he or she wanted salvation or because he or she wanted forgiveness. Example: "For salvation," "Salvation," "Because I wanted to be saved," "To confirm my decision to ask forgiveness for my sins," "Because I wanted my sins to go," "Because I allow Jesus in my heart."	7
The respondent wanted to be set free from demonic activity. Example: "To receive delivery from the evil."	1
The respondent repeated the prayer because of peer pressure. Example: "Because everybody was repeating the prayer, so I did too."	1
The respondent repeated the prayer because he or she "liked it." Example: "Because I liked it," "Because I like to pray," "Because I liked."	19
The respondent prayed because he or she loves Jesus. Example: "Because I love Jesus," "Because I love Christ," "Because Jesus loves me."	4
The respondent wanted to receive grace. Example: "I needed grace," "I wanted the grace of God."	3
The respondent supplied a nonsense answer or an answer that did not answer the question.	9
Other reasons that respondents gave include: "To thank God," "Because I lift Jesus in my life," "To feel good," "To change my life," "It is amazing to pray," "to be strong," "Improvement in life," "Because God is here," "I thought it was interesting," "It was not impossible," "To receive delivery from the evil."	29

Survey Question #5: Do You Need Healing?

The fifth survey question was, "Were you sick, or in need of healing, when you arrived here tonight?" Of 171 responses on Friday night, 76 answered, "No" (44.4%) and 95 answered, "Yes" (55.6%). Of 476 responses on Saturday night, 244 answered, "No" (51.3%) and 232 answered, "Yes" (48.7%).

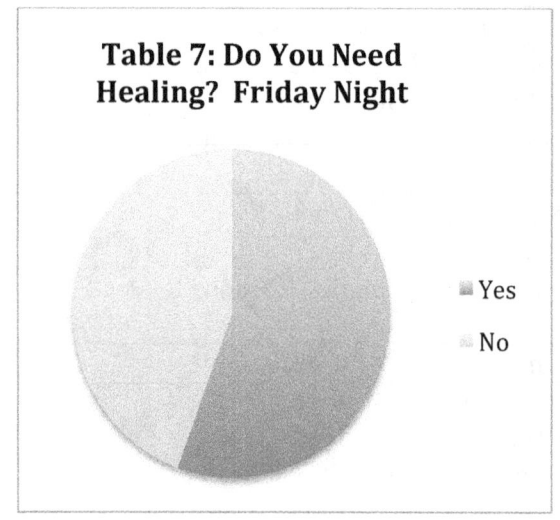

Survey Question #6: Do You Feel Better?

The sixth survey question was written as a statement, "My body feels better now than when I arrived." The Likert Scale was used for the responses.

Table 9. Do You Feel Better? Friday Night

Strongly Agree	Agree	Undecided	Disagree	Strongly Disagree
56 (36.1%)	63 (40.6%)	29 (18.7%)	5 (3.2%)	2 (1.3%)

Table 10. Do You Feel Better? Saturday Night

Strongly Agree	Agree	Undecided	Disagree	Strongly Disagree
128 (33.3%)	159 (41.4%)	57 (14.8%)	28 (7.3%)	12 (3.1%)

Of the 95 people on Friday night who answered "yes" to the question of whether they arrived with pain in the their bodies, 35 agreed and 37 strongly agreed that their body felt better. Ten said they were "not sure" if they felt better. Thirteen did not answer.

Of the 232 people on Saturday night who answered "yes" to the question of whether they arrived with pain in the their bodies, 89 "strongly agreed" and 93 "agreed" that their body felt better. Thirty-one said they were "not sure" if they felt better. Two said they "disagreed" and 9 "strongly disagreed" that they felt better. Seven left this answer blank.

Survey Question #7: Is It A Miracle?

The seventh survey question was written as a statement, "I would say the improvement in my body is a miracle." The Likert Scale was used for the responses.

Table 11. Is It A Miracle? Friday Night

Strongly Agree	Agree	Undecided	Disagree	Strongly Disagree
53 (35.8%)	56 (37.8%)	29 (19.6%)	7 (4.7%)	3 (2%)

Table 12. Is It A Miracle? Saturday Night

Strongly Agree	Agree	Undecided	Disagree	Strongly Disagree
138 (36.6%)	141 (37.4%)	60 (15.9%)	30 (8%)	8 (2.1%)

Of the 72 people on Friday night who answered "yes" to the question of whether they arrived with pain in their bodies and said that they felt better, 64 (88.89%) strongly agreed or agreed that they had received a miracle. Three said they were not sure, and 5 did not answer. Of the 182 people on Saturday night who answered "yes" to the question of whether they arrived with pain in their bodies and said that they felt better, 176 (96.7%) "strongly agreed" or "agreed" that they had received a miracle. 3 said they were "not sure" if it was a miracle. Two said they "definitely disagreed" it was a miracle and 1 left the answer blank.

Survey Question #8: How Did You Hear About This Meeting?

The eighth survey question was, "How did you hear about this meeting?" Multiple answers were allowed. On Friday night, a total of 173 people answered question eight. Fifty-seven heard about the meeting from a friend; 22 were invited by a family member; 48 saw a poster; and 41 received a flyer. Thirty-eight saw an advertisement on Facebook; 26 learned about the meeting on Instagram. Twenty-nine responded to a message on WhatsApp; 50 heard about the meeting on the radio; and 11 heard about the meeting from a sound car.

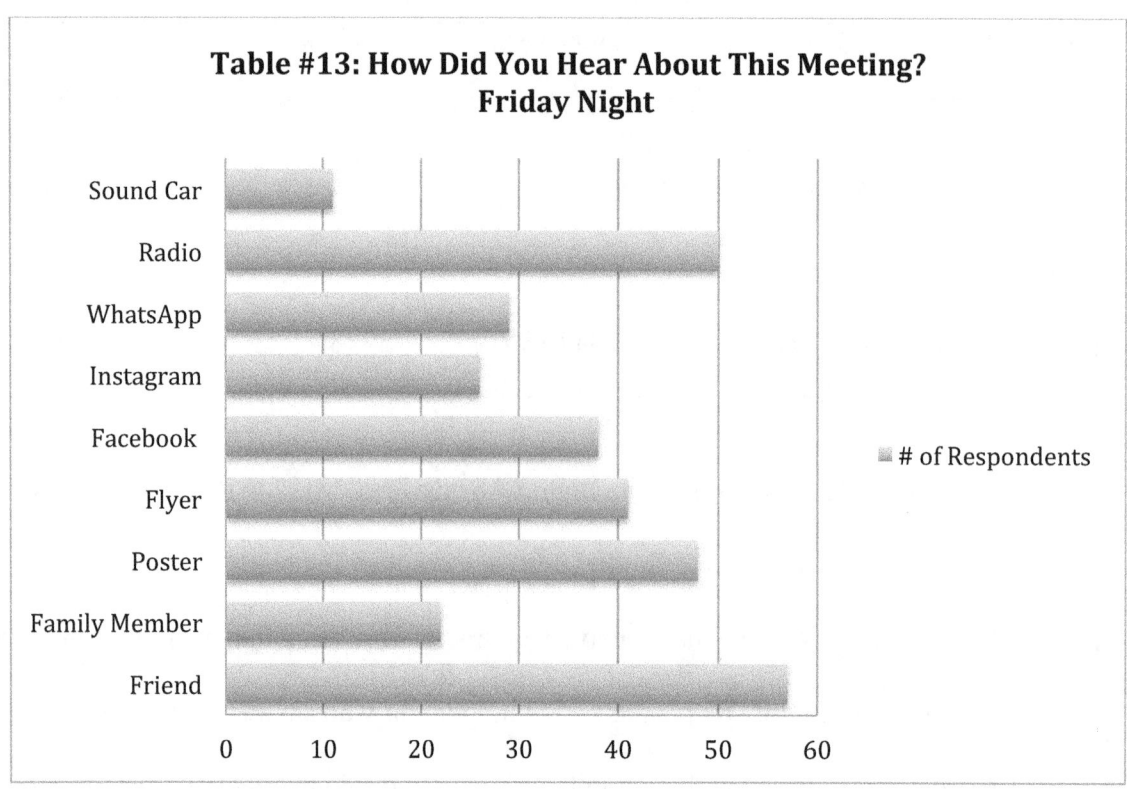

On Saturday night, a total of 466 people answered question eight. One hundred sixty-three heard about the meeting from a friend; 79 were invited by a family member; 123 saw a poster; 132 received a flyer' and 84 saw an advertisement on Facebook. Forty-one learned about the meeting on Instagram; 63 responded to a message on WhatsApp; 127 heard about the meeting on the radio; and 4 heard about the meeting from a sound car.[1]

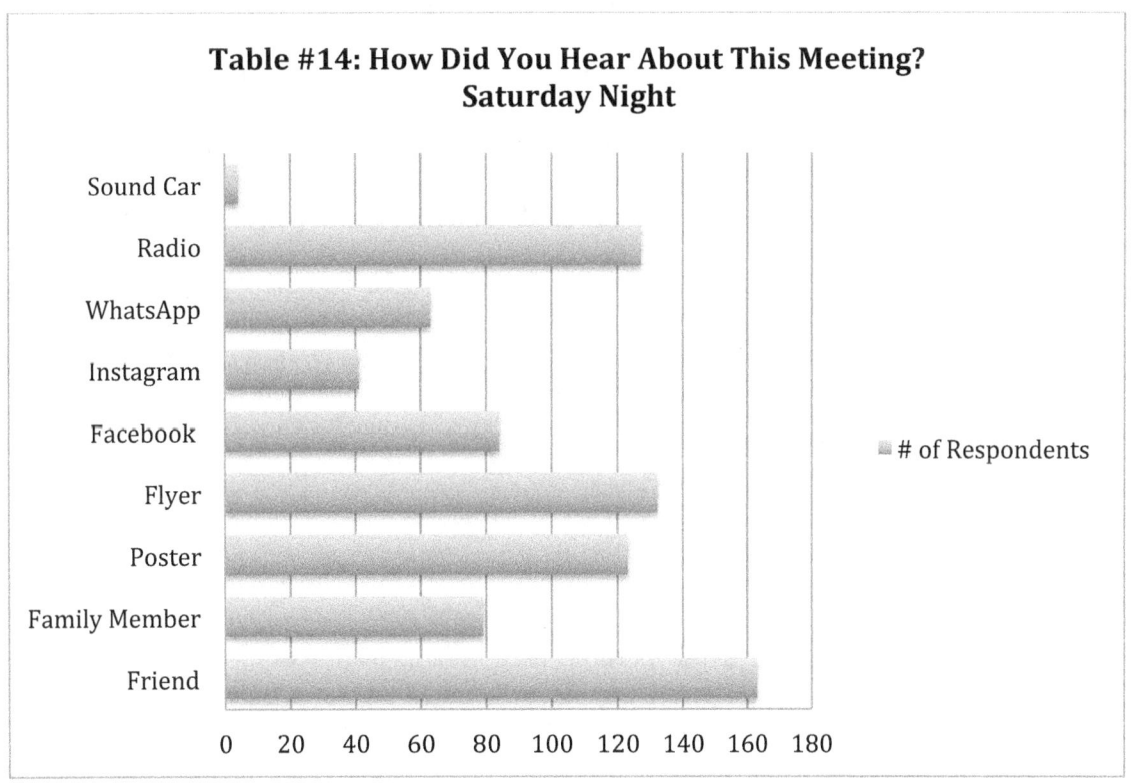

---

[1]Sound cars were accidently not included as an option on the written survey. Four people wrote in "sound car." If "sound car" had been included as an option, the number of people who would have chosen this option would likely have increased.

All of the marketing strategies used to promote this event proved to be successful[2] but the two that worked best were radio[3] and personal invitations.[4]

Survey Question #9: Why Did You Come to This Meeting?

The ninth survey question was, "Why did you come to this meeting?" Multiple answers were allowed. On Friday night, 169 responded to the question. 41 chose "My friend invited me." Thirty-seven said they were curious about what was happening; 29 wanted to hear the music; 55 said they needed a miracle; and 46 said they wanted to see miracles. Twenty-three came because their pastor told them they should come. Forty-one came because they are curious about God; 2 did not know why they came' and 26 gave another reason why they came. These "other" answers include: "I like to participate," "I am searching for more of God," "because I seek the Lord," "because I wanted to go," "because Jesus invited me," and "to seek God."

---

[2]All of the advertising methods used created awareness for some people who were surveyed. There was no advertising method that stood out as being completely unsuccessful. Many respondents indicated they had been exposed to three or more different methods of advertising. The advertising was deemed successful since it was hard to go anywhere in the town without being exposed to the advertising. It is suspected that the reason more people did not come to the crusade was not for lack of advertising, but because of a theological opposition to attending an evangelical event. In retrospect, it would have been helpful to ask people afterwards in the town why they did not attend.

[3]Apparently, a lot of people in the town listen to the radio. Advertising on Facebook, What's App, and Instagram also proved effective, but radio outperformed social media in the questionnaires.

[4]There was special emphasis in the months prior to the crusade placed on encouraging the local believers to pray for and invite people to the crusade.

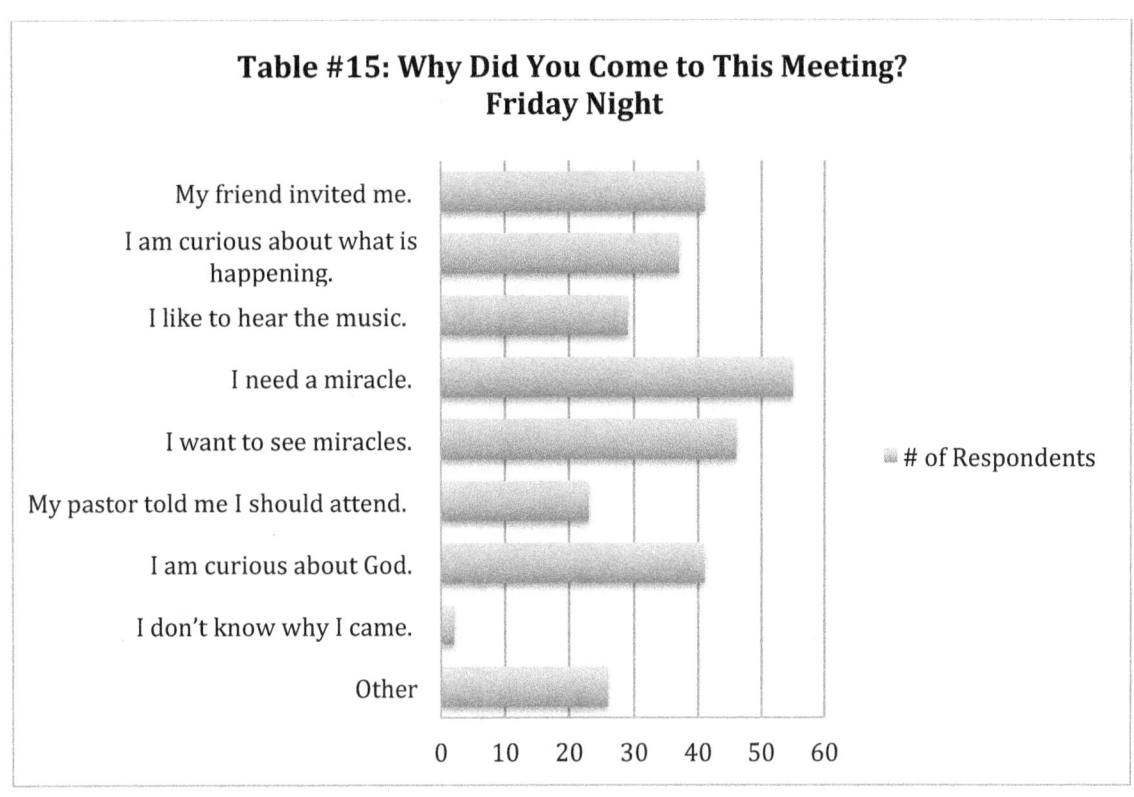

On Saturday night, 460 responded to the question, "Why did you come to this meeting?" One hundred seven chose "My friend invited me." Seventy-seven said they were curious about what was happening; 44 wanted to hear the music; 116 said they needed a miracle; and 106 said they wanted to see miracles. Sixty-one came because their pastor told them to come; 112 came because they are curious about God; 6 did not know why they came; and 66 gave another reason why they came. These "other" answers include: "Jesus called me," "to seek the presence of God," "because I am an evangelical," "because I wanted to," "because my wife invited me," "I came to seek God," "because I had a need," and "because someone asked me."

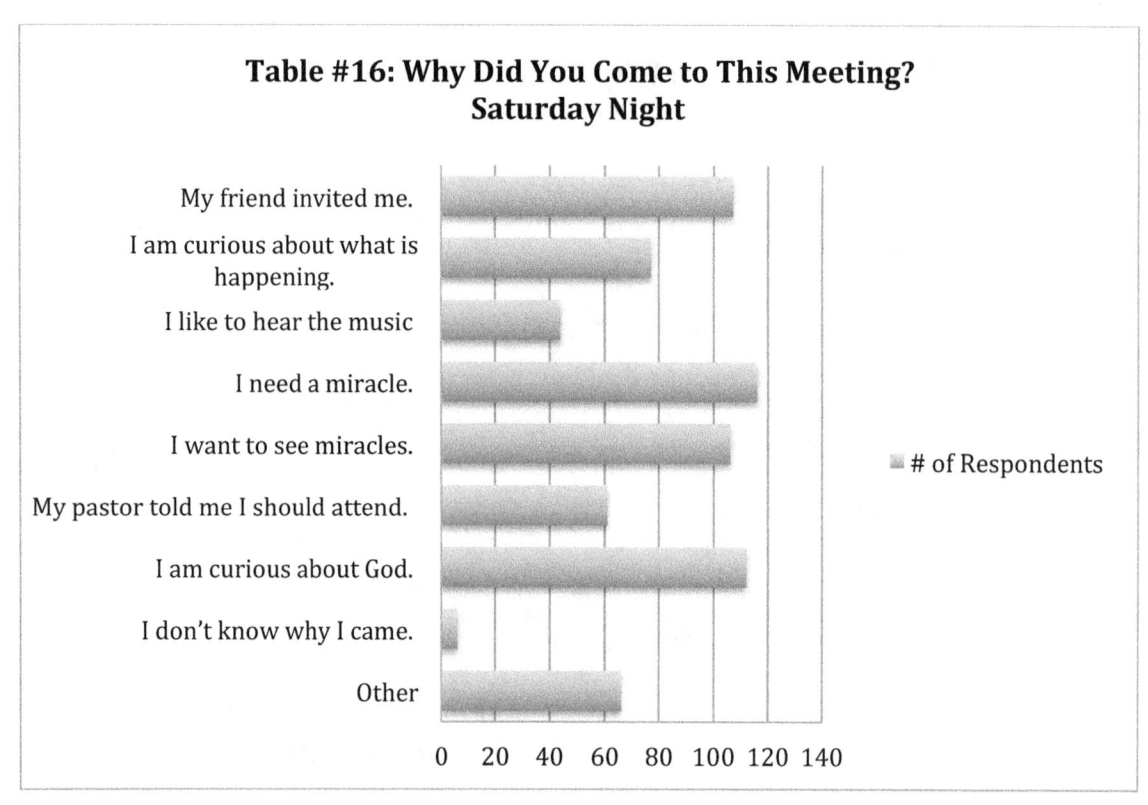

Survey Question #10: Distance Traveled

The tenth survey question was, "How long did it take you to travel to the meeting tonight?" The purpose of this question was to discover the radius of the impact of the crusade.

Table 17. How Far Did You Come? Friday Night

5 min or less	6-10 min	11-15 min	16-30 min	31-44 min	45 min +
26 (14.9%)	37 (21.1%)	45 (25.7%)	40 (22.9%)	11 (6.3%)	16 (9.1%)

Table 18. How Far Did You Come? Saturday Night

5 min or less	6-10 min	11-15 min	16-30 min	31-44 min	45 min +

| 67 (14.1%) | 125 (26.4%) | 107 (22.6%) | 97 (20.5%) | 41 (8.6%) | 37 (7.8%) |

People came to the event from a variety of distances, but it is unsurprising that fewer people came from farther away. For the Mode of Transportation in the next question there should have been more people who came by church bus, but a truck driver's strike in the week prior to the crusade made it difficult to arrange transportation.

Survey Question #11: Mode of Transportation

The eleventh question was, "How did you come to the meeting tonight?"

Table 19. Mode of Transportation? Friday Night

Car	Public Transportation	Church Bus	Motorcycle	Bicycle	Walking	Other
62 (35.6%)	11 (6.3%)	16 (9.2%)	52 (29.9%)	1 (0.6%)	30 (17.2%)	2 (1.2%)

Table 20: Mode of Transportation? Saturday Night

Car	Public Transportation	Church Bus	Motorcycle	Bicycle	Walking	Other
182 (38.6%)	42 (8.9%)	52 (11%)	129 (27.4%)	4 (0.8%)	59 (12.5%)	3 (0.6%)

Survey Question #12: What Is Your Religion?

On Friday, 37 people said they were Catholic (24.5%). Ninety-five said they were Christian /evangelical (62.9%). Fifteen people said they had no religion (9.9%). Four people chose "other" (2.8%). Of these "other" responses, two said they used to be a Christian, and two said they are atheists.

On Saturday, 86 people said they were Catholic (18.3%). Three hundred forty said they were Christian /evangelical (72.5%). Thirty-one people said they had no religion (6.6%), and 12 people chose "other."

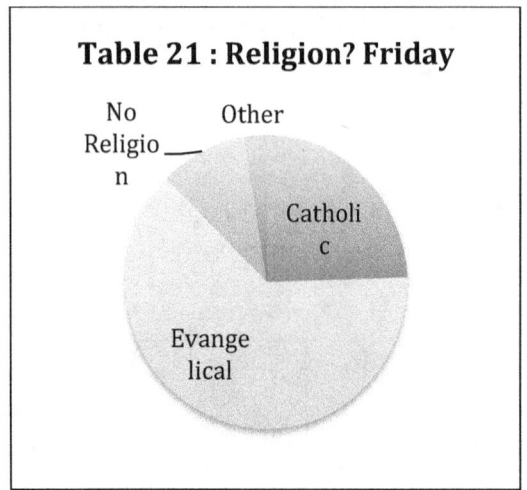

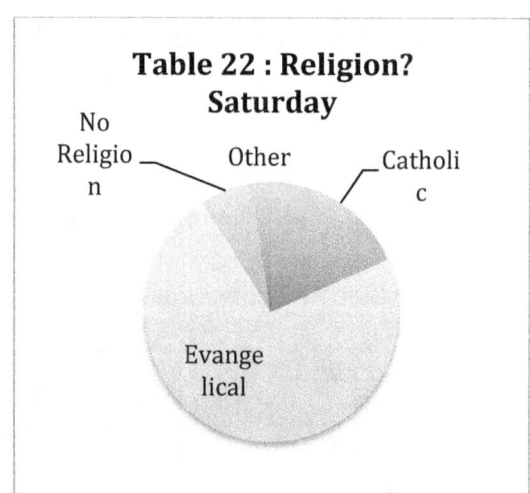

Survey Question #13: Are You Part of a Church?

On Friday, 108 people responded that they are part of a church (72.5%) and 41 people said they are not part of a church (27.5%). On Saturday, 378 people responded that they are part of a church (82.4%) and 81 people said they are not part of a church (17.6%).

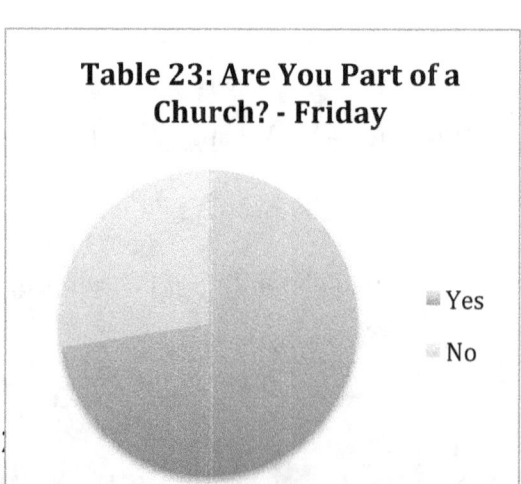

Survey Question #14: What Church Do You Attend?

The fourteenth question of the survey was an open-ended question asking, "What church do you attend?" A wide variety of responses were recorded including representatives from all nine churches that participated in the crusade, the Roman Catholic church, the Universal Church, the World Church, and the Mormon church.

Survey Question #15: How Often Do You Attend Your Church?

On Friday night, 149 people responded to the question, "How often do you attend your church?"

Table 25. How Often Do You Attend Your Church? Friday Night

Never	1-2 times per year	6-12 times per year	1-2 times per month	Every Sunday	2 or more times per week
6 (4%)	24 (16.1%)	10 (6.7%)	15 (10.1%)	22 (14.8%)	72 (48.3%)

Table 26. How Often Do You Attend Your Church? Saturday Night

Never	1-2 times per year	6-12 times per year	1-2 times per month	Every Sunday	2 or more times per week
23 (5%)	57 (12.5%)	18 (3.9%)	44 (9.6%)	78 (17.1%)	237 (51.9%)

Of the 40 people on Friday night who attend church twelve times per year or less, 31 prayed with the preacher for salvation, 8 did not, and 1 did not answer. Of these 40, 26 said they "strongly agreed" or "agreed" they would visit a church if invited, 2 said they were "not sure" if they would visit a church if invited and 12 left the question blank. Of the 98 people on Saturday night who attend church twelve times per year or less, 77 prayed with the preacher for salvation, 20 did not, and 1 did not answer.

On Saturday night, 50 out of 86 people (58.13%) who identified as Catholic indicated that they attended church less than once per month. Thirty-three out of 340 (9.7%) who identified as Evangelical indicated that they attended church less than once per month. This shows that the Catholics who attended the crusade go to church less than the Evangelicals who attended the crusade. This is likely because the devout Catholics who regularly attend their church heard the Archbishop when he told his parishioners not to go to the crusade. But, it also suggests that some who are nominally Catholic are in need of further evangelization. Twenty-seven of 43 (62.79%) who answered "no religion" or "other" attended church less than once a month. So, the frequency of church attendance between the Catholics who attended the crusade and those with "no religion" was statistically similar.

Survey Question #16: Would You Visit a Church If You Were Invited?

Question sixteen was only supposed to be asked to those who do not attend a church. The question was, "If invited, I would be willing to visit a church to receive additional prayer." The Likert Scale was used for the responses. On Friday night, 63 responses to this question were received.

Table 27: Would You Visit a Church If You Were Invited? Friday Night

Strongly Agree	Agree	Undecided	Disagree	Strongly Disagree
30 (47.6%)	25 (39.7%)	6 (9.5%)	2 (3.2%)	0

On Saturday night, 215 responses to this question were received.

Table 28. Would You Visit a Church If You Were Invited? Saturday Night

Strongly Agree	Agree	Undecided	Disagree	Strongly Disagree
80 (37.2%)	111 (51.6%)	14 (6.5%)	9 (4.2%)	1 (0.5%)

Pastor's Pre-Crusade Survey

Pre-Crusade Pastor's Survey Questions 1-4

A total of nine churches participated in the Caicò Crusade. The first three questions on the pastor's pre-survey were: What is the average weekly attendance at your church? How many members does your church have? How many people did your church baptize in the past year?

Table 29. Size of Local Churches

Name of Church	Weekly Attendance	# of Members	# Baptized
Church #1	800	800	71
Church #2	60	50	5
Church #3	50	80	17
Church #4	60	80	13
Church #5	150	142	16
Church #6	130	100	20
Church #7	25	35	8
Church #8	25	35	5
Church #9	50	35	5

Total weekly attendance of all the churches combined is 1,350. Total membership of all the churches combined is 1,357. Total combined number baptized in the past year is 160.

The evangelical church in Caicó is small. In a city of 66,246, there are only 1,357 members claimed by nine evangelical churches. This is about 2% of the population. Although the vast majority of the population in Caicó considers themselves to be Roman Catholic, the next survey question show that the existence of a significant amount of sinful behavior in the city demonstrates the great need for additional evangelism in this city.

Pre-Crusade Pastor's Survey Question 5: Biggest Spiritual Needs

The fifth question the pastors answered was, "What do you think are the biggest spiritual needs in your city?" The question was open-ended.

Response #1: Prayer, evangelism, reading the Bible
Response #2: Everything
Response #3: Breakthrough (prostitution, idolatry, addictions, suicidal spirits), spiritual healing (trauma, abuse, etc.) and the restoration of how man sees God.
Response #4: Evangelism and discipleship
Response #5: Living faith in Christ, based on the Bible. Greater involvement with the community and the church
Response #6: Seminar
Response #7: Freedom from the world
Response #8: Prayer and evangelism
Response #9: Revival

The local pastors of Caicó have a variety of concerns. They see a need for more prayer, evangelism, and Bible reading. They are concerned about prostitution, idolatry, addiction, abuse, and suicidal spirits. They want to reach out to their community. They want to see revival in their churches.

Pre-Crusade Pastor's Survey Question 6: Is Your Church Evangelistic?

The sixth question was presented as a statement, "Our church is an evangelistic church that preaches frequently about the need for evangelism." The answers followed the Likert Scale. Three churches "strongly agreed" (33%), six churches "agreed" (66%), no churches "disagreed" or were "unsure."

Table 30. Is Your Church Evangelistic?

Strongly Agree	Agree	Undecided	Disagree	Strongly Disagree
3 (33%)	6 (66%)	0	0	0

Pre-Crusade Pastor's Survey Question 7: Evangelistic Methods Used

The seventh question was, "What evangelistic methods does your church use to tell people about Jesus?" The question was open-ended.

Response #1: Evangelistic services, personal evangelism, visits, etc.
Response #2: Personal evangelism
Response #3: Cell groups, evangelistic campaigns (using disciples in the cell groups), ministerial networks and celebration service
Response #4: Houses of peace, "cell group work"
Response #5: Evangelism groups in neighborhoods
Response #6: Outdoor services
Response #7: We seek to demonstrate the transformation of the people.
Response #8: Campaigns, evangelistic services and personal invitations
Response #9: Personal evangelism and small groups

Pre-Crusade Pastor's Survey Questions 8-12

Table 31. Questions About Evangelism Practices

Name of Church	Our church conducts special services to reach the unsaved.	Our church goes outside the church to do an evangelistic outreach in our community.	Churches should be more aggressive in sharing their faith with others.	My church should be more aggressive in sharing their faith with others.	Our church plans to participate in the crusade in Caicó.
Church #1	Very Frequently	Very Frequently	Strongly Agree	Strongly Agree	Strongly Agree
Church #2	Occasionally	Occasionally	Agree	Agree	Strongly Agree
Church #3	Frequently	Occasionally	Strongly Agree	Strongly Agree	Strongly Agree
Church #4	Frequently	Occasionally	Strongly Agree	Strongly Agree	Strongly Agree
Church #5	Occasionally	Occasionally	Strongly Agree	Strongly Agree	Strongly Agree
Church #6	Very Frequently	Frequently	Strongly Agree	Strongly Agree	Strongly Agree
Church #7	Frequently	Frequently	Agree	Agree	Strongly Agree
Church #8	Frequently	Frequently	Agree	Agree	Strongly Agree
Church #9	Occasionally	Rarely	Strongly Agree	Strongly Agree	Strongly Agree

Overall, the evangelical churches of Caicó consider themselves to be evangelistic. According to their responses, they preach about evangelism on a regular basis and they use a variety of methods for reaching out to the lost including evangelistic services, personal evangelism, personal visits, house of peace, cell groups, and outdoor services. Some of the churches engage in evangelism frequently and some infrequently, but all the churches agreed their churches should be more evangelistic. This is why every church "strongly agreed" to participate in the crusade. The churches viewed the crusade as an opportunity to mobilize their members to be involved in evangelism.

Pre-Crusade Pastor's Survey Question 13: How is Your Church Participating in the Crusade?

The thirteenth question was, "How is your church participating in the crusade?" The pastors were asked to circle all the answers that applied. Eight churches said they plan to send church members to serve as ushers, counselors, prayer, and security. Seven churches helped to pass out flyers. Seven churches planned to invite neighborhoods. Five churches participated in pre-crusade outreaches. Nine churches attended leadership meetings and seven churches anticipated attending planning meetings.

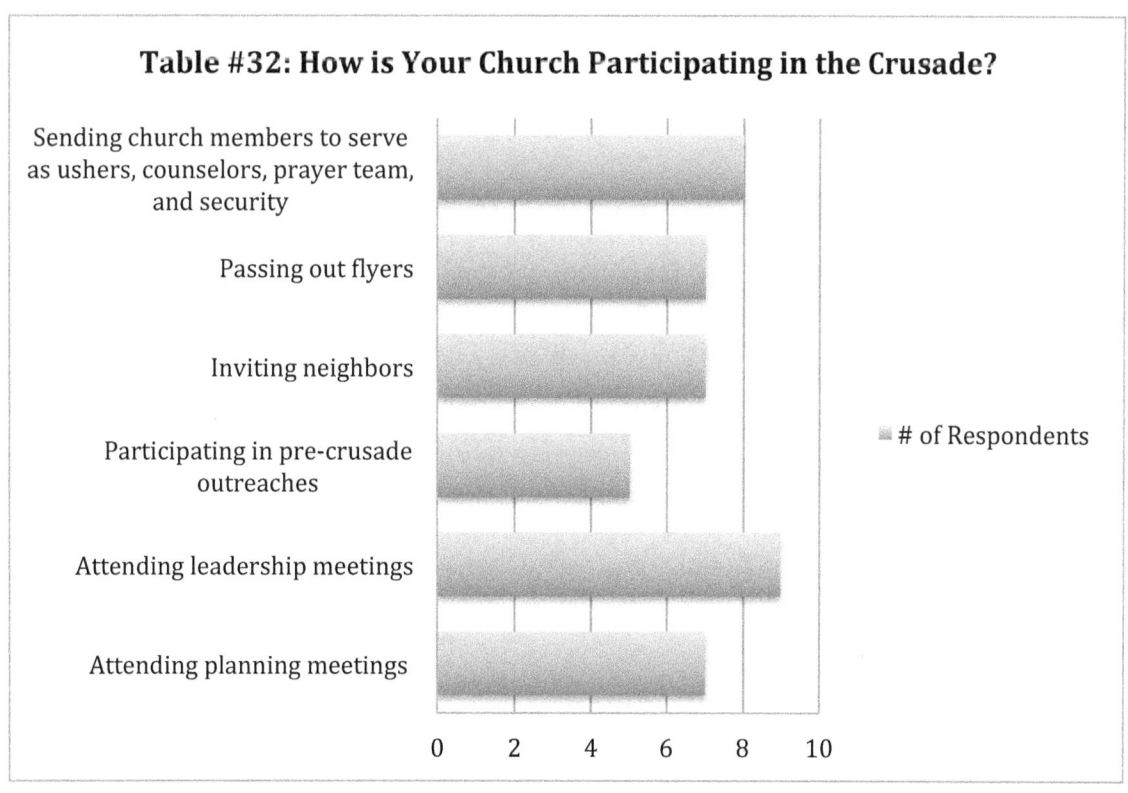

Pre-Crusade Pastor's Survey Question14: Number of Volunteers

The fourteenth question on the pastor's survey was, "How many people is your church sending to participate in the crusade?" This question measures how many people in each church plan to volunteer at the crusade.

Table 33. Number of Volunteers

Name of Church	How many people is your church sending to participate in the crusade?	Ushers	Counselors	Prayer Team	Security
Church #1	800	NA	NA	NA	NA
Church #2	50	15	10	10	10
Church #3	80	30	15	7	8
Church #4	100	5	5	5	2
Church #5	130	60	10	10	10
Church #6	80	30	10	10	10
Church #7	100	5	2	2	1
Church #8	35	30	15	10	5
Church #9	NA	10	NA	NA	NA

Pre-Crusade Pastor's Survey Question 15: Excitement About the Crusade

Question fifteen was presented as a statement, "I am excited about the crusade that is taking place in Caicó" and the answers followed the Likert Scale. Eight churches responded. Six churches "strongly agreed" with the statement (75%) and two churches "agreed" (25%) None of the respondents disagreed or were unsure.

Table 34: Excitement About the Crusade

Strongly Agree	Agree	Undecided	Disagree	Strongly Disagree
6 (75%)	2 (25%)	0	0	0

Pre-Crusade Pastor's Survey Question 16: What Will Be Accomplished?

The sixteenth question on the pre-crusade pastor's survey was, "What do you hope will be accomplished by the crusade in Caicó?" The question was open-ended.

Response #1: An awakening of the church and a great harvest of souls
Response #2: Lives
Response #3: Many lives for Jesus and our city being impacted with the power of the Lord to heal and set people free
Response #4: Many souls being saved
Response #5: Conversion of souls
Response #6: Evangelism being preached and the awakening of the local church
Response #7: Souls for the kingdom
Response #8: Yes
Response #9: Souls

Pre-Crusade Pastor's Survey Question 17: Concerns about the Crusade

Question fifteen was presented as a statement, "I have some concerns about the crusade taking place in Caicó" and the answers followed the Likert Scale.

Table 35. I Have Concerns About the Crusade.

Strongly Agree	Agree	Undecided	Disagree	Strongly Disagree
1 (11%)	4 (44%)	2 (22%)	0	2 (22%)

Pre-Crusade Pastor's Survey Question 18: Concerns About the Crusade

The eighteenth question on the pre-crusade pastor's crusade was "What are your concerns about the crusade coming to Caicó?" The question was open-ended.

Response #1: Christians that are not engaged
Response #2: Expectations that are too high
Response #3: None
Response #4: What we hope for is that everything would happen as planned.
Response #5: That we should give the necessary support to the success of the crusade
Response #6: May the local church not miss this great opportunity of having our city reached for Jesus.
Response #7: My concern is post-crusade that we keep the souls that we were able to win.
Response #8: I don't talk about concerns, but about the purpose of souls.
Response #9: Lack of people to do discipleship after

The pastors did have some concerns about the crusade. These concerns can be split into three categories. One pastor felt that expectations were way too high. Three pastors expressed the concern that the local church would miss or not take full advantage of this opportunity. Two pastors expressed concern about the need to disciple people after the crusade. The remaining two pastors did not have any concerns at all. None of these concerns were theological in nature, nor did they prevent these pastors from participating.

Pastor's Post-Crusade Survey

On Sunday evening, the day after the crusade was finished, the local pastors were asked to complete a Post-Crusade Survey. There were ten respondents, one more church responding than completed the Pre-Crusade Survey.

Post-Crusade Pastor's Survey Questions 1-3: Number of Participants

The first several questions on the post-crusade survey of the pastors covered how many people from each church attended the crusade, participated in the crusade, and how they participated?

Table 36. Number of Participants

Name of Denomination	How many people from your church attended the crusade?	How many people from your church participated in the crusade?	Ushers	Counselors	Prayer Team	Security
Church #1	35	25	10	5	10	0
Church #2	500-600	150	139	20	24	17
Church #3	60	40	37	2	1	0
Church #4	100	60	50	3	3	4
Church #5	50	50	6	NA	2	0
Church #6	Unknown	50	13	13	13	0
Church #7	50	50	6	2	4	0
Church #8	20	25	16	0	2	2
Church #9	120	NA	120	5	2	0
Church #10	NA	NA	5	1	2	2

A total of 1,035+ people from the churches attended the crusade. At least 575 people from the churches volunteered at the crusade. Of the 1,357 church members in the city, 76.27% of them attended the crusade and 42.37% of the church members participated as volunteers at the crusade.

Post-Crusade Pastor's Survey Questions 4-5: Number of People Invited and Number of Visitors

The fourth question was, "How many people who do not currently attend your church did your church members invite to the crusade?" The fifth question was, "How many new visitors did your church have on the Sunday after the crusade?"

Table 37. Number of People Invited and Number of Visitors

Name of Denomination	How many people who do not currently attend your church did your church members invite to the crusade?	How many new visitors did your church have on the Sunday after the crusade?
Church #1	50	4
Church #2	<200	62 reported by text message.
Church #3	100	14
Church #4	150	3
Church #5	30	3
Church #6	Unknown	4
Church #7	30	3
Church #8	100	15
Church #9	400	2
Church #1	400	2

The total number of people that churches invited to the crusade was more than 1,430. The total number of visitors to local churches on the day after the crusade was more than 112.

Post-Crusade Pastor's Survey Question 6: Follow Up?

The sixth question was stated as, "Our church is planning to participate in the follow-up of new believers who got saved at the crusade." The answers followed the Likert Scale.

Table 38. Our Church is Planning to Participate in the Follow-Up of New Believers

Strongly Agree	Agree	Undecided	Disagree	Strongly Disagree
8 (88.9%)	1 (11.1%)	0	0	0

Post-Crusade Pastor's Survey Question 7: What Were the Positive Effects?

The seventh question was, "What were some of the positive effects of the crusade?" Ten open-ended responses were recorded.

Responses #1-2: Spiritual revival.
Response #3: Salvation of souls, spiritual and ministerial strengthening
Response #4: It brought an awakening to the church's commitment to evangelism
Response #5: Conversion, healing and mobilization
Response #6: Saved souls, unity of the churches, awakening of the Christians to preach the gospel
Response #7: Uncertain
Response #8: More people saved to disciple and baptize, excitement
Response #9: Revival for the churches of our city
Response #10: Revival for the churches

Post-Crusade Pastor's Survey Question 8: Were There Any Negative Effects?

Question eight was, "Were there any negative effects from the crusade? What were they?" Five respondents answered, "No." Two did not answer. The other three answers were:

Response #8: None for me
Response #9: Frivolity
Response #10: We still don't know

Post-Crusade Pastor's Survey Question 9: Would You Change Anything?

The ninth question was, "Is there anything with the crusade that you wish had happened differently?" Four answered "No," two did not answer. The other answers were:

Response #7: The teams should have been formed in a more proportional way so that the church could participate in all teams and the distribution of conversion cards should be by neighborhood/region so the church could do a more efficient follow-up.
Response #8: I found everything well-organized.
Response #9: Children's event was poorly organized and executed.
Response #10: It could be more days.

Post-Crusade Pastor's Survey Question 10: Was the Crusade Worthwhile?

The tenth question was expressed as a statement, "The crusade was worth the time, money, and preparation that went into it." The answers followed the Likert Scale.

Table 39. Was the Crusade Worthwhile?

Strongly Agree	Agree	Undecided	Disagree	Strongly Disagree
8 (80%)	2 (20%)	0	0	0

Post-Crusade Pastor's Survey Question 11: Another Crusade

The eleventh question was expressed as a statement, "I would like to see another crusade in my city in the future." The answers followed the Likert Scale.

Table 40. Another Crusade

Strongly Agree	Agree	Undecided	Disagree	Strongly Disagree
9 (90%)	1 (10%)	0	0	0

Post-Crusade Pastor's Survey Question 12: Are Crusades Effective?

The eleventh question was expressed as a statement, "Mass evangelism is an effective method to reach people in Brazil." The answers followed the Likert Scale.

Table #41: Are Crusades Effective?

Strongly Agree	Agree	Undecided	Disagree	Strongly Disagree
9 (90%)	1 (10%)	0	0	0

Pastor's Post-Crusade Survey: Three Months Later

Post-Crusade Pastor's Survey, Three Months Later, Question 2: Weekly Attendance

The second question was, "What is the average weekly attendance at your church?"

Table 42. Average Weekly Attendance

	Number in Attendance
Church #1	40-50
Church #2	70
Church #3	60
Church #4	150
Church #5	100
Church #6	30
Church #7	60

| Church #8 | 40 |
| Church #9 | 1,000 |

Post-Crusade Pastor's Survey, Three Months Later, Question 3: Follow Up

The third question was expressed as a statement, "Our church followed-up on new believers who got saved at the crusade." The answers followed the Likert Scale.

Table 43. Did Your Church Follow Up on New Believers?

Strongly Agree	Agree	Undecided	Disagree	Strongly Disagree
4	2		2	1

Post-Crusade Pastor's Survey, Three Months Later, Question 4: Number of New Believers

The fourth question was, "How many new believers participated in your follow-up program?" The total number of people who participated in the follow up program was 30.

Table 44. Number of New Believers in Follow Up Program

	Number in Follow Up Program
Church #1	10
Church #2	0
Church #3	2
Church #4	4
Church #5	3
Church #6	3
Church #7	8
Church #8	0
Church #9	N/A

Post-Crusade Pastor's Survey, Three Months Later, Question 5: How was follow up done?

The fifth question was "Please describe how your church followed up on the new believers."

Church #1: Fridays with handouts for new converts
Church #2: There were no new converts
Church #3: We have already worked with discipleship and cells
Church #4: Sunday Bible School
Church #5: Through visits and in the Bible School
Church #6: Through the copy that was distributed in the Crusade, and Bible School
Church #7: Plan of salvation
Church #8: N/A
Church #9: N/A

Post-Crusade Pastor's Survey, Three Months Later, Questions 6, 8, 9: Post-Crusade Church Involvement

The sixth, eighth, and ninth questions were expressed as statements and the answers followed the Likert Scale.

Table 45. Questions About Post-Crusade Church Involvement

Question	Strongly Agree	Agree	Undecided	Disagree	Strongly Disagree
6. My church grew in attendance since the crusade took place.	2 (22.2%)	4 (44.4%)	0	2 (22.2%)	1 (11.1%)
8. My church has become more active in evangelism since the crusade.	3 (33.3%)	3 (33.3%)	0	2 (22.2%)	1 (11.1%)

| 9. My church members are more spiritually alive since the crusade took place. | 3 (33.3%) | 3 (33.3%) | 1 (11.1%) | 2 (22.2%) | 0 |

Post-Crusade Pastor's Survey, Three Months Later, Question 7: How Many Joined the Church?

The seventh question was, "How many people joined your church because of the crusade?" It was an open-ended question that could be answered with a number. The total number of people who joined the local churches was reported to be fifty which represents an increase of 3.68% in local church membership.

Table 46. How Many People Joined Your Church?

	How many people joined your church because of the crusade?
Church #1	15
Church #2	0
Church #3	2
Church #4	10
Church #5	3
Church #6	6
Church #7	6
Church #8	0
Church #9	8

Post-Crusade Pastor's Survey, Three Months Later, Question 10: Positive Aspects of Crusade

The tenth question was open-ended, "Three months later, what would you say are some of the positive effects of the crusade?"

Church #1: Pleasure of members for the gospel and more prayer
Church #2: In our church there was no change.
Church #3: Activation and awakening to evangelism
Church #4: It brought a great revival.
Church #5: Greater awareness of responsibility for the evangelization of the unreached.
Church #6: Spiritual revival and numeric growth
Church #7: The planting of a new church is the rural area of Vila Sabugi
Church #8: Impact on the city in terms of positioning, a large number of people for the church to reach and disciple.
Church #9: N/A

Post-Crusade Pastor's Survey, Three Months Later, Question 11: Negative Aspects of Crusade

The eleventh question was open-ended, "Were there any negative effects from the crusade? What were they?"

Church #1: None that I heard
Church #2: No comments
Church #3: No
Church #4: No
Church #5: No, none
Church #6: No
Church #7: No
Church #8: Not that I realize
Church #9: Not that I know

Post-Crusade Pastor's Survey, Three Months Later, Question 12: Was the Crusade Worthwhile?

The twelfth question was expressed as a statement, "The crusade was worth the time, money, and preparation that went into it." The answers followed the Likert Scale.

Table 47. Was the Crusade Worthwhile?

Strongly Agree	Agree	Undecided	Disagree	Strongly Disagree
4 (44.4%)	3 (33.3%)	1 (11.1%)	1 (11.1%)	0

In the Post-Crusade Pastor's Survey Question 10 immediately after the event, 8 (80%) "strongly agreed," and 2 (20%) "agreed" that the crusade was worthwhile.[1]

Post-Crusade Pastor's Survey, Three Months Later, Question 13: Another Crusade?

The thirteenth question was expressed as a statement, "I would like to see another crusade in my city in the future." The answers followed the Likert Scale.

Table 48. I Would Like to See Another Crusade in my City in the Future.

Strongly Agree	Agree	Undecided	Disagree	Strongly Disagree
7 (77.8%)	2 (22.2%)	0	0	0

In the Post-Crusade Pastor's Survey Question 11 immediately after the event, 9 (90%) "strongly agreed" and 1 (10%) "agreed" they would want to see another crusade.

Post-Crusade Pastor's Survey, Three Months Later, Question 14: Are Crusades Effective?

The fourteenth question was expressed as a statement, "Mass evangelism is an effective method to reach people in Brazil." The answers followed the Likert Scale.

---

[1] On the question "Was the crusade worthwhile?" one pastor changed his answer to from "Strongly Agree" to "Disagree." He was asked what caused this change in his opinion. He explained, "One of my branch churches just left my denomination and joined another denomination. The pastor of my branch church became friends with the pastor of the other denomination while passing out flyers for the crusade together." Because of the loss of one of his branch churches, this pastor went from feeling that the crusade was worthwhile to being bitter about the results of the event.

Table 49. Mass Evangelism is an Effective Method to Reach People in Brazil

Strongly Agree	Agree	Undecided	Disagree	Strongly Disagree
3 (33.3%)	5 (55.6%)	0	1 (11.1%)	0

In the Post-Crusade Pastor's Survey Question 12 immediately after the event, 9 (90%) "strongly agreed" and 1 (10%) "agreed" with this question.

Church's Post-Crusade Survey

The purpose of administering a post-crusade survey to the local churches was to measure the attendance of local believers at the crusade and their level of involvement in both promoting the crusade and volunteering at the crusade. The survey gave the researcher insight into who was invited and whether they came. Respondents were also asked if the crusade had an impact on their lives, their churches, and their city.

Post-Crusade Church Survey Question 1: Age of Church Members

Table 50. Average Age of Churches Surveyed

Name of Church	Average Age of Church
Church #1	27.5
Church #2	33.6
Church #3	34.8
Church #4	32.2
Church #5	37.9
Church #6	29.3
Church #7	35
Average Age of All Churches Combined	32.9

Post-Crusade Church Survey Question 2: Gender

Of the 263 respondents to the question about gender, 120 (45.6%) were male, and 143 (54.4%) were female.[2]

Table 51. Gender of Church Members

Name of Church	Male	Female
Church #1	13 (38.2%)	21 (61.8%)
Church #2	29 (43.9%)	37 (56.1%)
Church #3	8 (40%)	12 (60%)
Church #4	24 (53.3%)	21 (46.7%)
Church #5	20 (64.5%)	11 (35.5%)
Church #6	23 (41.8%)	32 (58.2%)
Church #7	3 (25%)	9 (75%)
Totals	120 (45.6%)	143 (54.4%)

Post-Crusade Church Survey Question 3: When Did You Go?

The third question the church members were asked was when they attended the crusade. The possible answers were "Thursday Night Youth Event," "Friday Night Crusade," "Saturday Night Crusade," and "Did Not Attend." Multiple answers were allowed so the total percentages will equal more than 100%. Among the seven churches surveyed, there were a total of 263 respondents. Of these respondents, 149 (56.6%) attended on Thursday night, 186 (70.7%) attended on Friday night, and 174 (66%) came on Saturday night. In addition, nine people wrote that they attended the children's festival

---

[2]The gender of the crowd was also more female than male. This suggests it is important for evangelists to make a deliberate effort to attract males to their events; but at the same time, the evangelist should recognize the need to communicate effectively with the females who are attending.

on Saturday morning[3]. Only 24 or 9.1% of the 263 church members surveyed did not attend at all.

Table 52. Services Attended

Name of Church	Thursday Night Youth	Friday Night Crusade	Saturday Night Crusade	Did Not Attend
Church #1	16 (47.1%)	28 (82.4%)	27 (79.4%)	0
Church #2	25 (37.9%)	39 (59.1%)	45 (68.2%)	11 (16.7%)
Church #3	11 (55%)	18 (90%)	11 (55%)	0
Church #4	38 (84.4%)	38 84.4%)	26 (57.8%)	0
Church #5	18 (58.1%)	20 (64.5%)	21 (67.7%)	2 (6.5%)
Church #6	38 (69.1%)	38 (69.1%)	41 (74.5%)	8 (14.5%)
Church #7	3 (25%)	5 (42%)	3 (25%)	3 (25%)
Totals:	149 (56.6%)	186 (70.7%)	174 (66%)	24 (9.1%)

Post-Crusade Church Survey Question 4: How did you participate in the crusade?

The purpose of the fourth question was to discover what role church members volunteered to play in the crusade. Of the 263 respondents, 54 (20.5%) served as ushers, 8 (3%) served as counselors, 14 (5.3%) were part of the prayer team of intercessors, 5 (1.9%) worked as security. 117 (44.5%) of the church members surveyed said they played no part in the crusade.

Table 53. Participation in the Crusade

Name of Church	Usher	Counselor	Prayer Team	Security	None	Total Respondents
Church #1	3 (13.6%)	0	3 (13.6%)	1 (4.5%)	15 (68.2%)	34

---

[3]Church #2 had 1 person, Church #4 had 6, and Church #6 had 2 people who went to the kid's crusade.

Church #2	11 (22.4%)	0	7 (14.3%)	0	31 (63.3%)	66
Church #3	1 (16.7%)	0	1 (16.7%)	0	4 (66.7%)	20
Church #4	10 (31.3%)	4 (12.5%)	2 (6.3%)	2 (6.3%)	14 (43.8%)	45
Church #5	9 (32.1%)	1 (3.6%)	1 (3.6%)	2 (7.1%)	15 (53.6%)	31
Church #6	18 (36.7%)	3 (6.1%)	0	0	28 (57.1%)	55
Church #7	2 (16.7%)	0	0	0	10 (83.3%)	12
Totals	54 (20.5%)	8 (3%)	14 (5.3%)	5 (1.9%)	117 (44.5%)	263

Post-Crusade Church Survey Question 5-6: Crusade Promotion

The fifth question was, "Did you pass out any flyers?" The sixth question was, "Did you share information about the crusade on social media?" These questions were designed to measure the involvement of the local churches in helping to promote the crusade. One hundred four (40.2%) out of 259 respondents said they helped by passing out promotional flyers. One hundred sixty-nine (65%) out of 260 respondents said they shared information about the crusade on social media.

Table 54. Crusade Promotion

Name of Church	5. Did you pass out any flyers?	6. Did you share information about the crusade on social media?
Church #1	7 Yes (20.6%) 27 No (79.4%)	26 Yes (76.5%) 8 No (23.5%)
Church #2	17 Yes (26.2%) 48 No (73.8%)	38 Yes (58.5%0 27 No (41.5%)
Church #3	8 Yes (60%) 12 No (40%)	15 Yes (75%) 5 No (25%)

Church #4	24 Yes (54.5%) 20 No (45.5%)	38 Yes (86.4%) 6 No (13.6%)
Church #5	11 Yes (37.9%), 18 No (62.1%)	19 Yes (63.3%) 11 No (36.7%)
Church #6	30 Yes (54.5%), 25 No (45.5%)	28 Yes (50.9%), 27 No (49.1%)
Church #7	7 Yes (58.3%), 5 No (41.7%)	5 Yes (41.7%), 7 No (58.3%)
Totals	104 Yes (40.2%) 155 No (59.8%)	169 Yes (65%) 91 No (35%)

Post-Crusade Church Survey Question 7, 9: Number of People Invited and Number Who Came

The seventh question was, "How many total people did you invite to the crusade?" and the ninth question was, "Of the people you invited, how many came?" These seven representative churches invited approximately 1,424 people and at least 566 (39.74%) of those invited came.

Table 55. Number of People Invited and Number Who Came

Name of Church	7. Total # of People Invited	9. Total # of People Who Came
Church #1	170	102
Church #2	234	83
Church #3	120	59
Church #4	548	145
Church #5	92	54
Church #6	201	101
Church #7	59 +	22
Totals	1,424	566

Post-Crusade Church Survey Question 8: Who Was Invited?

The eighth question was, "Who did you invite to the crusade?"

Table 56. Who Was Invited?

Name of Church	Friends	Family	Neighbor	Co-Worker	Fellow Student	Random
Church #1	17	14	9	2	2	6
Church #2	39	31	10	13	4	11
Church #3	8	12	8	7	1	2
Church #4	39	32	26	22	9	10
Church #5	20	14	8	3	3	6
Church #6	31	21	10	5	10	11
Church #7	5	7	5	3	1	3
Totals	159	131	76	55	30	49

Post-Crusade Church Survey Question 10-12: Rides, Salvation, and Miracles

Table 57. Rides, Salvation, and Miracles

Name of Church	10. Did you give someone a ride to the crusade?	11. Did anyone you invited pray with the preacher for salvation?	12. Do you know of anyone who received a miracle at the crusade?
Church #1	11 Yes (67.6%) 23 No (32.4%)	17 Yes (53.1%) 15 No (46.9%)	32 Yes (94.1%) 2 No (5.9%)
Church #2	14 Yes (22.6%) 48 No (77.4%)	26 Yes (48.1%) 28 No (51.9%)	49 Yes (76.6%) 15 No (23.4%)
Church #3	2 Yes (10%) 18 No (90%)	9 Yes (45%) 11 No (55%)	20 Yes (100%) 0 No
Church #4	23 Yes (52.3%) 21 No (47.7%)	28 Yes (36.4%) 16 No (63.6%)	45 Yes (100%) 0 No
Church #5	9 Yes (32.1%) 19 No (67.9%)	14 Yes (56%) 11 No (44%)	25 Yes (80.6%) 6 No (19.4%)
Church #6	10 Yes (19.2%) 42 No (80.8%)	18 Yes (36%) 32 No (64%)	44 Yes (81.5%) 10 No (18.5%)
Church #7	1 Yes (8.3%) 11 No (91.7%)	11 Yes (100%) 0 No	10 Yes (83.3%) 2 No (16.7%)
Totals	70 Yes (27.8%) 182 No (72.2%)	123 Yes (52.1%) 113 No (47.9%)	225 Yes (86.5%) 35 No (13.5%)

Post-Crusade Church Survey Question 13: Miracles Witnessed

The thirteenth question was, "Please tell us about the miracle that happened." It was an open-ended question. A wide variety of miracles were reported. Most of the testimonies were repetitious because they came from those who testified on the platform. It is not known if these recipients of miracles were personally known by the respondent or whether the respondent only witnessed the testimony that was shared from the platform.

Table 58. Miracles Witnessed

Type of Miracle	Number of People Who Mentioned It
Deaf or Mute People Healed[4]	Deaf (100), Mute (12)
Blind People Healed	12
Person in Wheelchair Walked	13
Leg Problems Healed, Knee Healed	Leg Problems (10), Walked on Crutches (3), Paralytic Walked (6), Knee Healed (2)
Lumps or Cyst in the Breast Disappeared	Lumps (5), Cyst in Breast (3)
Throat healed	6
A pain in the arm healed	8
Asthma, Breathing Problems Healed	Asthma (4), Breathing Problems (7), Respiratory problems (1)
Cancer Healed	3

Of the 263 respondents to the church survey, twenty-one (7.98%) specified they knew someone who received a miracle. Here are their testimonies:

Testimony #1: My cousin was deaf since 1 year old and she was cured.

---

[4]On Friday night, three deaf people who attended a local school for the deaf were healed. Their testimony on the platform made a deep impression on the audience. One hundred twelve people mentioned the miracle of the deaf/mutes who began to speak.

Testimony #2: A colleague of mine from the school who was deaf was healed and began to listen to the glory of the Lord. It showed that Jesus is still the same.

Testimony #3: A cousin of mine who did not listen in time heard again.

Testimony #4: A deaf person in my husband's family listened again.

Testimony #5: My nephew was freed from spirits; he heard voices.

Testimony #6: The person I invited only said that God had healed her, did not specify the problem.

Testimony #7: My mother, [Name Withheld], was healed. She had an accident five years ago, and she felt a lot of pain in her spine and legs…Thank You, my God…

Testimony #8: My sister-in-law was healed of an issue in the throat.

Testimony #9: My sister-in-law was healed of an issue in the throat, people healed of deafness and girl who did not walk was healed.

Testimony #10: Sister of my church was healed of a lump in the bosom, another sister was healed of an issue in the throat.

Testimony #11: My friend was deaf and silent and began to hear and to speak.

Testimony #12: A friend was healed; he was deaf from birth.

Testimony #13: My sister in Christ, she had a problem with her breathing and was healed in the name of Jesus.

Testimony #14: Friends who had health problems were healed.

Testimony #15: My mother had an accident five years ago and always had pain and could not bend down. After the prayer she was healed.

Testimony #16: The lady that I invited, had pains in the column, and she said that she felt something burning in the place of the pains, and that after that she did not feel any more pains.

Testimony #17: My co-worker had several days with her left foot with numbness and at the moment of prayer she was cured.

Testimony #18: My aunt was cured of depression.

Testimony #19: Deaf people from a church that I attended listened again.

Testimony #20: The boy who studies at the school near my house is walking again.

Testimony #21: Many people I meet have received miracles.

People also reported the miracles they had received in their own bodies. Of the 263 respondents to the church survey, 13 (4.94%) reported a personal testimony. These included:

Personal Testimony #1: I Suffered from asthma for a long time and could not breathe properly but was healed.

Personal Testimony #2: Me and my husband. I had a fever for 6 days and I prayed and God healed me. And my husband received healing from a hernia in the esophagus.

Personal Testimony #3: Yes, I had a pain in the stomach and God made a miracle and healed me.

Personal Testimony #4: People with lots of pain (including myself) were healed. I did not feel any more pains, God bless!

Personal Testimony #5: I had chronic pain in my left arm and the Lord healed me.

Personal Testimony #6: I was healed of a hernia in the esophagus. I prayed and felt my chest burn and I believed that God healed me.

Personal Testimony #7: I was cured of a pain that was on my back.

Personal Testimony #8: I could bend my knee.

Personal Testimony #9: I had asthma three years ago and I started to breathe through my mouth.

Personal Testimony #10: I was healed in my vision, I had glaucoma.

Personal Testimony #11: I was healed of a very strong pain in my kidney.

Personal Testimony #12: I was healed.

Personal Testimony #13: I struggled with anxiety and I feel better.

Post-Crusade Church Survey Question 14: Individual Impact

The fourteenth question was a statement, "The crusade impacted my life." 247 church members responded.

Table 59. Individual Impact

Name of Church	Strongly Agree	Agree	Undecided	Disagree	Strongly Disagree
Church #1	25 (73.5%)	9 (26.5%)	0	0	0
Church #2	37 (62.7%)	16 (27.1%)	4 (6.8%)	2 (3.4%)	0
Church #3	12 (66.7%)	6 (33.3%)	0	0	0
Church #4	40 (88.9%)	5 (11.1%)	0	0	0
Church #5	18 (58.1%)	11 (35.5%)	0	1 (3.2%)	1 (3.2%)
Church #6	31 (62%)	16 (32%)	3 (6%)	0	0
Church #7	4 (40%)	2 (20%)	4 (40%)	0	0
Totals	167 (67.6%)	65 (26.3%)	11 (4.4%)	3 (1.2%)	1 (0.4%)

Post-Crusade Church Survey Question 15: Church Impact

The fifteenth question was a statement, "The crusade impacted my church." 246 church members responded.

Table 60. Church Impact

Name of Church	Strongly Agree	Agree	Undecided	Disagree	Strongly Disagree
Church #1	22 (64.7%)	9 (26.5%)	3 (8.8%)	0	0
Church #2	34 (57.6%)	16 (27.1%)	9 (15.3%)	0	0
Church #3	11 (33.3%)	6 (61.1%)	1 (5.6%)	0	0
Church #4	40 (88.9%)	5 (11.1%)	0	0	0
Church #5	19 61.3%)	8 (25.8%)	4 (12.9%)	0	0
Church #6	33 (67.3%)	14 (28.6%)	2 (4.1%)	0	0
Church #7	4 (40%)	5 (50%)	1 (10%)	0	0
Totals	163 (66.3%)	63 (25.6%)	20 (8.1%)	0	0

Post-Crusade Church Survey Question 16: City Impact

The final question was a statement, "The crusade impacted my city." 253 church members responded.

Table 61. City Impact

Name of Church	Strongly Agree	Agree	Undecided	Disagree	Strongly Disagree
Church #1	26 (76.5%)	8 (23.5%)	0	0	0
Church #2	41 (66.1%)	19 (30.6%)	2 (3.2%)	0	0
Church #3	11 (61.1%)	7 (38.9%)	0	0	0
Church #4	38 (84.4%)	6 (13.3%)	1 (2.2%)	0	0
Church #5	20 (64.5%)	9 (29%)	2 (6.5%)	0	0
Church #6	37 (69.8%)	15 (28.3%)	1 (1.9%)	0	0
Church #7	3 (30%)	6 (60%)	1 (10%)	0	0
Totals	176 (69.6 %)	70 (27.7%)	7 (2.8%)	0	0

Chapter Summary

This chapter documents the answers to six different surveys administered to attendees at a crusade, local pastors who participated in the crusade, and the members of local churches. The results of these surveys are presented in a sequential, logical order. Sixty-one tables and graphs are used to present the answers in a clear and concise way. The next chapter will evaluate the meaning of these responses.

CHAPTER 6

RESPONSES TO FINDINGS

Introduction

This chapter will begin by interpreting the answers to the surveys that were documented in the previous chapter by focusing on four different areas of interest: salvation, miracles, church involvement, and follow-up. Conclusions will then be made based on the research conducted, and theological reflections will be made. Recommendations will be provided on ways the research could have been improved. Suggestions will be given concerning further research that could be conducted. Finally, this chapter will conclude with a summary of what has been learned during this research project.

Interpretation of Results

There are four major areas of this study that lead to valuable insights. These areas are the prayer of salvation, miracles, the local church involvement in the crusade, and follow-up. All four areas are worth looking at in depth.

The Prayer of Salvation

The primary purpose of an evangelistic crusade is the salvation of the lost. The evangelist measures his or her success or failure based on the number of people who are rescued from hell and ushered into heaven.[1]

So what happened at the crusade in Caicó, Brazil? The results could be reported in several different ways. On both nights, over eighty percent of the crowd repeated the salvation prayer with the evangelist.[2] Acts 2:21 says, "Everyone who calls on the name of the Lord shall be saved." It is this researcher's theological opinion that being saved is as simple as crying out to Jesus for salvation.[3] The high percentage of people repeating

---

[1]The reporting of the numbers of people saved is often how the evangelist justifies his or her existence and how he or she raises money for the next event. The evangelist is responsible for proclaiming the Gospel and the Holy Spirit is responsible for drawing people to God. In reality, evangelists cannot save anyone, but modern-day evangelists often report the results from their crusades as if the salvation of the people is dependent upon their efforts. This emphasis is caused in large part by the need to report results to the evangelist's backers. D. L. Moody was known for asking businessmen to give him money (see Winter, 125-126). Businessmen are driven by the bottom line, and they want to see what their investment is producing. Ever since Moody's time, evangelists have often spoken the language of business in reporting on their results.

[2]On the question, "Did you repeat the prayer with the preacher tonight?" on Friday night, 154 respondents replied "Yes" (87.5%) and 22 respondents replied "No" (12.5%). On Saturday night, 395 respondents replied "Yes" (82.6%) and 83 respondents replied "No" (17.4%).

[3]Crying out to Jesus is the beginning of salvation (Acts 2:21), but it is not the end. Salvation will eventually lead to full repentance, water baptism, being filled with the Holy Spirit (Acts 2:38), becoming a disciple of Christ (Matthew 28:19), doing good works (Ephesians 2:10), and producing the fruit of a Christian life (John 15:5).

the prayer of salvation indicates that a remarkable number of people at this evangelistic event desired to be saved.[4]

However, the fourth question (which was open-ended), "Why did you repeat the prayer with the preacher tonight?" shows there were actually many different reasons why people repeated the prayer. Some people repeated it because they wanted to put their faith in Christ, but others prayed because they wanted a miracle. The preacher was very clear in his message that repeating the prayer would lead to forgiveness of sins and salvation, but for the most part, people did not reflect this understanding in their open-ended answers as to why they prayed. This was a disappointment to the evangelist who was preaching.[5]

---

[4]Over the course of his ministry, the researcher has led just over two million people in a prayer of salvation. When he preaches, he aims for 100% involvement in the prayer of salvation. Usually he would say, "If you want Jesus to forgive your sins, please repeat this prayer after me." He does not limit the prayer to those who are making a "first-time decision" to follow Christ; rather, he asks people to make a "this-time decision" to trust Christ for salvation and forgiveness of sins.

[5]One factor that could have influenced how people answered this question is that there were multiple prayers that were prayed at the event. At the beginning of the message, the evangelist opened with prayer; during the altar call, the evangelist led the audience in a prayer of salvation; and finally, there were prayers for healing and prayers for casting out demons. It is possible that the variety of answers came because of the variety of prayers.

Even though many people did not specifically pray for salvation or forgiveness of sins,[6] they did indicate that they prayed because they have faith in God.[7] The answer the evangelist wanted to hear from people in response to this question was, "I wanted Jesus to forgive my sins," but the most common answer he received was, "Because I have faith in God." Since "faith in God" is an essential part of salvation these answers could mean the respondents wanted salvation. It suggests that the respondents were more focused on the positive aspects of the Gospel message rather than on the negative aspects of being aware of personal sin. More questioning would be needed to clear up this point.

Another factor influencing what people were praying for could have been the emphasis on miracles in both the advertising[8] and in the preaching. The second most common answer to the question "Why did you pray?" was, "Because I needed a miracle."[9] The open-ended nature of the question made it hard for people to answer the question in a way that would have indicated whether they wanted forgiveness of sins or a miracle or both. The researcher wishes he had given a list of possible reasons for people

---

[6]On Saturday night, seven people indicated in the open-ended answers that they wanted salvation or because they wanted forgiveness of sins. If the question was worded differently, it would have produced different results. For example, the researcher could have asked a "yes" or "no" question: Did you repeat the prayer because you wanted to ask Jesus to forgive your sins?

[7]On Saturday night, one hundred and twenty people indicated that they prayed because they have "faith" (Survey Question 4).

[8]The event was advertised as a "Crusade of Faith and Miracles."

[9]On Saturday night, ninety-eight people prayed because they needed a "miracle" or a "healing" (Survey Question 4).

to pray and allowed people to make multiple choices. This would have produced more helpful answers.

Perhaps the lack of people saying they were praying for salvation indicates there were not many people getting saved at the event. However, a total of 641 people filled out decision cards at the crusade as a sign of their decision to follow Jesus.[10] In a city that has 1,357 evangelical believers,[11] this represents a 43% increase in the number of Christians in the city, assuming that each person who completed a decision card is properly discipled.

It proved to be difficult to know who was already saved and who made a first time commitment to follow Christ. On Saturday night, 18.3% of the crowd said they were Catholic,[12] 72.5% of the crowd said they were evangelical, and only 6.6% of the crowd

---

[10]The evangelist told the crowd, "If you have chosen to follow Jesus tonight for the first time, I invite you to come to the front to meet with a counselor." Those who came forward were met by a local church member trained to be a prayer counselor. They proceeded to pray with the individual, to answer any questions they had about salvation, to fill out a decision card with the individual's information, and to give the individual a follow-up book.

[11]Pre-Crusade Pastor's Survey Question 3.

[12]There is a deep antagonism between the Roman Catholic Church and the evangelical church in Caicó, Brazil. During the crusade in Caicó on Thursday night (the same night as the crusade youth outreach), the Catholic cathedral held a procession in order to honor St. Anne, the patron saint of Caicó. At the end of the procession, the archbishop gave a sermon and said, "Do everything you can to oppose the crusade. We should not accept their kind in our city. Do not go to the crusade and do everything you can to expel them from our city." This opposition from the archbishop directly impacted the attendance of the crusade.

said they had no religion.[13] Since the purpose of an evangelistic event is to reach the lost, it seems at first glance that the fact that over 90% of the crowd already considers themselves to be Christian means that the event was mostly preaching to the choir.

However, the next question, "Are you part of a church?" shows that 17.6% of the respondents did not consider themselves to belong to a formal church.[14] The next open-ended question concerned what church they attended and this question shows that some of the people attend unorthodox (Mormon)[15] or semi-orthodox churches (Universal)[16] that may be considered evangelical but may not embrace a full spectrum of Christian beliefs.[17] The final question about church attendance shows that 21.4% of the crowd

---

[13] Survey Question 12.

[14] Survey Question 13.

[15] The Church of Jesus Christ of Latter Day Saints (Mormon Church) follows the teachings of Joseph Smith, who allegedly received another Gospel of Jesus Christ written on tablets of gold from the angel Moroni. (Joseph Smith, *Pearl of Great Price*, Joseph Smith History (Salt Lake City, Utah: Church of Jesus Christ of Latter-Day Saints, 1981), 1:34). The vast majority of Christian denominations consider Mormon beliefs unorthodox. In Caicó, the Mormon Church maintains a church building identical to hundreds of other churches they have in cities across Latin America, right down to a basketball court hidden behind a locked gate and a strip of perfectly manicured grass beside the parking lot.

[16] The *Igreja Universal do Reino de Deus*, often called the Universal Church, does not teach universalism, despite its name. It is considered a Neo-Pentecostal denomination, and it is known for a heavy emphasis on Prosperity. They have been criticized for promising blessings in exchange for extravagant offerings.

[17] Survey Question 14.

attends church sporadically (less than once a month) so the ratio of regular church attendees and irregular church attendees was about 80/20.[18]

There are three aspects of religion: one's beliefs, where one belongs, and one's behavior.[19] The fact that 20% of the crowd attends church infrequently is one indication of their spiritual state and could indicate that 20% of the crowd was in need of salvation. This 80/20 ratio was disappointing to the evangelist because ideally an evangelistic event should have a 60/40 ratio or even a 50/50 ratio. However, while the event was not as successful as it could have been, it is still a success because those 20% do need to hear the Gospel and a total of 641 people (14.9% of a crowd of 4,300) filled out decision cards indicating a desire to follow Christ. Every evangelistic event is different and based on this researcher's experience, in some countries (and even in Brazil) it is possible to have a much higher percentage of the crowd who rarely or never attend a Christian church.

A typical testimony of someone who prayed for salvation in Caicó is that of a thirty-three-year-old Catholic woman who attends church 1-2 times per year.[20] She repeated the prayer of salvation with the preacher because she says, "I have faith." She arrived with pain in her body and she agreed that she felt better after prayer and was sure she had received a miracle. She was invited by a member of her family and she came

---

[18]Survey Question 15.

[19]Allan Billings proposed this triangular formulation of believing, belonging, and behaving as a way of measuring a person's religious involvement in 2001. See Evert Van De Poll, *Europe and the Gospel: Past Influences, Current Developments, Mission Challenges* (London: Verista, 2013), 290-91.

[20]Respondent 440 on Saturday evening.

because she needed a miracle. She walked 16-30 minutes to the crusade. She strongly agrees that she would be willing to visit a local church for additional prayer if someone invites her. It is interesting that this woman who prayed for salvation came to the crusade because she needed a miracle in her life. The subject of miracles is a second important emphasis of this research project.

Miracles

When Philip the Evangelist preached in Samaria, there were many miracles (Acts 8:6-7) and the crusade in Caicó, Brazil witnessed many miracles too.[21] About fifty percent of the crowd came with pain in their bodies. A remarkably high percentage of people who came with pain in their bodies felt better after prayer and most of them felt like they had received a miracle.[22] This result suggests that healing can play an important role in Biblical evangelism.

A typical testimony is that of a twenty-four-year-old female who came with pain in her body. She agrees that she feels better after prayer and is sure that she has received a miracle. She heard about the crusade from a friend and a family member, she saw a poster, received a flyer, and saw information on Facebook and Instagram, and she heard about the crusade on the radio. She came because she wanted to see a miracle. She came

---

[21] Post-Crusade Church Survey Question 13.

[22] Of those in the crowd, 48.7% of the crowd reported that they arrived with pain in their bodies, while 78.5% of those who came with pain in their bodies felt better after the healing prayer. Of the 182 people on Saturday night who answered "yes" to the question of whether they arrived with pain in their bodies and said that they felt better, 176 (96.7%) "strongly agreed" or "agreed" that they had received a miracle. (Survey Questions 5-7)

by church bus from 16-30 minutes away. She considers herself to be evangelical from the Assembly of God church, but she only attends church one-to-two times per year. She repeated the salvation prayer and she strongly agrees that she would visit a church for additional prayer if invited.[23]

Another testimony is that of a sixty-six-year-old man who repeated the prayer of salvation because he says, "I believe in God." He came with pain in his body and he agrees that he feels better and he agrees that it is a miracle. He saw a poster and received a flyer about the crusade. He came because he wanted to see a miracle and because his pastor asked him to participate. He arrived by car from 16-30 minutes away. He is an evangelical member of the Assembly of God church who attends church two or more times per week.[24]

Advertising the miracle power of God played an enormous role in convincing people to come to the crusade.[25] A desire for miracles also played a significant role in the responsiveness of the people to repeat the prayer of the salvation.[26] The miracles that

---

[23]Respondent #466 on the Saturday night survey.

[24]Respondent #403 on the Saturday night survey.

[25]On the question, "Why did you come to this meeting?" 55 out of 169 (32.54%) respondents on Friday night and 116 out of 460 (25.22%) on Saturday night said they came because they needed a miracle, and another 46 out of 169 (27.22%) on Friday and 106 out of 460 (23%) on Saturday said they came because they wanted to see miracles. So, on Friday night 59% and on Saturday 48% came because of an interest in miracles. (Survey Question 9)

[26]On the open-ended question, "Why did you pray?" 98 respondents mentioned a need for "healing" or the desire to receive a "miracle." Example of what they wrote include: "Because I needed a miracle," "I needed to be healed," "Because my daughter needed to be healed" (Survey Question 4).

happened in Caicó made an impression on the believers who attended the crusade.[27] Many of those who came to the crusade personally knew someone who was healed[28] or were healed themselves.[29] The power of God was clearly manifested and visible to the church members who attended the crusade.[30]

The emphasis on miracles at a crusade is a uniquely Pentecostal / Charismatic / Spirit-Empowered practice. Pentecostals believe that Jesus Christ is the same yesterday, today, and forever (Hebrews 13:8). They believe that the same miracles that happened in the ministry of Jesus can still occur today. As noted in Chapter 3, praying for the sick in the crusade context was developed by missionary evangelist T.L. Osborn as a way to prove that Jesus is alive to people of other religions. The Spirit-Empowered believer believes that the instruction Jesus gave to the seventy-two in Matthew 10:8 to "heal the sick, cleanse the lepers, raise the dead, and cast out demons" extends to believers today and should be part of fulfilling the Great Commission (Matthew 28:20). Although some Christian theologians (known as cessationists) deny that miracles can happen today, the

---

[27] When asked, "Do you know of anyone who received a miracle at the crusade?" 225 (86.5%) of respondents to the survey of local church members replied in the affirmative (Post-Crusade Church Survey Question 12).

[28] Of the 263 respondents to the church survey, 21 (7.98%) specified they knew someone who received a miracle (Post-Crusade Church Survey Question 13).

[29] Of the 263 respondents to the church survey, 13 (4.94%) reported a personal testimony (Post-Crusade Church Survey Question 13).

[30] On Friday night, three deaf people who attended a local school for the deaf were healed. Their testimony on the platform made a deep impression on the audience. After the crusade, 112 of the local church members mentioned the miracle of the deaf/mutes who began to speak (Post-Crusade Church Survey Question 13).

experience of Spirit-Empowered believers is that miracles can and do happen today for those who believe. There are great evangelists in history (D.L. Moody, Billy Graham, Luis Palau) who never emphasized miracles in their ministries yet were used powerfully by God to lead countless thousands to Christ. But the experience of Pentecostal evangelists like Oral Roberts, T.L. Osborn, and Reinhard Bonnke show that miracles can play a valuable role in the ministry of the evangelist. The experience of this researcher in Caicó, Brazil and the numerous miracles that were reported there reaffirm the important role that an emphasis on miracles can play in evangelism.

Church Involvement

Another factor in the success of the Caicó crusade was the enthusiastic participation of the local churches.[31] All nine of the churches that participated in the crusade did so by sending church members to serve in various ways[32] because they were excited about the event.[33] The reason the churches participated is because they were hoping to see many people get saved and to see a revival among their church members.[34] Overall, the level of participation by the local churches was high. They participated in a variety of ways.

---

[31] A total of 1,035+ people from the churches attended the crusade. At least 575 people from the churches volunteered at the crusade.

[32] Pastor's Pre-Crusade Survey Question 13-14.

[33] Pastor's Pre-Crusade Survey Question 15.

[34] Pastor's Pre-Crusade Survey Question 16.

First, the churches participated by attending the event. Questions on two different surveys measured the level of church attendance. According to the pastors' estimate, 76.27% of the 1,357 church members in the city[35] attended the crusade[36] and according to the church members themselves 90.9% of the church members attended.[37] The disparity between these numbers is small and could be attributed to the lack of preciseness in the pastor's survey. Regardless, a large percentage of the local church members attended the crusade at least once. The highest percentage of church members who attended was on Friday night (70.7%),[38] but the biggest crowd was on Saturday night. This suggests that the crowd on Saturday night had a higher percentage of unbelievers.

Second, the churches participated by serving at the event. According to the pastors, 42.37% of the church members participated as volunteers at the crusade[39] and according to the church members, 44.5% participated.[40] Again, the disparity between these numbers is small and could be attributed to the lack of preciseness in the pastor's survey.

---

[35]Pre-Crusade Pastor's Survey Questions 2-3

[36]Post-Crusade Pastor's Survey Question 1.

[37]Post-Crusade Church Survey Question 3.

[38]Post-Crusade Church Survey Question 3.

[39]Post-Crusade Pastor's Survey Question 2.

[40]Post-Crusade Church Survey Question 4.

Third, the churches participated by inviting people to come to the event. On average, every church member invited at least one person to the crusade.[41] In practice, some church members invited lots of people and others did not invite any.[42] More church members used social media to promote the crusade (65%) than who actually passed out flyers (40.2%).[43] This might reflect a larger trend in society towards social media becoming more important as a method of influencing people. This suggests evangelists should focus more attention on reaching people through social media.

The church members who were surveyed invited around 1,424 people and at least 566 (39.74%) of those invited came to the crusade.[44] Of the 466 people who were surveyed on Saturday night, 242 heard about the meeting because of a friend or family member who invited them to come.[45] This illustrates the importance of involving the local church in inviting people to the crusade. Advertising alone cannot make an evangelistic event successful; it is vital for local church members to invite the lost. Thus, an important part of conducting a crusade is training and motivating the local believers to be involved in personal evangelism. Mass evangelism should be an extension of personal evangelism. The mass crusade done well should activate the local church to be involved

---

[41] Pastor's Post-Crusade Survey Questions 4-6.

[42] Post-Crusade Church Survey Question 7.

[43] Church's Post-Crusade Survey Questions 5-6.

[44] Church's Post-Crusade Survey Questions 7-9. This data correlates with the Post-Crusade Pastor's Survey Question 4, which says the total number of people that churches invited to the crusade was more than 1,430.

[45] Survey Question 8.

in one-on-one evangelism. Mass evangelism is most successful when it is connected with personal evangelism done by the local church.

Only 27.8% of the church members gave a ride to a friend or family member.[46] However, the researcher finds that only 38.6% of the attendees came by car.[47] This indicates that a high percentage of the church members do not own a car and thus could not give a ride to a friend. This question would have provided more valuable information if the researcher had asked, "Did you bring a friend to the crusade?"

52.1% of the church members surveyed invited someone who they said prayed with the evangelist for salvation.[48] This reinforces the importance of involving the local church in promoting the crusade. Since many of the people who got saved are already known by church members, it is speculated that there is a higher probability that they will be discipled. It is believed that there is positive correlation between the involvement of the members of the local church and the retention of the fruit of the crusade.

One example of a church member who was involved is a thirty-five-year-old female[49] who attended all three nights of the crusade and served as a counselor. She distributed flyers but did not share about the crusade on social media. She invited two family members and both of them came. She gave them a ride and they both prayed for

---

[46]Church's Post-Crusade Survey Question 10.

[47]Crusade Survey Question 11.

[48]Church's Post-Crusade Survey Question 11.

[49]Respondent #15 from church Church 3.

salvation. One person who came with her said she was cured from an unspecified disease. The woman felt that the crusade impacted her life, her church, and her city.

Follow Up

The fourth area of interest is follow up of new believers. On the crusade survey the researcher asked the people who do not currently attend a church if they would be willing to visit a church in order to received additional prayer. The vast majority of the respondents indicated in the affirmative.[50] This suggests there is an open door to disciple people after an evangelistic event is over because if a church can get someone to visit, then the church can start the discipleship process during that visit.

A total of 641 people filled out decision cards during the crusade. Immediately after the crusade was over the decision cards were divided up among the participating churches. On Sunday morning each person who completed a decision card was called and invited to come to church that evening (in Caicó, the main church service occurs on Sunday evening). Each church then invited the new believers to join a discipleship group to discuss the new believer's book that was passed out at the crusade. The day after the crusade, 112 of the people who filled out decision cards visited one of the local churches.[51]

---

[50]Eighty people "strongly agreed" they would be willing to visit a church (37.2%), and 111 "agreed" they would visit a church (51.6%). Fourteen were not sure if they would visit (6.5%), while 9 "disagreed" that they would visit a church (4.2%). One "strongly disagreed" that he would be willing to visit a church (0.5%) (Survey Question 16).

[51]Post-Crusade Pastor's Survey Questions 5.

All the churches planned to follow up on the new believers[52] but three months later it was discovered that not all the churches actually did so.[53] The churches who did follow up did so in a variety of ways including cell groups, special meetings, and Bible school classes.[54] The total number of people who participated in the follow up program was 30.[55] A total of at least 50 new people joined the local churches because of the crusade.[56]

So, 14.9% (641) of the crowd of 4,300 filled out decision cards and 4.6% (30) of those who filled out decision cards participated in the follow up process and 7.8% (50) of those who filled out decision cards joined a local church. These new members represent church growth of 3.68%.[57] These numbers suggest that more emphasis on follow up is needed after the crusade is over.

---

[52]The day after the crusade, on the statement, "Our church is planning to participate in the follow-up of new believers who got saved at the crusade," eight pastors "strongly agreed" and one pastor "agreed." None disagreed. (Post-Crusade Pastor's Survey Question 6).

[53]On the statement, "Our church followed-up on new believers who got saved at the crusade," four pastors "strongly agreed," two "agreed," two "disagreed," and one "strongly disagreed." (Post-Crusade Pastor's Survey, Three Months Later, Question 3).

[54]Post-Crusade Pastor's Survey, Three Months Later, Question 5

[55]Post-Crusade Pastor's Survey, Three Months Later, Question 4

[56]Post-Crusade Pastor's Survey, Three Months Later, Question 7

[57]Fifty new members added to the original 1,357 church members in the city.

Overall Impact

When discussing the positive aspects of the crusade seven of the pastors mentioned "revival," "excitement" among the churches, and "awakening." Three mentioned the "salvation of souls." Two mentioned an increase in "commitment to evangelism." One mentioned the "unity of the churches" and one mentioned "spiritual strengthening."[58] None of the pastors mentioned any significant negative aspects of the crusade.[59] One pastor would have changed the way the follow up cards were distributed, one thought the children's event was poorly organized, and one thought the crusade should have lasted longer.[60] Overall, the pastors were happy with the results of the crusade. All the pastors "agreed" or "strongly agreed" that the crusade was worth the time, money, and preparation,[61] and they all wanted another crusade to come to their city.[62] Ninety percent of the pastors felt that crusades are an effective method of evangelism and only one was unsure,[63] although these numbers trended downward when the pastors were asked the same question three months later.[64] The church members who

---

[58] Pastor's Post-Crusade Survey Question 7

[59] Pastor's Post-Crusade Survey Question 8

[60] Pastor's Post-Crusade Survey Question 9

[61] Pastor's Post-Crusade Survey Question 10

[62] Pastor's Post-Crusade Survey Question 11

[63] Pastor's Post-Crusade Survey Question 12

[64] Post-Crusade Pastor's Survey, Three Months Later, Questions 12-14.

were surveyed felt the crusade had an impact on them individually, on the churches involved, and on the city of Caicó.[65] These overall positive responses suggest that at least in the context of a small city in northeast Brazil, crusades are an effective method of evangelism.

There are a lot of numbers in this study, but the truth is that numbers are important. God even named a whole book in the Bible, "Numbers." The reality is that every number represents a story. Every statistic stands for a person. At the crusade in Caicó, Brazil many people were touched by God, saved, and healed and the numbers tell the story of what God did.

Conclusions

A survey is an effective method of capturing a snapshot picture of an evangelistic event. Polls are used to measure opinions about politics, entertainment, shopping trends, and television watching habits. There is no reason they cannot provide valuable insight on religious attitudes and behavior. Evangelists should conduct more surveys at their events in order to sharpen their methods and messages. The methods used for the research in this paper can be used for future research projects of a similar nature.

The way a question is asked can determine how it is answered.[66] It is important to carefully target each question toward a specific research subject. Care must be taken that

---

[65]Church's Post-Crusade Survey Questions 14-16

[66]The researcher would change the open-ended question asking why people prayed to a closed question with several options, in order to get a more precise result.

the researcher's prejudice and assumptions do not accidentally render the survey results less meaningful.

The surveys in this project were completed by using face-to-face interviews. The information gained from an interview is only as good as the interviewer who asks the questions. It is important to make sure the interviewers who help collect the data are well trained and understand the purpose of the information they are collecting. In addition, there is a danger that some information collected in face-to-face interviews is inaccurate because of a desire to please the interviewer. In some cases it would be better to allow the participant to fill out a questionnaire instead of having an interviewer fill out the questionnaire.

It was difficult to collect a truly random sample in the environment of an evangelistic event. People who were fully engaged in the event were more likely to answer questions, while those who just wanted to watch were less willing to complete an interview. This might have skewed results.

Open-ended questions are better than closed questions in gauging opinions. But, evaluating open-ended questions is extremely time-consuming when the answers must be translated into a second language. Due to the difficulties involved, this type of survey should only have closed questions. In future surveys, this researcher will only use closed questions.

Theological Reflection

Evangelism is an expression of the heart of the Triune God. In the beginning of time, God created Adam and Eve because He wanted to have fellowship with them.

Every day He would walk and talk with them. But when they sinned, this fellowship was broken. God promised a Savior who would come to restore what had been lost (Gen 3:15). When the perfect time arrived (Gal 4:4), God sent His only Son that whosoever believes in Him would not perish but would have everlasting life (John 3:16). Jesus died on a wooden cross to pay the price for sin (Rom 6:23). But, Jesus did not stay dead. After three days, Jesus rose from the dead (Acts 2:24) and He is alive today, ready to save humanity from the curse of sin. This good news is known as the "*evangel*."

Evangelism is the supreme task given by Christ to the Church. Between the time of His resurrection and His ascension, Jesus commanded His disciples to preach the Gospel to the whole world on multiple occasions (Matt 28:19; Mark 16:15; Luke 24:47; John 20:21; Acts 1:8). This command to evangelize continues to have urgency for the Church today.

Evangelism is done by believers who are sent to preach good news to the lost. The method God has prescribed for people to be saved is the sending of preachers.[67] God desires for every person to be saved (1 Tim 2:4). But, not all are saved. In order for people to be saved, they must call upon the name of the Lord (Acts 2:21, Rom 10:13). In order for people to call upon the name of Jesus, they must believe that Jesus died on the cross for their sins and rose from the dead (Rom 10:8-9). In order to believe, they must hear the Gospel. In order for them to hear, there must be someone who preaches to them. In order for a preacher to preach, he or she must be sent (Romans 10:14-15). The

---

[67]The word "preacher" is not meant to imply professional clergy. Any believer who is willing to share the Gospel through the spoken word could be called a "preacher." The command to "go into all the world and preach" (Mark 16:15) was given to every believer, not just to the evangelist or pastor.

evangelist is one who is sent with a mission to preach good news to those who need Jesus.

Evangelism is reliant upon the work of the Holy Spirit. No one can say, "Jesus is Lord" except by the Holy Spirit (1 Cor 12:3). No one can come to Jesus unless the Father draws him (John 6:44). There is a divine partnership between God and the preacher who both work together to bring sinners to salvation. Converting the sinner is God's work; preaching the Gospel is the evangelist's task. The evangelist's role is to communicate the Gospel clearly, and God's job is to save the sinner.

Evangelism is the delight of heaven. When a sinner repents, all of heaven rejoices (Luke 15:7,10). If one repentant sinner causes heaven to rejoice, there is even greater celebration when a multitude of sinners repent. When Jesus was on earth, He ministered both to individuals (John 4:4-26) and to multitudes (Matt 4:25; 5:1; 7:28; 8:1; 15:30; 19:2; 22:23; 23:1). Philip the evangelist also ministered to an individual (Acts 8:2-38), and to multitudes (Acts 8:5-8). Both individual evangelism and mass evangelism are viable methods for sharing the Gospel. Mass evangelism is a Biblical method of evangelism that has been used throughout church history to draw people to Christ and it continues to be a useful and fruitful tool for preaching the Gospel in modern times.

Recommendations

Recommendations to improve the project: First, it would be valuable to be able to interview those under the age of eighteen. This study was seriously impaired by the IRB rules which dictate that no one under eighteen years of age can be studied without signed permission from their parents. The information collected would have been far more accurate if the researcher had been able to administer surveys to the many teenagers who attended the event.

Recommendations for further research: It would be beneficial to conduct research on several more crusades. While every mass evangelism event has some similarities, they also have many differences. Different cities, countries, languages, and religions would produce a variety of results. The results at this crusade are unique and cannot be extrapolated to fit every evangelism event.

Recommendations for implementation in ministry: This project produced many results that will directly assist this researcher in future mass evangelism events. The data from the surveys affirmed the importance of miracles in evangelism and the importance of involving the local church in reaching the lost. Another important finding is the increasing importance of using social media to reach people even in the context of a developing nation.

Suggestions for Future Studies: Since the greatest criticism the evangelist receives is in the area of follow up, a future study on how the churches of Brazil follow up on converts would be enlightening. Ideally, this study would track those who fill out decision cards over a twelve-month period to see what their spiritual journey looks like. Do the people who get saved at a crusade end up joining a church and becoming disciples or do they fall away from the faith?

A study aimed at improving church participation in personal witnessing would also be beneficial. A soul-winning seminar could be done in conjunction with a pre-test and a post-test to measure an increase in knowledge about the importance of witnessing and to measure an increase in the motivation of local church members for witnessing. This teaching could be combined with a survey after the crusade to find out if the soul-winning seminar is an effective tool for bringing the lost to hear the Gospel.

This study asked subjective questions about whether people felt better after the healing prayer. A follow up study looking for medical proof of miracles would be interesting. Do the physical healings last or are they simply the result of a placebo effect?

Summary of Chapter and Project

The researcher is an evangelist who conducts large evangelistic events. He decided to do this research project on mass evangelism because many people in both the academic world and in the church world have criticized the use of mass evangelism and said it is an ineffective waste of time, effort, and resources. However, after completing this project, this researcher is convinced that much of this criticism is misplaced.

Chapter 1 explained the nature of the problem. Chapter 2 provided a Biblical, theological, historical, cultural, and personal examination of mass evangelism. It was demonstrated that the use of mass evangelism has a solid Biblical precedent and a theological raison d'être. The historical research revealed that mass evangelism has been an essential component of many moves of God throughout history. In Chapter 3, a review of the literature highlighted a variety of sources that affirm the use of mass evangelism.

In Chapter 4, a research plan is described. The goal of this research was to conduct a series of surveys at a mass evangelism event in the nation of Brazil. In Chapter 5, the results of these surveys are revealed. In this final chapter, the implications of these surveys are examined and a conclusion is provided. The investigation into the Biblical, theological, and historical background of mass evangelism, the review of literature, and the research conducted at an actual event of mass evangelism agree that mass evangelism is an effective and viable way to lead people to Jesus.

APPENDIX A

CRUSADE SURVEY

Appendix A - Survey of Attendees at a Mass Evangelistic Event in Caicó, Brazil

1. What is your age? _____

2. What is your gender?
    [ ] Male   [ ] Female

3. Did you repeat the prayer with the preacher tonight?
    [ ] Yes
    [ ] No

4. Why did you repeat the prayer with the preacher tonight?
_____

5. Were you sick or in need of healing, when you arrived here tonight?
    [ ] Yes
    [ ] No

6. My body feels better now than when I arrived.

Strongly Agree   Agree   Undecided   Disagree   Strongly Disagree

7. I would say the improvement in my body is a miracle.

Strongly Agree   Agree   Undecided   Disagree   Strongly Disagree

8. How did you hear about this meeting? (Check all that apply)
    [ ] My friend told me about the meeting.
    [ ] A family member invited me.
    [ ] I saw a poster about the event.
    [ ] I was given a flyer about the event.
    [ ] I saw the meeting advertised on Facebook.
    [ ] I heard about the event on television.
    [ ] I heard about the event on the radio.

9. Why did you come to this meeting? (Check all that apply)
    [ ] My friend invited me.
    [ ] I am curious about what is happening.
    [ ] I like to hear the music.
    [ ] I need a miracle.
    [ ] I want to see miracles.

[ ] My pastor told me I should attend.
[ ] I am curious about God.
[ ] I don't know why I came.
[ ] Other _____

10. How long did it take you to travel to the meeting tonight?
    [ ] 5 minutes or less
    [ ] 6-10 minutes
    [ ] 11-15 minutes
    [ ] 16-30 minutes
    [ ] 31-44 minutes
    [ ] 45 or more minutes

11. How did you come to the meeting tonight?
    [ ] Car
    [ ] Public Transportation
    [ ] Church Bus
    [ ] Motorcycle
    [ ] Bicycle
    [ ] Walking
    [ ] Other

12. What is your religion?
    [ ] Catholic
    [ ] Christian / Evangelical Christian
    [ ] No religion
    [ ] Other _____

13. Are you part of a church?
    Yes   No

14. If yes, what church do you attend?

---

15. How often do you attend your church?
    [ ] Never
    [ ] 1 or 2 times per year
    [ ] 6-12 times each year
    [ ] 1 or 2 times each month
    [ ] Every Sunday

[ ] 2 or more times each week

If you do not attend a church, please answer this question:

16. If invited, I would be willing to visit a church to receive additional prayer.

Strongly Agree   Agree   Undecided   Disagree   Strongly Disagree

APPENDIX B

PRE-CRUSADE PASTOR'S SURVEY

Appendix B – Pre-Crusade Pastor's Survey

1. Church Affiliation or Denomination: _____

2. What is the average weekly attendance at your church? _____

3. How many members does your church have? _____

4. How many people did your church baptize in the past year? _____

5. What do you think are the biggest spiritual needs in your city?
_____
_____
_____
_____

6. Our church is an evangelistic church that preaches frequently about the need for evangelism.

Strongly Agree   Agree   Undecided   Disagree   Strongly Disagree

7. What evangelistic methods does your church use to tell people about Jesus?

_____
_____
_____
_____

8. Our church conducts special services to reach the unsaved.

Very Frequently   Frequently   Occasionally   Rarely   Never

9. Our church goes outside the church to do an evangelistic outreach in our community.

Very Frequently   Frequently   Occasionally   Rarely   Never

10. Churches should be more aggressive in sharing their faith with others.

Strongly Agree   Agree   Undecided   Disagree   Strongly Disagree

11. My church should be more aggressive in sharing their faith with others.

Strongly Agree Agree Undecided Disagree Strongly Disagree

12. Our church plans to participate in the crusade in Caicó.

Strongly Agree Agree Undecided Disagree Strongly Disagree

13. How is your church participating in the crusade? (Circle all that apply)

Sending church members to serve as ushers, counselors, prayer team, and security
Hanging banners
Passing out flyers
Inviting neighbors
Participating in pre-crusade outreaches
Attending leadership meetings
Attending planning meetings

14. How many people is your church sending to participate in the crusade?

Ushers _____

Counselors _____

Prayer Team _____

Security _____

15. I am excited about the crusade that is taking place in Caicó?

Strongly Agree Agree Undecided Disagree Strongly Disagree

16. What do you hope will be accomplished by the crusade in Caicó.

_____
_____
_____
_____
_____

17. I have some concerns about the crusade taking place in Caicó.

Strongly Agree Agree Undecided Disagree Strongly Disagree

18. What are your concerns about the crusade coming to Caicó?
_____

APPENDIX C

POST-CRUSADE PASTOR'S SURVEY

Appendix C – Post-Crusade Pastor's Survey

1. Church Affiliation or Denomination: _____

2. How many people from your church attended the crusade? _____

3. How many people from your church participated in the crusade?

Ushers _____

Counselors _____

Prayer Team _____

Security _____

4. How many people who do not currently attend your church did your church members invite to the crusade? _____

5. How many new visitors did your church have on the Sunday after the crusade?
_____

6. Our church is planning to participate in the follow-up of new believers who got saved at the crusade?

Strongly Agree   Agree   Undecided   Disagree   Strongly Disagree

7. What were some of the positive effects of the crusade?
_____
_____
_____
_____
_____

8. Were there any negative effects from the crusade? What were they?
_____
_____
_____

_____
_____
_____
_____

9. Is there anything with the crusade that you wish had happened differently?

_____
_____
_____
_____
_____

10. The crusade was worth the time, money, and preparation that went into it.

Strongly Agree   Agree   Undecided   Disagree   Strongly Disagree

11. I would like to see another crusade in my city in the future.

Strongly Agree   Agree   Undecided   Disagree   Strongly Disagree

12. Mass evangelism is an effective method to reach people in Brazil.

Strongly Agree   Agree   Undecided   Disagree   Strongly Disagree

APPENDIX D

POST-CRUSADE PASTOR'S SURVEY, 3 MONTHS LATER

Appendix D – Post-Crusade Pastor's Survey – Three Months Later

1. Church Affiliation or Denomination:_____

2. What is the average weekly attendance at your church? _____

3. Our church followed up on new believers who got saved at the crusade.

Strongly Agree   Agree   Undecided   Disagree   Strongly Disagree

4. How many new believers participated in your follow up program? _____

5. Please describe how your church followed up on the new believers.
_____
_____
_____
_____

6. My church grew in attendance since the crusade took place.

Strongly Agree   Agree   Undecided   Disagree   Strongly Disagree

7. How many people joined your church because of the crusade? _____

8. My church has become more active in evangelism since the crusade.

Strongly Agree   Agree   Undecided   Disagree   Strongly Disagree

9. My church members are more spiritually alive since the crusade took place.

Strongly Agree   Agree   Undecided   Disagree   Strongly Disagree

10. Three months later, what would you say are some of the positive effects of the crusade?
_____
_____
_____
_____
_____

11. Were there any negative effects from the crusade? What were they?

_____
_____
_____
_____
_____

12. The crusade was worth the time, money, and preparation that went into it.

Strongly Agree   Agree   Undecided   Disagree   Strongly Disagree

13. I would like to see another crusade in my city in the future.

Strongly Agree   Agree   Undecided   Disagree   Strongly Disagree

14. Mass evangelism is an effective method to reach people in Brazil.

Strongly Agree   Agree   Undecided   Disagree   Strongly Disagree

APPENDIX E

POST-CRUSADE CHURCH'S SURVEY

Appendix E – Post-Crusade Survey of Church Members

1. What is your age? _____

2. What is your gender?
    [ ] Male   [ ] Female

3. I attended the crusade. (Circle all that Apply)

    Thursday Night Youth Concert

    Friday Night

    Saturday Night

    I did not attend the crusade.

4. I participated in the crusade as a:

    Usher

    Counselor

    Prayer Team

    Security

    Other

    None

5. Did you pass out any flyers?
    Yes   No

6. Did you share information about the crusade on social media?
    Yes   No

7. How many total people did you invite to the crusade?
_____

8. Who did you invite to the crusade? (Circle all that apply)
    Friends
    Family
    Neighbors

       Co-workers
       Fellow students
       Random people on the street

9. Of the people you invited, how many came?
_____

10. Did you give someone a ride to the crusade?
    Yes   No

11. Did anyone you invited pray with the preacher for salvation?
    Yes   No

12. Do you know of anyone who received a miracle at the crusade?
    Yes   No

13. Please tell us about the miracle that happened.
_____
_____
_____
_____

14. The crusade impacted my life.

Strongly Agree   Agree   Undecided   Disagree   Strongly Disagree

15. The crusade impacted my church.

Strongly Agree   Agree   Undecided   Disagree   Strongly Disagree

16. The crusade impacted the city.

Strongly Agree   Agree   Undecided   Disagree   Strongly Disagree

BIBLIOGRAPHY

Books

Allison, Lon, and Mark Anderson. *Going Public with the Gospel.* Downer's Grove, IL: InterVarsity Press, 2003.

Ammerman, Nancy T., Jackson W. Carroll, Carl S. Dudley, and William McKinney, eds. *Studying Congregations.* Nashville, TN: Abingdon Press, 1998.

Asbury, Francis. *The Journal of Francis Asbury.* Vols. 2 and 3. New York, NY: Methodist Episcopal Church, 1821.

Barna, George. *Marketing the Church.* Colorado Springs, CO: Nav Press, 1988.

Becker, U. "Gospel, Evangelize, Evangelist," *The New International Dictionary of New Testament Theology.* Vol. 2. Edited by Colin Brown. Grand Rapids, MI: Zondervan, 1971. 107-115.

Belcher, Joseph. *George Whitefield. A Biography with Special Reference to His Labors in America.* New York: American Tract Society, 1857.

Bennett, David. *The Altar Call: Its Origins and Present Usage.* Lanham, MD: University Press of America, 2000.

Bonnke, Reinhard. *Evangelism by Fire.* Laguna Hills, CA: Reinhard Bonnke, 1993.

Broocks, Rice. *God's Not Dead.* Nashville, TN: W Publishing, 2013.

Carroll, H. K. *A Religious Encyclopedia, or, Dictionary of Biblical, Historical, Doctrinal, and Practical Theology.* Vol 3. Edited by Philip Schaff. Edinburgh: T. & T. Clark, 1884. .

Cartwright, Peter. *The Autobiography of Peter Cartwright: The Backwoods Preacher.* Cincinnati: L. Swormstedt & A. Poe, 1859.

Cartwright, Peter. *Autobiography of Peter Cartwright.* Nashville, TN: Abingdon, 1956.

Cherry, Jason. *The Culture of Conversionism and the History of the Altar Call.* Athens, AL: JEC, 2016.

Clement. *Recognitions of Clement.* In Vol. 8 of *The Ante-Nicene Fathers.* Edited by Alexander Roberts and James Donaldson, 1885, Reprint. Peabody, MA: Hendrickson, 1995.

Clendenen, E. R. "Jonah, Book of." *Holman Illustrated Bible Dictionary.* Edited by C. Brand, C. Draper, A. England, S. Bond, & T. C. Butler. Nashville, TN: Holman Bible Publishers, 2003. Logos Bible Software Version 5.2 2014). (April 20, 2019).

Comfort, Ray. *Hell's Best Kept Secret.* Springdale, PA: Whitaker House, 1989.

Conkin, Paul K. *Cain Ridge: America's Pentecost.* Madison, WI: University of Wisconsin Press, 1990.

De Oliveira, Joanyr. *The Assemblies of God in Brazil: An Illustrated Historical Summary.* Edited by Richard Hoover. Rio De Janeiro: Assemblies of God Publishing House, 1997.

Dodd, C. H. *The Apostolic Preaching and Its Developments.* New York, NY: Harper and Row, 1964). https://postbarthian.com/2012/10/15/the-apostolic-preaching-and-its-developments-by-c-h-dodd/ (29 March 2019).

Dorsett, Lyle W. *A Passion for Souls: The Life of D. L. Moody.* Chicago, IL: Moody, 1997.

Dowie, John Alexander. *The Gospel of Divine Healing and How I Came to Preach It.* Chicago: Zion Publishing, 1874.

_____. "Talks with Ministers on Divine Healing." "God's Way of Healing." In *Leaves of Healing*, Vol. II. N.p. Chicago: Zion Publishing, 18 October 1895.

Drummond, Lewis A. *The Evangelist: The Worldwide Impact of Billy Graham.* Nashville, TN: Word Publishing, 2001.

Edwards, Jonathan. *Sinners in the Hands of an Angry God.* Boston: S. Kneeland and T. Green, 1741.

_____. *Distinguishing Marks of a Work of the Spirit of God.* Upper Moorfields J. Paramore, 1741

Ellenwood, Lee K., ed. "Quotations on Mission." *The Living Pulpit* 16, no. 3 (2007): 45. *ATLA Religion Database with ATLASerials*, EBSCOhost (5 December 2017).

The Encyclical Epistle of the Church at Smyrna Concerning the Martyrdom of the Holy Polycarp, In vol. 1 of *Ante-Nicene Fathers,* Edited by Alexander Roberts and James Donaldson, 1885. Reprint, Peabody, MA: Hendrickson, 1995.

Eusebius. *The Church History of Eusebius.* In Vols. 1, 3 of *The Nicene and Post-Nicene Fathers.* Edited by Philip Schaff and Henry Wace, 1886. Reprint. Peabody, MA: Hendrickson, 1995.

Finney, Charles G. *Memoirs.* New York: Fleming H. Revell, 1876.

_____. *Lectures on Revivals of Religion.* Old Tappan, NJ: Fleming H. Revell, 1868.

Friedrich. *"Euangelion." Theological Dictionary of the New Testament.* Vol. 2. Edited by Gerhard Kittel. Grand Rapids, MI: Eerdmans, 1987. 707-737.

Godwin, David E. *Church Planting Methods.* Desota, TX: Lifeshare Communications, 1984.

Graham, Billy. *Just As I Am: The Autobiography of Billy Graham.* San Francisco, CA: HarperCollins Worldwide, 1997.

Green, Michael. *Evangelism in the Early Church.* Grand Rapids, MI: Eerdmans, 2003.

Grudem, Wayne A., ed. *Are Miraculous Gifts for Today?* Grand Rapids, MI: Zondervan, 1996.

Hadaway, Kirk. *Church Growth Principles: Separating Fact from Fiction.* Nashville, TN: Broadman Press, 1991.

Harrell David Edwin, Jr. *All Things Are Possible: the Healing and Charismatic Revivals in Modern America.* Bloomington, IN: Indiana Univ. Press, 1975.

Howell, Don N., Jr. "Mission in Paul's Epistles: Genesis, Pattern, and Dynamics." In *Mission in the New Testament: An Evangelical Approach*, ed. William Larkin Jr. and Joel F. Williams, 63-91. Maryknoll, NY: Orbis, 1998.

Huston, Sterling W. *Crusade Evangelism and the Local Church.* Minneapolis, MN: Billy Graham Evangelistic Association, 1996.

Hybels, Bill, and Mark Mittelberg. *Becoming a Contagious Christian.* Grand Rapids, MI: Zondervan, 1994.

Irenaeus. *Against Heresies.* Book 1. In Vol. 1 of *The Ante Nicene Fathers.* Edited by Alexander Roberts and James Donaldson. Revised by A. Cleveland Coxe.

Buffalo: Christian Literature Company, 1885. Reprint, Peabody, MA: Hendrickson, 1995.

Koo, Hongnak. *The Impact of Luis Palau on Global Evangelism.* Grand Rapids, MI: Credo Communications, 2010.

Larkin, William, Jr., and Joel F. Williams, eds. *Mission in the New Testament: An Evangelical Approach.* Maryknoll, NY: Orbis, 1998.

Larkin, William, Jr. "Mission in Acts." In *Mission in the New Testament: An Evangelical Approach*, ed. William Larkin Jr. and Joe F. Williams, 170-185. Maryknoll, NY: Orbis, 1998.

Lewis, Sinclair. *Elmer Gantry.* New York, NY: Signet Classics, 2007.

Liardon, Roberts. *God's Generals: Why They Succeeded and Why Some Fail.* New Kensington, PA: Whitaker House, 1996.

_____ . *John G Lake: The Complete Collection of his Life Teachings.* Tulsa, OK: Albury, 1999.

Mcloughlin, William G., Jr. *Modern Revivalism: Charles Finney to Billy Graham.* Eugene, OR: Wipt & Stock, 2005.

Miller, Basil. *Ten Famous Evangelists.* Grand Rapids, MI: Zondervan, 1949.

Osborn, Tommy Lee and Daisy Osborn. *Faith Library in 23 Volumes: 20th Century Legacy of Apostolic Evangelism.* Tulsa: OSFO International, 1997.

_____ . *Healing the Sick: A Living Classic.* Tulsa, OK: Harrison House, 1992.

_____ . *The Gospel According to T.L. and Daisy.* Tulsa, OK: Osborn Publishers, 1985

_____ . *The Message that Works.* Tulsa, OK: Osborn Publishers, 1997.

Origen. *Against Celsus.* In Vol. 4 of *The Ante-Nicene Fathers.* Edited by Alexander Roberts and James Donaldson, 1885. Reprint. Peabody, MA: Hendrickson, 1995.

Palau, Kevin. *Unlikely: Setting Aside our Differences to Live out the Gospel.* New York, NY: Howard, 2015.

Palau, Luis, and David Sanford. *Calling America and the Nations to Christ.* Nashville, TN: Thomas Nelson, 1994.

Peters, George W. *A Biblical Theology of Missions*. Chicago, IL: Moody Press, 1972.

Petersen, Jim. *Living Proof: Sharing the Gospel Naturally*. Colorado Springs, CO: NavPress, 1989.

Pippert, Rebecca Manley. *Out of Salt Shaker*. Downers Grove, IL: InterVarsity, 1999.

Pollock, John. *The Billy Graham Story*. Grand Rapids, MI: Zondervan, 2003.

Rackham, Richard Belward. *The Acts of the Apostles: An Exposition*. London, England: Methuen, 1901.

Roberts, Oral. *Expect a Miracle: My Life and Ministry*. Nashville, TN: Thomas Nelson, 1995.

_____. *God Still Heals Today*. Tulsa: Oral Roberts. 1984.

_____. *If You Need Healing, Do These Things*. Tulsa: Oral Roberts. 1969.

_____. *The Miracle of Seed-Faith*. Tulsa, OK: Oral Roberts Evangelistic Association, 1982.

_____. *Expect a New Miracle Every Day*. Tulsa, OK: Oral Roberts Evangelistic Association, 1963.

_____. *God is a Good God*. Tulsa, OK: Bobbs-Merrill Company, 1960.

Robertson, A. T. *Word Pictures in the New Testament* (Ac 8:5). Nashville, TN: Broadman Press, 1933. Logos Bible Software Version 5.2 2014). (April 20, 2019).

Salter, Darius L. *America's Bishop: The Life of Francis Asbury*. Nappanee, IN: Francis Asbury Press, 2003.

Scharpff, Paulus. *History of Evangelism*. Translated by Helga Bender Henry. Grand Rapids, MI: Eerdmans, 1966.

Senior, Donald and Carroll Stuhlmueller. *The Biblical Foundation for Missions*. Maryknoll, NY: Orbis, 1984.

Smith, Joseph. *Pearl of Great Price*. Salt Lake City, Utah: Church of Jesus Christ of Latter-Day Saints, 1981.

Street, R. Allen. *The Effective Invitation*. Grand Rapids, MI: Kregel, 2004.

Synan, Vinson. *The Century of the Holy Spirit*. Nashville, TN: Thomas Nelson, 2001.

Templeton, Charles B. *Farewell to God: My Reasons for Rejecting the Christian Faith*. Toronto, Ontario: McClelland & Stewart, 1996.

Terry, John M. *Evangelism: A Concise History*. Nashville, TN: Broadman & Holman, 1994.

Thomas, William. *An Assessment of Mass Meetings as a Method of Evangelism – Case Study of Eurofest'75 and the Billy Graham Crusade in Brussels*. Amsterdam, Editions Rodopi N.V., 1977.

Tuttle, Robert G. *The Story of Evangelism*. Nashville, TN: Abingdon, 2006.

Van De Poll, Evert. *Europe and the Gospel: Past Influences, Current Developments, Mission Challenges*. London: Verista, 2013.

Vondey, Wolfgang. *Pentecostal Theology: Living the Full Gospel*, Systematic Pentecostal and Charismatic Theology Series. London: Bloomsbury T&T Clark, 2017.

Wagner, C. Peter. *Strategies for Church Growth*. Ventura, CA: Regal Books, 1987.

_____. *Church Planting for a Greater Harvest*. Ventura, CA: Regal Books, 1990.

Wesley, John. "Wesley Begins Field-Preaching." *Journal of John Wesley*. (15 March 1739): N.p. Christian Classics Ethereal Library. https://www.ccel.org/ccel/wesley/ journal.vi.iii.i.html (18 March 2018).

Wright, Christopher J. H. *The Mission of God: Unlocking the Bible's Grand Narrative*. Downers Grove, IL: InterVarsity, 2006.

Periodicals

Beeke, Joel R. "Calvin's Evangelism." *Mid-America Journal of Theology* 15 (2004): 69. *ATLA Religion Database with ATLASerials*, EBSCOhost (6 November 2017).

"Billy's Victory in London." *Time* 88, no. 3, (15 July 1966): N.p. *Academic Search Complete*, EBSCOhost (5 September 2017).

Boehm, Nathan. "Daniel Boone Associated with Revival." *Word Nuggets*, 23 April 2010. N.p. https://wordnuggets.wordpress.com/2010/04/23 /daniel-boone-associated-with-revival/ (18 March 2018).

Bonnet, *Letters of Calvin*, 3:134. Quoted in Joel R. Beeke. "Calvin's Evangelism." *Mid-America Journal of Theology* 15 (2004): 73. *ATLA Religion Database with ATLASerials*, EBSCOhost (6 November 2017).

Cassidy, Michael. "Limitations of Mass Evangelism and Its Potentialities," *International Review of Mission* 65, no. 258 (1976): 202-215. *ATLA Religion Database with ATLASerials*, EBSCOhost (1 September 2017).

Cook, Guillermo. "The Protestant Predicament: From Base Ecclesial Community to Established Church: A Brazilian Case Study," *International Bulletin of Missionary Research* 8, no. 3 (1984): 98-102. *ATLA Religion Database with ATLASerials*, EBSCOhost (6 November 2017).

Crawford, Dan R. "Crusade Evangelism and the Local Church." *Missiology* 15, no. 3 (1987): 375. *ATLA Religion Database with ATLASerials,* EBSCOhost (22 December 2017).

de Mello, Manoel. "Participation Is Everything: Evangelism from Viewpoint of a Brazilian Pentecostal." *International Review of Mission* 60, no. 238 (1971): 245-248. *ATLA Religion Database with ATLASerials*, EBSCOhost (November 6, 2017).

George, Sherron Kay. "Brazil: An 'Evangelized' Giant Calling for Liberating Evangelism." *International Bulletin of Missionary Research* 26, no. 3 (2002): 104-109. *ATLA Religion Database with ATLASerials*, EBSCOhost (6 November 2017).

Gonçalves, Antônio de Campos. "Evangelism in Brazil Today: Its Significance and Results." *International Review of Mission* 48, no. 191 (1959): 302-308. *ATLA Religion Database with ATLASerials*, EBSCOhost (6 November 2017).

Matthews, Ed. "Mass Evangelism: Problems and Potentials." *Journal of Applied Missiology* 4, no.1, (N.d.): n.p. http://web.ovu.edu/missions/jam/massive1.htm (1 June 2016).

Mota, Jorge Cesar. "Evangelism and Unity in Brazil." *The Ecumenical Review* 5, no. 2 (1953): 155-158. *ATLA Religion Database with ATLASerials,* EBSCOhost (6 November 2017).

Smith, Harold B., et al., eds. "Is Mass Evangelism Dead?" *Christianity Today,* July 2007, 54. *ATLA Religion Database*, EBSCOhost (19 June 2016).

Vondey, Wolfgang, 2017. "Soteriology at the Altar: Pentecostal Contributions to Salvation as Praxis." *Transformation* 34 (3) (N.d.): 223–38. doi:10.1177/0265378816675831.). (March 30, 2019)

Williams, Andrew Ray (2019) "Water Baptism in Pentecostal Perspective: A Bibliographic Evaluation," *Spiritus: ORU Journal of Theology*: 4, no. 1 (2019): , Article 9. https://digitalshowcase.oru.edu/spiritus/vol4/iss1/9. (April 20, 2019).

Zelia, Soares. "Popular Piety and Evangelism in Brazil." *International Review of Mission* 82, no. 327 (1993): 401-410. *ATLA Religion Database with ATLASerials*, EBSCOhost (6 November 2017).

Other Sources

Ahibuogwu, Solomon Uche. "Increasing the Knowledge of Evangelism Among International Groups." D.Min. proj., Oral Roberts University, 2013.

"Aimee Semple McPherson." *Amazonaws.com.* N.d. https://s3.amazonaws.com /foursquare.org/wp-content/uploads/2018/10/08153920/ AimeeSempleMcPherson Bio.pdf (April 20, 2019).

"Appendix A: Oral Roberts University Historical Information." *www.oru.edu.* N.d. http://www.oru.edu/pdfs/pres-seach-committee/appendix_a.pdf (April 20, 2019).

Bang, Yong Koo. "A Study of Child-parents Evangelism Methods for Students Living with Unbelieving Parents." D.Min. proj., Oral Roberts University, 1999.

Bauer, Scott G. "Mission for a Multitude: A Strategy for Mobilizing 1000 People for Mass Evangelism." D. Min. proj., Oral Roberts University, 1995.

"Benjamin Franklin on Rev. George Whitefield." *National Humanities Center.* 1739. N.p. http://nationalhumanitiescenter.org/pds/becomingamer /ideas/text2/ franklinwhitefield.pdf/ (18 March 2018).

Billy Graham Museum, Wheaton, IL Sign on wall. (February 20, 2015).

"Brazil," *CIA World Factbook*, 1 September 2017. N.p. "https://www.cia.gov/library /publications/the-world-factbook/geos/br.html (1 September 2017).

"Brazil Hopes Truck Strike Ends," Yahoo News, n.p, (29 May 2018). https://www.yahoo.com/news/brazil-hopes-end-truck-strike-eighth-day-141557061.html (September 4, 2018).

"Brazil Takes Stock of a Week Long Strike and Its Not Pretty," *Bloomberg News*. May 28, 2018. N.p. https://www.bloomberg.com/news/articles/2018-05-28/brazil-takes-stock-of-a-week-long-strike-and-it-s-not-pretty/ (4 September 2018).

Broocks, Rice, Jr. "The Gift of the Evangelist." D. Miss. proj., Fuller Theological Seminary, School of Intercultural Studies, 2010.

Charry, Gloria I. "Increasing Evangelism through Training in Intercession." D.Min. proj., Oral Roberts University, 2001.

Chappell, Paul G. "The Divine Healing Movement in America." Ph.D. diss., Drew University, Madison, NJ, 1983.

"Christ the Healer." *Healing and Revival*. N.d. http://healingandrevival.com/BioBosworth.htm. (3 April 2019).

Fannin, Linda Lee. "Changing Attitudes about Evangelism Among Young Adult Leaders in Hungary." D.Min. proj., Oral Roberts University, 2013.

Flick, Stephen. "D. L. Moody's Lost Opportunity." N.d. N.p. https://christianheritagefellowship.com/d-l-moodys-lost-opportunity/ (18 March 2018).

Giovannetti, William A. "A Strategy for Linking Crusade Evangelism with Church Planting." D. Min. proj., Fuller Theological Seminary, 1996.

Greenway, Adam Wade. "The Integration of Apologetics and Evangelism in the Ministry of Ruben Archer Torrey." PhD Diss., Southwestern Baptist Theological Seminary, 2007.

"Historia." 20 January 2014. N.p. *Municipe de Caico*. http://caico.rn.gov.br/pagina.php?codigo=3/ (19 November 2018).

Hofstede, Geert. "The Six-D Model of National Culture." *About Geert Hofstede*. N.d. N.p. https://geerthofstede.com/culture-geert-hofstede-gert-jan-hofstede/6d-model-of-national-culture/ (October 8, 2018).

_____. "10 Minutes with Geert Hofstede on Indulgence versus Restraint." *YouTube video*, 9:33. Posted March 2015. https://www.youtube.com/watch?v=zQj1VPNPHlI. (March 29, 2019).

_____. "10 Minutes with Geert Hofstede on Power Distance." *YouTube video*, 11:27. Posted November 2014. https://www.youtube.com/watch?time_continue=3&v=DqAJclwfyCw. (March 29, 2019).

_____. "10 Minutes with Geert Hofstede on Uncertainty Avoidance." *YouTube video,* 15:26. Posted March 2015. https://www.youtube.com/watch?time_continue=1&v=fZF6LyGne7Q. (March 29, 2019)

_____. "10 Minutes with Geert Hofstede on Indulgence versus Restraint." *YouTube video,* 9:33. Posted March 2015. https://www.youtube.com/watch?time_continue=1&v=V0YgGdzmFtA. (March 29, 2019).

King, Daniel. "Pre-Crusade Survey of Local Church Pastors." Caicó, Brazil. 25 May 2018.

King, Robert James. "The Impact of a Children's Crusade on the Conversion Process in Mexico." D.Min. proj., Oral Roberts University, 2002.

Koak, Jang Geun Koak. "Training for Effective Evangelism." D.Min. proj., Oral Roberts University, 2002.

Kovar, Claudia. "Victory in Eastern Europe/Daugherty Spreads Word to Albania." *TulsaWord.com.* 14 July 1993. https://www.tulsaworld.com/archives/victory-in-eastern-europe-daugherty-spreads-world-to-albania/article_c68ede10-e9ed-50bb-ba8f-03dd1f1ec774.html/ (10 September 2018).

Koo, Hongnak. "The Impact of Luis Palau on Global Evangelism: An Evaluation of His Evangelistic Theology and Strategy." PhD Diss., Southwestern Baptist Theological Seminary, 2008.

Lindsey, Dennis Gordon. "The History and Global Impact of Christ for the Nations Institute." D.Min. proj., Oral Roberts University, 2014.

Loescher, Randall Scott. "Recruiting, Assessing, Training and Deploying Church Planters in Open Bible Churches' Central Region." D.Min. proj., Oral Roberts University, 2001).

Mairembam, Manichouba Singh. "Increasing the Knowledge of Person to Person Evangelism among the Meiteis of Manipur." D.Min. proj., Oral Roberts University, 2008.

Mayton, Kenneth. "Research Resources." Class handout from DMIN 786 Principles of Research, Oral Roberts University, 2016.

Morrow, William Brad. "Mass Evangelism and its Effect on Church Planting: A Filipino Case Study." PhD Diss., The Southern Baptist Theological Seminary, 2003.

Noh, Lee Ho. "Increased Knowledge of Believers about Evangelism." D.Min. proj., Oral Roberts University, 2007.

"Nokolaus von Zinzendorf." *Christianity Today,* n.d., n.p. http://www.christianitytoday.com/history/people/denominationalfounders /nikolaus-von-zinzendorf.html/ (19 March 2018).

O'More, R. Michael. "A Model for Empowering the Laity for Personal/relational Evangelism at Woodlawn Church." D.Min. proj., Oral Roberts University, 1999.

"Osborn Ministries International." *Osborn.org*. N.d. https://osborn.org/about/osborn-ministries-international (April 20, 2019).

"Our Story. The History and Future of the Foursquare Church." *Foursquare.* N.d. N.p. https://www.foursquare.org/about/ aimee_semple_mcpherson/ (19 March 2018).

Packer, J. I. Paper on Whitfield presented to the Whitefield Fraternal, May 1994, at the College Church in Wheaton. IL. Quoted in William A. Giovannetti, "A Strategy for Linking Crusade Evangelism with Church Planting," (DMIN proj., Fuller Theological Seminary, 1996). https://oralroberts.idm.oclc.org/login?url=https://search. proquest.com/docview/304351317?accountid=12997. (November 21, 2017).

Park, Jin-Gu. "A Study on the Person to Person Evangelism Training of Laity." D.Min. proj., Oral Roberts University, 1995.

Park, Kwang Sung. "Increasing the Awareness of Evangelism Opportunities among New Converts in Korean Immigrant Church." D.Min. proj., Oral Roberts University, 2006.

Prakash, Edith Dhana. "A Critical Investigation of Tommy Lee Osborn's Work in India: Its Impact and Implications." PhD Diss., Regent University, 2013.

Rose, Desmond Herbert, "Assessing Evangelism Explosion III in the Rural Context." D.Min. proj., Oral Roberts University, 2000.

Roth, Sid. "Sid Roth Welcomes Billy Joe Daugherty." *Sid Roth Hosts It's Supernatural.* 4 September 2009. N.p. http://www.itssupernatural.org/sid-roth/sid-roth-welcomes-billy-joe-daugherty/ (10 September 2018).

"The World Factbook: Brazil." *The Word Factbook*. 13 November 2017. N.p. https://www.cia.gov/library/publications/the-world-factbook/geos/br.html/ (13 November 2017).

Thomas, William. *An Assessment of Mass Meetings as a Method of Evangelism – Case Study of Eurofest'75 and the Billy Graham Crusade in Brussels.* Amsterdam: Editions Rodopi N.V., 1977.

Touthang, Seikhokam. "Increasing the Knowledge of Asian Immigrants About Evangelism." D.Min. proj., Oral Roberts University, 2005.

Winter, Terry Walter Royne. "Effective Mass Evangelism: A Study of Jonathan Edwards, George Whitefield, Charles Finney, Dwight L. Moody, and Billy Graham." D. of Pastoral Th. proj., Fuller Theological Seminary, 1968.

ORAL ROBERTS UNIVERSITY
INSTITUTIONAL REVIEW BOARD
HUMAN SUBJECTS REVIEW
APPROVAL STATUS FORM

Approval Date: 5/16/2018   **IRB #:** SP2018-17

Proposal Title/Subject: *Appraising the Impact of an Evangelistic Campaign in Caico, Brazil*

Principal Investigator(s): Daniel King

Reviewed and Processed as:
[ ] Exempt   [X] Expedited   [ ] Full Board

Approval Status Recommended by Reviewer(s):

ALL APPROVALS MAY BE SUBJECT TO REVIEW BY FULL INSTITUTIONAL REVIEW BOARD AT NEXT MEETING.

APPROVAL STATUS PERIOD VALID FOR ONE CALENDAR YEAR AFTER WHICH A CONTINUATION OR RENEWAL REQUEST IS REQUIRED TO BE SUBMITTED FOR BOARD APPROVAL.

ANY MODIFICATIONS TO APPROVED PROJECT MUST ALSO BE SUBMITTED FOR APPROVAL.

Comments, Modifications/Conditions for Approval or Reasons for Deferral or Disapproval are as follows:

Total Project Period: May 17, 2018 to June 30, 2018

Signature: _____   5-16-2018
Chair of Institutional Review Board   Date

cc: Faculty Sponsor
      Dean of School

VITA

Daniel King

Candidate for the Degree of

Doctor of Ministry

(Church Ministry Leadership)

Title: APPRAISING THE IMPACT OF AN EVANGELISTIC CAMPAIGN IN CAICÓ, BRAZIL

Biographical:

    Personal Data: Born in Tulsa, Oklahoma, February 4, 1979, the son of Robert and Susan King

    Education: Graduated from Home School, El Paso, Texas, 1997; received a Bachelor of Arts degree with a New Testament concentration from Oral Roberts University, Tulsa, Oklahoma; received a Master of Divinity from Oral Roberts University, Tulsa, Oklahoma; completed requirements for the Doctorate of Ministry Degree at Oral Roberts University, Tulsa, Oklahoma, in December of 2018.

    Professional Experience: Full-time missionary evangelist from 2002-2018. Visited over seventy nations to preach the Gospel. Conducted over one hundred evangelistic campaigns. Led over two million people in a salvation prayer. Author of over twenty books with over six hundred thousand books in print.

    Professional Organizations: Ordained Minister, Victory Leadership Network. Founder of The Soul Winner's Alliance, Member of the Next Generation Alliance, Founding Member of the Global Council for the Global Evangelist Network of Empowered 21. Member of the International Convention of Faith Ministries, International Director of the Fellowship of Covenant Ministries International.

    Permanent Address: King Ministries International, PO Box 701113 Tulsa, OK, 74170, www.kingministries.com, 1-877-431-4276

Contact the Author:

Daniel King daniel@kingministries.com

King Ministries International

PO Box 701113 Tulsa, OK 74170 USA

King Ministries Canada

PO Box 3401 Morinville, Alberta T8R 1S3 Canada

Visit us online at:

www.kingministries.com

Product Hotline:

1-877-431-4276

www.ingramcontent.com/pod-product-compliance
Lightning Source LLC
Chambersburg PA
CBHW081151290426
44108CB00018B/2515